SEX AND SPORTS

This book addresses one of the most controversial and polarizing topics of recent years: transgender girls' inclusion in girls' sports. The book explores legal precedent and medical science and explains why neither can answer the question of how eligibility rules should be drawn for girls' sports. The decision is, at core, a political one, necessarily reflecting social values and priorities. The book examines positions from the right and left that have dominated the public debate, revealing their ideological commitments and logical weak points. With the goal of helping readers clarify their own positions, rather than advocacy for a particular viewpoint, the book provides a framework for thinking about this issue that focuses on the discrete benefits organized sports provides to participants and society more broadly and considers how such benefits can be most fairly and justly allocated to girls and boys – both transgender and cisgender.

KIMBERLY A. YURACKO is Judd and Mary Morris Leighton Professor of Law at Northwestern Pritzker School of Law. She has written extensively about sex discrimination in sports, education, employment and tort law. In 2022, Yuracko received a John Simon Guggenheim Foundation fellowship to write this book. Her prior book, *Gender Nonconformity and the Law*, was published in 2016.

SEX AND SPORTS

Transgender Rights and the Culture War Over Girls' Sports

KIMBERLY A. YURACKO
Northwestern Pritzker School of Law

Shaftesbury Road, Cambridge CB2 8EA, United Kingdom

One Liberty Plaza, 20th Floor, New York, NY 10006, USA

477 Williamstown Road, Port Melbourne, VIC 3207, Australia

314–321, 3rd Floor, Plot 3, Splendor Forum, Jasola District Centre, New Delhi – 110025, India

Cambridge University Press is part of Cambridge University Press & Assessment, a department of the University of Cambridge.

We share the University's mission to contribute to society through the pursuit of education, learning and research at the highest international levels of excellence.

www.cambridge.org
Information on this title: www.cambridge.org/9781009649247
DOI: 10.1017/9781009649216

© Kimberly A. Yuracko 2026

This publication is in copyright. Subject to statutory exception and to the provisions of relevant collective licensing agreements, no reproduction of any part may take place without the written permission of Cambridge University Press & Assessment.

When citing this work, please include a reference to the DOI 10.1017/9781009649216

First published 2026

A catalogue record for this publication is available from the British Library

Library of Congress Cataloging-in-Publication Data
Names: Yuracko, Kimberly A., 1969– author
Title: Sex and sports / Kimberly A. Yuracko, Northwestern Pritzker School of Law.
Description: Cambridge, United Kingdom ; New York, NY : Cambridge University Press, 2026. | Includes bibliographical references and index.
Identifiers: LCCN 2025048404 (print) | LCCN 2025048405 (ebook) | ISBN 9781009649193 hardback | ISBN 9781009649216 ebook
Subjects: LCSH: Transgender women – Legal status, laws, etc. | Transgender people – Legal status, laws, etc. | Sports for women – Law and legislation | Sexual minorities and sports | Gender identity in sports | Sports – Sociological aspects | Gender identity – Moral and ethical aspects | Feminism and sports
Classification: LCC K3242.3 .Y87 2026 (print) | LCC K3242.3 (ebook)
LC record available at https://lccn.loc.gov/2025048404
LC ebook record available at https://lccn.loc.gov/2025048405

ISBN 978-1-009-64919-3 Hardback
ISBN 978-1-009-64924-7 Paperback

Cambridge University Press & Assessment has no responsibility for the persistence or accuracy of URLs for external or third-party internet websites referred to in this publication and does not guarantee that any content on such websites is, or will remain, accurate or appropriate.

For EU product safety concerns, contact us at Calle de José Abascal, 56, 1°, 28003 Madrid, Spain, or email eugpsr@cambridge.org.

To Sacha, Katja and Ron

CONTENTS

Acknowledgments   *page* viii

   Introduction   1
1. The Law   7
2. The Science   37
3. The Argument for Inclusion   54
4. The Argument for Exclusion   82
5. A Pragmatic Proposal for Women's Sports   99

   Conclusion   140

Index   143

ACKNOWLEDGMENTS

I thank Mark Kelman for encouraging me to write on this topic and for many discussions throughout the process. I had written early in my career about what antidiscrimination law requires with regard to sex-segregated sports. At that time, the treatment of transgender athletes was not an issue and the question of the day was how schools must allocate opportunities and resources to male and female students who differed in terms of their athletic abilities and interests. The question of what it means to treat people who are different in relevant respects fairly and equally has driven my scholarly writing throughout my career. It is what attracted me to the current topic and brought me back full circle to a focus on sports after years of writing about antidiscrimination in employment, education and tort law. Mark has been my teacher and mentor throughout this intellectual journey and my close friend through the unpredictable journey of life.

This book was several years in the writing and portions of the book were previously published in the *American Journal of Law & Equality* and in the *Villanova Law Review*. I am grateful to many people for their generous contributions. I would like to thank Zach Clopton, Don Herzog, Randall Kennedy, Andrew Koppelman, Mac McCorkle, Max Schanzenbach, Julie Suk and faculty workshop participants at Fordham Law School and University of Michigan Law School for reading and commenting on earlier drafts or providing resources and insights that were critical to the work. I am grateful to my excellent research assistants, Sylvie Gizzi, May Hiatt, Irena Huang, Lucy Choi Jung, Mackai Nguyen, Paris Souza and Jingjing Wang, to my wonderful library liaison Jesse Bowman and to my extraordinary faculty assistant Jane Brock. I am also grateful to the Guggenheim Foundation and to the Judd and Mary Morris Leighton professorship at Northwestern Pritzker School of Law, both of which provided generous support for this project.

Finally, I would like to thank my children, Sacha and Katja, and my partner, Ron Dunkel, for their love and support through this project and all others. Writing is often solitary, sometimes frustrating. I am forever and always grateful for their joy, laughter, dreams and the busyness of our day-to-day life.

Introduction

In 2012, then Vice President Joe Biden proclaimed discrimination against transgender individuals to be the "civil rights issue of our time."[1] The Obama administration and, subsequently, the Biden administration took the position that discrimination against transgendered individuals was a prohibited form of sex discrimination and interpreted federal antidiscrimination statutes in accordance with this view. In 2020, the Supreme Court agreed, holding that in the employment context, where careers are open to talents, and men and women compete directly against each other for rewards, transgender individuals could not simply be excluded from the tournament.

Yet, for the Obama and Biden administrations, equality for transgender individuals required not only ending their exclusion from coed spaces but demanding their inclusion in sex-segregated spaces on the basis of gender identity. In the context of education, this meant requiring that schools generally permit transgender girls to participate on the sports teams – and use the bathrooms and locker rooms – associated with their gender identity, not their biological sex. It was this demand for transgender inclusion in sex segregated spaces, far more than the call for nondiscrimination in unisex contexts like employment, that proved controversial.

---

[1] See Donovan Slack, *Biden says Transgender Discrimination "Civil Rights Issue of Our Time,"* POLITICO44 BLOG (Oct. 30, 2012), https://shorturl.at/jaEhs; *Vice President Joe Biden: Transgender Discrimination "Civil Rights Issue of Our Time,"* TRANSGENDER LAW CENTER (Oct. 31, 2012), https://shorturl.at/LORGJ. For a discussion of what the term "transgender" means to activists, see DAVID VALENTINE, IMAGINING TRANSGENDER: AN ETHNOGRAPHY OF A CATEGORY 33 (2007); *see also Frequently Asked Questions about Transgender People,* NAT'L CTR. FOR TRANSGENDER EQUAL., https://shorturl.at/e7UHX (explaining that transgender people "are people whose gender identity is different from the gender they were thought to be at birth" and one's "gender identity" is one's "internal knowledge of your own gender"). "Cisgender" refers to "[a] person whose gender identity matches the gender they were assigned at birth." *LGBTQ+Glossary,* IT GETS BETTER PROJECT, https://itgetsbetter.org/glossary/.

The issue of transgender women's participation in women's sports captured national attention in 2021 when Lia Thomas, a student-athlete at Penn, joined the women's varsity swim team after previously swimming for two years on the men's team. Thomas had taken female hormones for one year, making her eligible, at that time, to participate on the women's team. Competing in the women's category, Thomas had tremendous success – even winning an NCAA Division I national championship – far outshining her more modest results in the men's category. Thomas' success in the pool – and her presence in the women's locker room – sparked widespread debate.

With Donald Trump's election in 2024, the political pendulum shifted dramatically. On his first day in office, President Trump issued an executive order announcing that the state would recognize only two sexes defined in terms of biology at birth.[2] He followed this order just two weeks later with one specifically and categorically barring transgender girls and women from women's sports in educational programs.[3]

Although the political winds have changed, the debate is far from over and policy is far from settled. This book provides a critical examination of the legal, scientific and ethical issues raised by transgender girls' inclusion in girls' sports. It challenges the absolutist positions that have dominated the popular and political discourse and offers a more nuanced framework for deciding when transgender girls and women should, and should not, be permitted to compete in women's sports.

While some of the analysis of this book will likely be useful in contexts other than sports, this book is, quite deliberately, narrow in scope. What is at stake when we think about transgender girls' and women's inclusion in female sports is different from what is at stake when we think about transgender women's inclusion in sex-segregated bathrooms, prisons or locker rooms. As a result, the framework for fairly allocating the relevant goods and benefits in each context will differ, and so too will our likely answers to questions of inclusion. Transgender rights are, in other words, appropriately contextual.

In broad strokes, the book is divided into three parts. The first part explores the legal and scientific issues raised by transgender girls' inclusion in girls' sports and explains why neither positive law nor medical science provides a clear answer to how eligibility rules should be drawn. Chapter 1

---

[2] See Executive Order, January 20, 2025, Defending Women from Gender Ideology Extremism and Restoring Biological Truth to the Federal Government.
[3] See Executive Order, February 5, 2025, Keeping Men Out of Women's Sports.

describes the multilayered, complicated and, at times, contradictory legal landscape governing school sports. At the federal level is Title IX, which prohibits discrimination on the basis of sex in educational programs that receive federal funding. At the state level are statutes which increasingly exclude transgender girls from girls' sports in the name of ensuring fair competition. Both are subject to the equal protection demands of the federal constitution. The chapter explains why antidiscrimination mandates are so indeterminate in sex-segregated contexts and why, as a result, whether and when transgender girls must be included in girls' sports is still very much an open question. Chapter 2 describes the science of sex and explains why it too cannot determine eligibility rules for girls' sports. There is, in fact, significant agreement among scientists and medical professionals about what determines sex and what factors matter most for athletic success. Nonetheless, eligibility rules are, and must be, fundamentally social choices. Only with social agreement about the meaning and purpose of women's sports, can science help with category assignments.

The second part of the book identifies the commitments and convictions underlying and motivating arguments for inclusion and exclusion of transgender girls and highlights their weaknesses. This part focuses on the most absolutist arguments on both sides. These positions are not strawmen, they are instead the views that have dominated public discourse and defined political action.

On the left, groups like the American Civil Liberties Union (ACLU), the National Women's Law Center and the National Organization for Women assert their unqualified support for transgender women's inclusion in women's sports. The ACLU proclaims unequivocally that "[t]rans girls are girls" and that trans girls have a right to participate on athletic teams consistent with their gender identity.[4] The National Women's Law Center likewise "firmly support[s] the inclusion of women and girls who are transgender in all aspects of school – including sports, restrooms, and locker rooms – as a matter of both civil rights law and of human rights."[5] The National Organization of Women explains that "'[d]ebate' about [t]rans [g]irls and [w]omen in [s]chool [s]ports [s]preads [t]ransphobia and [b]igotry."[6] Doubters, those who question whether transgender

---

[4] *Four Myths about Trans Athletes Debunked*, ACLU, www.aclu.org/news/lgbtq-rights/four-myths-about-trans-athletes-debunked.
[5] Press Release, National Women's Law Center Intervenes in Defense of Transgender College Athletes, https://shorturl.at/u6hne.
[6] Angie Veliz, *"'Debate' about Trans Girls and Women in School Sports Spreads Transphobia and Bigotry through the False Lens of 'Fairness,'"* NOW, https://shorturl.at/GCT9R.

women should be fully included in women's spaces, have been condemned, often viciously. Even the socially powerful and otherwise politically progressive have been subject to withering attacks. The treatment of J.K. Rowling, author of the Harry Potter books, is particularly noteworthy. In a series of tweets and longer writings, Rowling expressed her belief in the importance of biological sex and of single-sex spaces for biological women. She received in response widespread condemnation from Hollywood, including from the young stars of her movies, online abuse and threats of violence.[7]

On the right, categorical exclusion of transgender girls and women from women's sports has become both a talking point and policy priority for the Republican Party. In addition to President Trump's executive order barring transgender girls from girls' sports, the Republican-controlled House of Representatives voted in January 2025 to amend Title IX to require transgender girls' exclusion.[8] Passage in the Senate is far less certain. At the state level, as of early 2025, twenty-five states have passed exclusionary eligibility rules for girls sports.[9]

Chapters 3 and 4 explain why both absolutist positions are a mistake. Arguments for blanket inclusion unpersuasively deny the existence and relevance of biological sex. They also place tremendous weight on the subjective pain experienced by transgender girls who are excluded from girls' sports, while ignoring the subjective pain experienced by cisgender girls forced to compete against them. Arguments for exclusion, by contrast, focus on the perceived unfairness to individual cisgender girls of being denied victories they might otherwise win, yet the arguments fail to explain why ensuring victories for cisgender girls requires that all trans girls be excluded or, moreover, why winning should determine eligibility rules for girls' sports at all ages and all levels. Arguments for both inclusion and exclusion rest too on controversial and often overlooked conceptions of human flourishing and personhood.

The third part of the book suggests a nuanced, empirically informed and pragmatic framework for determining eligibility lines for girls' sports.

---

[7] *J.K. Rowling Writes about Her Reasons for Speaking Out on Sex and Gender Issues* (Jun. 10, 2020), www.jkrowling.com/opinions/j-k-rowling-writes-about-her-reasons-for-speaking-out-on-sex-and-gender-issues/; Abby Gardner, *A Complete Breakdown of the J.K. Rowling Transgender-Comments Controversy*, GLAMOUR (Sept. 3, 2024), https://shorturl.at/yIfoP.
[8] H.R. 28 – Protection of Women and Girls in Sports Act of 2025, www.congress.gov/bill/119th-congress/house-bill/28/text.
[9] Katie Barnes, *Transgender Athlete Laws by State: Legislation, Science, More*, ESPN (Aug. 24, 2023), https://shorturl.at/AO8pS.

Central to it is the belief that questions of transgender girls' inclusion in girls' sports should be answered by identifying the benefits and goods that come from athletic participation and then drawing eligibility rules with an eye to maximizing these benefits for transgender and cisgender girls and boys alike. I identify three primary benefits of sports – basic benefits, special benefits and group benefits. The basic benefits are the physical and psychological benefits that athletic participants get from athletic endeavors. The special benefits are the distinct set of goods – sometimes tangible sometimes not – that go to the small group of winners. The group benefits are the goods that organized sports confer on those who do not themselves play but who identify with the winners. Nonparticipants who identify socially with athletic winners receive benefits in the form of self-esteem, role-modeling and social status that comes from the celebration of female athletes and the recognition of women as strong autonomous agents.

Although the benefits of sport attach to all levels of play, they attach to different levels in different degrees. At the early childhood and recreational levels, the basic benefits predominate as both the reason and the reward for play. At more elite levels, the special and group benefits of sports become more pronounced. At each level of play, eligibility rules should be drawn so as to maximize the benefits of sports for girls and women – both transgender and cisgender – recognizing that under some circumstances the interests of the two groups will in fact diverge.

This book is more analysis than argument, more philosophical than political. Its goal is not to "win" an argument, but to deepen the conversation by speaking to a range of audiences. First and foremost, I hope this book will speak to those who are themselves or through their family members grappling directly with these issues as athletic participants. Second, I hope it will speak to policymakers who are shaping at the federal, state or organizational level, eligibility rules for women's sports. Finally, I hope the book will speak to judges. Courts will ultimately have to decide what policies are consistent with statutory and constitutional requirements. In July 2025, the Supreme Court accepted cert in two cases challenging absolute and categorical bans on transgender girls' participation in girls' sports.[10] These cases are important though their result is likely to be narrow. Whether the Supreme Court holds that absolute

---

[10] West Virginia v. B.P.J., 2025 WL 1829164 (July 3, 2025); Little v. Hecox, 2025 WL 1829165 (July 3, 2025). In January 2026, just before this book went to press, the Supreme Court heard oral argument in both cases.

exclusions of transgender girls from girls' sports are impermissible or permissible, lower courts will continue to face challenges to a broad and diverse range of less restrictive laws and policies. Deciding these cases will require courts to assess and understand the social benefits of sports, the goals of sex segregation in this context and the impact of transgender girls' inclusion at different levels and ages of play. These are precisely the questions of this book. The answers are genuinely hard and the stakes truly high. We all deserve a more thoughtful discussion.

1

The Law

The positive law governing transgender girls' participation in school sports in America falls into three categories. First, there is federal statutory law – most importantly Title IX – and the regulations, guidance letters and executive orders that interpret it. Second, there is state law, which has increasingly been used to define eligibility rules for girls' and women's sports in terms of reproductive biology at birth. Finally, there is constitutional law, most critically the Equal Protection Clause of the Fourteenth Amendment, which constrains states directly and constrains the federal government indirectly via incorporation into the Fifth Amendment.[1] There is, necessarily, a hierarchy. Administrative interpretations and executive orders must be faithful to the statute they interpret. State law must defer to federal law. Both federal and state law must obey constitutional requirements. Courts, of course, are the final arbiters of compliance.

This chapter begins with a focus on federal antidiscrimination law, describing the shifting, often flip-flopping, interpretations of Title IX's mandate for girls' sports. The chapter next describes the range of state laws addressing transgender girls' participation in girls' sports enacted in the shadow of the chaos and instability of federal law. Finally, the chapter examines judicial rulings about what Title IX and the Equal Protection Clause require in this context.

1.1 Federal Law

Title IX of the Education Amendments of 1972 is rightfully at the center of discussions about whether transgender girls may be included in girls' sports. Title IX provides quite simply: "No person in the United States shall, on the basis of sex, be excluded from participation in, be denied the

---

[1] Bolling v. Sharpe, 347 U.S. 497, 500 (1954).

benefits of, or be subjected to discrimination under any education program or activity receiving Federal financial assistance."[2] Title IX applies to all public schools and, because almost all private universities receive some federal funding – most often in the form of research grants or student financial aid – to almost all private colleges as well.[3]

Nonetheless, this section begins with a prior statute, Title VII of the Civil Rights Act of 1964. Title VII prohibits discrimination in employment on the basis of sex, race, color, religion and national origin. When it was initially passed, Title VII excluded educational institutions, leaving unchecked widespread discrimination against female faculty and students. In 1972, Congress not only extended Title VII to apply to employment in educational institutions, it also passed Title IX of the Education Amendments to prohibit educational discrimination against girls and women more broadly.[4] Title IX was both modeled after Title VII and designed to fill its holes. When interpreting Title IX, courts regularly look to Title VII case law for interpretive guidance.[5] It is difficult, as a result, to understand how agencies and courts are currently interpreting Title IX, or to anticipate how they are likely to do so in the future, without understanding Title VII.

1.1.1 Title VII

Before Title VII's passage, many jobs in America were formally sex-segregated.[6] Employers openly and unabashedly excluded women

---

[2] 20 U.S.C. § 1681 (2018).
[3] *See, e.g.*, Richard Vedder, *There Are Really Almost No Truly Private Universities*, FORBES (Apr. 8, 2018, 8:00 AM) https://shorturl.at/rX8Cd; R. SHEP MELNICK, THE TRANSFORMATION OF TITLE IX: REGULATING GENDER EQUALITY IN EDUCATION 4 (2018) ("Since every public elementary, middle, and high school in the country and virtually every college and university – private as well as public – receives federal money, these thousands of institutions are all subject to the rules established by the courts and by the Department of Education's Office for Civil Rights (OCR) under Title IX").
[4] Kristen M. Galles, *Filling the Gaps: Women, Civil Rights, and Title IX*, 31 HUM. RTS. MAG. 16 (July 1, 2004), https://shorturl.at/yfJUt.
[5] Title IX Legal Manual, U.S. DEP'T OF JUST. C.R. DIV. (2015), https://perma.cc/3D2U-F2DM ("It is generally accepted outside the sexual harassment context that the substantive standards and policies developed under Title VII apply with equal force to employment actions brought under Title IX").
[6] SHARON WHITNEY, THE EQUAL RIGHTS AMENDMENT: THE HISTORY AND THE MOVEMENT 18–20 (1984); DEBORAH L. RHODE, JUSTICE AND GENDER: SEX DISCRIMINATION AND THE LAW 58 (1989).

from desirable high-paying jobs that were reserved for men.⁷ The story of Justice Sandra Day O'Connor's inability to find a law firm job other than as a legal secretary after graduating third in her class from Stanford Law School in 1952 is now well known and almost quaintly anachronistic.⁸ Her experience, however, was typical of the time.⁹ Just as African Americans were routinely excluded from jobs and even from whole industries,¹⁰ women were confined to "pink collar" jobs and often barred from the more prestigious and profitable positions reserved for men.¹¹ Indeed, private discrimination was in some cases required by state law. "By the mid-1960s 26 states prohibited women from working in certain jobs, and 19 states had hours regulations for women workers."¹² Women were statutorily excluded from jobs that required heavy lifting,¹³ as well as from work as diverse as bartending,¹⁴ shining shoes and

---

[7] Diane L. Bridge, *The Glass Ceiling and Sexual Stereotyping: Historical and Legal Perspectives of Women in the Workplace*, 4 VA. J. SOC. POL'Y & L. 581, 599 (1996) (describing, for example, a Westinghouse manual from the early 1900s which provided that "the lowest paid male job was not [to] [sic] be paid a wage below that of the highest paid female job, regardless of the job content and value to the firm") (emphasis omitted) (quoting RAY MARSHALL & BETH PAULIN, EMPLOYMENT AND EARNINGS OF WOMEN: HISTORICAL PERSPECTIVE, IN WORKING WOMEN: PAST, PRESENT, FUTURE (Karen S. Koziara et al. eds., 1987)) (citations omitted) (also quoting the International Ladies' Garment Workers' Union contract from 1913, which limited women to the less skilled jobs and provided that "the highest paid female could not earn more than the lowest paid male").

[8] NANCY MAVEETY, JUSTICE SANDRA DAY O'CONNOR: STRATEGIST ON THE SUPREME COURT 13 (1996); Mary Jo White, *The 2022 Sandra Day O'Connor Medal of Honor Recipient: Mary Jo White*, 26 SETON HALL J. LEGIS. & PUB. POL'Y 262, 266 (2002).

[9] Barbara Allen Babcock, *Foreword: A Real Revolution*, 49 U. KAN. L. REV. 721 (2000) (describing the "open and rank discrimination" faced by female lawyers when she graduated from Yale Law School in 1963); RHODE, *supra* note 6 at 55 (noting that "[a]n extensive survey of law school graduates and administrators in the mid-1960s reported almost two thousand separate occasions on which employers had disclosed policies against hiring women").

[10] Albemarle Paper Co. v. Moody, 422 U.S. 405, 409 (1975) (employer had operated a racially segregated plant reserving high-pay and high-skilled jobs for whites); Griggs v. Duke Power Co., 401 U.S. 424, 426–28 (1971) (employer had refused to hire blacks for any but its lowest-paying jobs).

[11] Bridge, *supra* note 7 at 599.

[12] KAREN J. MASCHKE, LITIGATION, COURTS, AND WOMEN WORKERS 5 (1989).

[13] Bowe v. Colgate-Palmolive Co., 416 F.2d 711, 717–18 (7th Cir. 1969) (referring to state laws excluding women from jobs which require lifting heavy weights); Rosenfeld v. S. Pac. Co., 293 F. Supp. 1219, 1223–29 (C.D. Cal. 1968) (ruling in favor of a female plaintiff's Title VII challenge to California's "hours and weights legislation" which barred women from jobs involving lifting of certain weights).

[14] Goesaert v. Cleary, 335 U.S. 464, 465–66 (1948) (upholding a Michigan statute prohibiting women from tending bar unless they were the wives or daughters of male owners).

legislative service.[15] Society viewed men as the primary labor market participants and wage earners. Women were viewed as peripheral market participants and supplemental wage earners seeking "pin money."[16] It was this kind of categorical group-based discrimination that was the Act's target.[17]

Not surprisingly, "sex" under Title VII was conceived of as biological sex. The Act prohibited discrimination based on biology, not gender expression. As the Ninth Circuit explained in the 1977 case of *Holloway v. Arthur Anderson & Co.*, "the term sex should be given the traditional

---

[15] RHODE, *supra* note 6 at 44 (explaining that "[d]uring the late nineteenth century, legislatures began passing an increasing volume of exclusionary laws, and by mid-twentieth century, women in half the states were banned from work ranging from shining shoes to legislative service").

[16] WHITNEY, *supra* note 6 at 14 (noting that during the Great Depression "the myth that most women were working simply to earn 'pin money' for luxuries took over" because "[o]nly men were recognized as legitimate breadwinners, and twenty-six state legislatures passed laws forbidding employers to hire married women").

[17] Representative Martha Griffiths argued that without including protections for sex in the Act, women would continue to be excluded from higher wage jobs. 110 CONG. REC. 2577–84 (1964), reprinted in U.S. EQUAL EMP'T OPPORTUNITY COMM'N, LEGISLATIVE HISTORY OF TITLES VII AND XI OF CIVIL RIGHTS ACT OF 1964 3210–19 (1968). Moreover, she argued that the prohibition of sex discrimination was needed to eradicate states' protective legislation that only served to entrench women's subordinate employment position. *Id.* at 3219. Griffiths argued that "some protective legislation was to safeguard the health of women, but it should have safeguarded the health of men, also. Most of the so-called protective legislation has really been to protect men's rights in better paying jobs." *Id.* Similarly, Representative St. George argued in favor of the amendment as a way to challenge restrictive protective labor laws that prevented "women from going into the higher salary brackets." *Id.* at 3221. St. George explained: "Women are protected – they cannot run an elevator late at night and that is when the pay is higher. They cannot serve in restaurants and cabarets at night – when the tips are higher – and the load ... is lighter." *Id.* at 3221. The Supreme Court has recognized the purposes behind Title VII. *See* Int'l Bhd. of Teamsters v. United States, 431 U.S. 324, 364 (1977) (noting that "a primary objective of Title VII is ... to achieve equal employment opportunity and to remove the barriers that have operated to favor white male employees over other employees"); Franks v. Bowman Transp. Co., 424 U.S. 747, 763 (1976) (explaining that the goal of Title VII was to "prohibit all practices in whatever form which create inequality in employment opportunity due to discrimination on the basis of race, religion, sex, or national origin"); Gen. Elec. Co. v. Gilbert, 429 U.S. 125, 160 (1976) (Brennan, J., dissenting) (arguing that the primary purpose of Title VII was "'to assure equality of employment opportunities and to eliminate those discriminatory practices and devices which have fostered [sexually] stratified job environments to the disadvantage of [women]'") (quoting McDonnell Douglas Corp. v. Green, 411 U.S. 792, 800 (1973)). *See also* Erickson v. Bartell Drug Co., 141 F. Supp. 2d 1266, 1269 (W.D. Wash. 2001) ("What is clear from the law itself, its legislative history, and Congress' subsequent actions, is that the goal of Title VII was to end years of discrimination in employment and to place all men and women, regardless of race, color, religion, or national origin on equal footing in how they were treated in the workforce").

definition based on anatomical characteristics."[18] The Seventh Circuit famously agreed in the 1984 case of *Ulane v. Eastern Airlines*. According to the Seventh Circuit:

> It is a maxim of statutory construction that, unless otherwise defined, words should be given their ordinary, common meaning. The phrase in Title VII prohibiting discrimination based on sex, in its plain meaning, implies that it is unlawful to discriminate against women because they are women and against men because they are men ... We agree with the Eighth and Ninth Circuits that if the term "sex" as it is used in Title VII is to mean more than biological male or biological female, the new definition must come from Congress.[19]

Title VII was very successful at ending such categorical forms of discrimination and, over time, discrimination became more subtle and more nuanced.

In the decades after the Act's passage, it became rare for employers to exclude all women (or men) from employment because of their biological status as such. Employers did, however, discriminate against and exclude particular subsets of women or men – namely those who performed their gender in ways the employer found unacceptable or deviant. An employer might, for example, refuse to hire women who appeared too masculine or tacitly condone harassment of a man deemed inappropriately feminine.

The Supreme Court's landmark case addressing stereotyping discrimination of this kind was *Price Waterhouse v. Hopkins*.[20] The case was brought by Ann Hopkins, who had worked in the Washington, DC, office of Price Waterhouse for five years when the partners in that office proposed her for partnership in 1982. Hopkins was one of eighty-eight candidates and the only woman. She was passed over for partnership and held for reconsideration the following year. The man who was assigned by Price Waterhouse to tell Hopkins why her candidacy had been held over told her that to improve her chances the following year, she should "'walk more femininely, talk more femininely, dress more femininely, wear makeup, have her hair styled, and wear jewelry.'"[21] Hopkins sued for sex discrimination. By the time the case reached the Supreme Court, the main questions had to do with burdens of responsibility. The lasting

---

[18] Holloway v. Arthur Anderson & Co., 566 F.2d 659, 662 (9th Cir. 1977).
[19] Ulane v. E. Airlines, Inc., 742 F.2d 1081, 1085, 1087 (7th Cir. 1984).
[20] Price Waterhouse v. Hopkins, 490 U.S. 228 (1989).
[21] *Price Waterhouse*, 490 U.S. at 235 (quoting Hopkins v. Price Waterhouse, 618 F. Supp. 1109, 1117 (D.D.C. 1985)).

impact of the case, however, flowed from the Court's pronouncement that sex stereotyping is a form of discrimination prohibited by Title VII. "As for the legal relevance of sex stereotyping," the Court explained, "we are beyond the day when an employer could evaluate employees by assuming or insisting that they matched the stereotype associated with their group, for '[i]n forbidding employers to discriminate against individuals because of their sex, Congress intended to strike at the entire spectrum of disparate treatment of men and women resulting from sex stereotypes.'"[22]

What followed from the Court's holding in *Price Waterhouse* was a number of lower court cases providing protection for male employees harassed because of perceived effeminacy or homosexuality as well as protection for transgender employees discriminated against for socially transitioning. In *Doe by Doe v. City of Belleville*, for example, the Seventh Circuit ruled that the harassment of two boys who were perceived by their male coworkers to be insufficiently masculine constituted sex discrimination under Title VII.[23] Relying directly on *Price Waterhouse*, the court explained that "a man who is harassed because his voice is soft, his physique is slight, his hair is long, or because in some other respect he exhibits his masculinity in a way that does not meet his coworkers' idea of how men are to appear and behave, is harassed 'because of' his sex."[24] Similarly, in *Centola v. Potter*, a Massachusetts district court relied on the sex stereotyping rationale to hold that a man harassed for his perceived effeminacy and homosexuality had presented evidence of sex discrimination sufficient to survive a motion for summary judgment.[25]

---

[22] *Price Waterhouse*, 490 U.S. at 251 (citations omitted). After the Supreme Court's decision, Hopkins's case wound its way back down to the district court and the court of appeals. Ultimately, Hopkins won elevation to the partnership at Price Waterhouse and also back pay. Hopkins v. Price Waterhouse, 920 F.2d 967 (D.C. Cir. 1990).

[23] Doe by Doe v. City of Belleville, 119 F.3d 563 (7th Cir. 1997). The Seventh Circuit's opinion in *Belleville* was vacated by the Supreme Court for further consideration in light of its decision in *Oncale v. Sundowner Offshore Servs., Inc.*, 523 U.S. 75 (1998). City of Belleville v. Doe by Doe, 523 U.S. 1001, 1001 (1998). The case then settled before there was a decision on remand. The Supreme Court's decision in *Oncale*, in which the Supreme Court held that same-sex sexual harassment could be actionable under Title VII, did nothing, however, to challenge or retract the gender stereotyping logic set forth in *Price Waterhouse*, on which the *Belleville* decision relied.

[24] *Belleville*, 119 F.3d at 581.

[25] Centola v. Potter, 183 F. Supp. 2d 403, 409–10 (D. Mass. 2002). The *Centola* court suggested that the sex stereotyping logic of *Price Waterhouse* should not only protect men harassed because of their perceived effeminacy but also men harassed because they choose to date men instead of women.

In *Smith v. City of Salem*, the sex stereotyping logic of *Price Waterhouse* was used for the first time to protect transgender workers.[26] Smith, a transgender female who worked as a lieutenant in the Salem Fire Department in Salem, Ohio, was threatened with termination when she began expressing a more feminine appearance at work. "Sex stereotyping based on a person's gender non-conforming behavior," the court explained, "is impermissible discrimination, irrespective of the cause of that behavior; a label, such as 'transsexual,' is not fatal to a sex discrimination claim where the victim has suffered discrimination because of his or her gender non-conformity."[27] Other courts followed suit.[28]

Price Waterhouse did not, however, wholly eliminate sex-specific workplace norms. In *Jespersen v. Harrah's Operating Company*, for example, the Ninth Circuit held that the sex stereotyping prohibition did not prohibit the casino from requiring that female but not male bartenders wear makeup.[29] Nor did *Price Waterhouse* say anything about how transgender workers should be assigned in sex-specific contexts. Courts were divided after *Price Waterhouse* on whether Title VII's prohibition on sex discrimination required employers to permit transgender workers to use the bathroom consistent with their gender identity or permitted employers to assign transgender employees to the bathroom consistent with their biological sex.[30]

---

[26] Smith v. City of Salem, Ohio, 378 F.3d 566, 568 (6th Cir. 2004).

[27] *Smith*, 378 F.3d at 575.

[28] *See, e.g.*, Rosa v. Park West Bank & Trust Co., 214 F.3d 213 (1st Cir. 2000); Schwenk v. Hargford, 204 F.3d 1187 (9th Cir. 2000); Glenn v. Brumby, 724 F. Supp.2d 1284 (N.D. Ga. 2010), aff'd, 663 F.3d 1312 (11th Cir. 2011). *See also* Schroer v. Billington, 577 F. Supp. 2d 293, 305 ("Ultimately, I do not think it matters for purposes of Title VII liability whether the library withdrew its offer of employment because it perceived Schroer to be an insufficiently masculine man, and insufficiently feminine woman, or an inherently gender-nonconforming transsexual."); Lopez v. River Oaks Imaging & Diagnostic Group, Inc., 542 F. Supp.2d 653, 660 (S.D. Tex. 2008) (denying defendant's motion for summary judgment and explaining that "Title VII is violated when an employer discriminates against an employee, transsexual or not, because he or she has failed to act or appear sufficiently masculine or feminine enough for an employer"); Creed v. Fam. Express Corp., 2007 WL 2265630, at *4 (N.D. Ind. Aug. 3, 2007) (noting that "Ms. Creed's allegation she was terminated after refusing to present herself in a masculine way permits the inference she was terminated as a result of [her employer's] stereotypical perceptions, rather than simply her gender dysphoria").

[29] Jespersen v. Harrah's Operating Co., 444 F.3d 1104 (9th Cir. 2006).

[30] *See* Kastl v. Maricopa Cnty. Cmty. Coll. Dist., 325 F. App'x 492, 493–94 (9th Cir. 2009) (holding that employer's ban on transsexual plaintiff's use of women's restroom for safety reasons did not constitute sex discrimination); Etsitty v. Utah Transit Auth., 502 F.3d 1215, 1224 (10th Cir. 2007) (holding that the employer's "legitimate" concerns about potential liability from having the transgender female plaintiff use women's public restrooms

The Court's next landmark decision for gender-nonconforming workers was *Bostock v. Clayton County*.[31] In *Bostock*, the Court consolidated three cases which raised the question of whether "an employer can fire someone simply for being homosexual or transgender."[32] The answer, the Court explained, was clear: "An employer who fires an individual for being homosexual or transgender fires that person for traits or actions it would not have questioned in members of a different sex. Sex plays a necessary and undisguisable role in the decision, exactly what Title VII forbids."[33] "[H]omosexuality and transgender status are inextricably bound up with sex," the Court explained, "[n]ot because homosexuality or transgender status are related to sex in some vague sense or because discrimination on these bases has some disparate impact on one sex or another, but because to discriminate on the these grounds requires an employer to intentionally treat individual employees differently because of their sex."[34]

The *Bostock* court was also clear, however, that it was not answering the question of how transgender workers must be assigned in sex-segregated contexts. "[E]mployers worry," the Court noted, that "under Title VII … sex-segregated bathrooms, locker rooms, and dress codes will prove unsustainable after our decision today."[35] But, the Court explained, "we do not prejudge any such question today … [W]e do not purport to address bathrooms, locker rooms, or anything else of the kind."[36]

1.1.2 Title IX

Title IX arose out of a series of hearings in 1970 organized by Representative Edith Green (Oregon),[37] focusing on discrimination in educational

---

justified its prohibition on her doing so and overcame any presumption of illegality). *But see* Roberts v. Clark Cnty. Sch. Dist., 215 F. Supp. 3d 1001, 1015 (D. Nev. 2016) (granting summary judgment for transgender plaintiff finding that school district "banned Roberts from the women's bathroom because he no longer behaved like a woman, [which] … alone shows that the school district discriminated against Roberts based on his gender and sex stereotypes"); Lusardi v. McHugh, EEOC Appeal No. 0120133395, 2015 WL 1607756 (Apr. 1, 2015) (holding that a federal agency that denied an employee access to the bathroom corresponding to the employee's gender identity discriminated on the basis of sex).

[31] Bostock v. Clayton Cnty., 590 U.S. 644 (2020).
[32] *Id*. at 651.
[33] *Id*. at 651–52.
[34] *Id*. at 660–61.
[35] *Id*. at 681.
[36] *Id*.
[37] Paula J. Snyder, *A Legislative and Judicial History of Title IX in Athletics* 30 (May 2008) (Ph.D. dissertation, Kent State University) (on file with author). *See also* 117 CONG. REC.

employment. The Act did not go through the normal committee process but was tucked into a broader omnibus education law where it did not generate much attention – a deliberate strategy by Title IX's supporters.[38] Indeed, Representative Green discouraged women's rights organizations from lobbying for the Act out of concern that doing so would only spark opposition.[39] Title IX passed both houses and was signed into law by President Richard Nixon on June 23, 1972. Athletics was barely mentioned.[40]

Title IX authorized federal agencies to "issu[e] rules, regulations, or orders of general applicability which shall be consistent with achievement of the objectives" of the Act.[41] The law also, however, included two unusual procedural requirements which significantly limited agency rulemaking. The first required presidential approval for all rules issued under Title IX.[42] The second, which was added in 1974, allowed Congress, without approval of the president, to invalidate any administrative regulation.[43] The latter provision was declared unconstitutional by the Supreme Court in 1983 in *INS v. Chahda*,[44] but the former remains in force, if not enforced.

While individual enforcement actions are permitted, Title IX's primary enforcement mechanism is the "power of the purse." The Office for Civil Rights (OCR) can threaten to withdraw federal funds from schools in violation of Title IX's mandate. When enacted, Title IX contained program-specific limitations providing that any termination of funding "shall be

---

39249–50 (1971) (Representative Green describing the "ample documentation" of discrimination against women in education gathered at subcommittee hearings); SUSAN WARE, TITLE IX: A BRIEF HISTORY WITH DOCUMENTS 3, 40 (2014). *See Discrimination Against Women: Hearings before Spec. Subcomm. on Educ. of Comm. on Educ. & Lab., H.R. on Sec. 805 of H.R. 16098*, 91st Cong., 2d Sess. (1970).

[38] WARE, *supra* note 37 at 3. See also MELNICK, *supra* note 3 at 41 (explaining that in the Senate, Title IX did not go through the normal committee process but was added to the omnibus bill on the floor by Senator Birch Bayh).

[39] WARE, *supra* note 37 at 41.

[40] *Id.* at 4 ("In the hearings and debate about the law, athletics [was] barely mentioned, other than an offhand remark by Senator Bayh that the law would not mean that football teams had to be coeducational").

[41] 20 U.S.C. § 1682.

[42] *Id.* ("No such rule, regulation or order shall become effective unless and until approved by the President."); *see also* MELNICK, *supra* note 3 at 42.

[43] General Education Provisions Act, Pub. L. No. 93-380, § 431(d)(1), 88 Stat. 567 (Aug. 21, 1974) (as amended at 20 U.S.C. § 1232(d)(1)); *See also* MELNICK, *supra* note 3 at 42.

[44] Immigr. & Naturalization Serv. v. Chadha, 462 U.S. 919, 944–58 (1983) (holding Congressional veto provision of Section 244(c)(2) of the Immigration and Nationality Act unconstitutional).

limited in its effect to the particular program, or part thereof, in which such noncompliance has been so found."[45] In 1984, in *Grove City College v. Bell*, the Supreme Court interpreted such provisions to mean that only the specific educational program or activity receiving federal financial assistance, not the entire college, would be subject to Title IX's mandate.[46] Since athletic departments did not receive federal funds, *Grove City College* meant that Title IX could not reach them. *Grove City College* was, however, short-lived. In 1988, Congress overrode the decision by enacting the Civil Rights Restoration Act of 1988 over President Reagan's veto. The Act made Title IX applicable to all programs within any institution receiving federal aid.[47]

Title IX's silence on what the Act meant for school sports both demanded and left ample room for administrative rulemaking.[48] In 1975, the secretary of health, education and welfare promulgated implementing regulations for Title IX.[49] The regulations provided that while Title IX typically required that girls and boys be measured against the same performance metric and be evaluated on the same criteria, this was not the case in the context of athletics, where a single competitive metric would largely exclude girls and women from participation. Instead, the regulations provided that "a recipient may operate or sponsor separate teams for members of each sex where selection for such teams is based upon competitive skill or the activity involved is a contact sport."[50] While the use of the word "may" in the regulations suggested that schools did not need to segregate athletic teams based on sex, an opinion letter from the OCR indicated otherwise. According to the OCR, "an institution would not be effectively accommodating the interests and abilities of women if it abolished all its women's teams and opened up its men's teams to women, but only a few women were able to qualify for the men's team."[51] Sex-segregated teams were, then, not only permissible but seemingly required in order to give female athletes

---

[45] 20 U.S.C. § 1682.
[46] Grove City Coll. v. Bell, 465 U.S. 555 (1984).
[47] Civil Rights Restoration Act of 1988, Pub. L. No. 100-259, 465 Stat. 28 (1988).
[48] In 1974, Congress enacted the Javits Amendment which required the Department of Health, Education and Welfare to propose regulations applying Title IX to college sports. *See* Education Amendments of 1974, Pub. L. No. 93-380, § 844, 88 Stat. 484, 612 (1974).
[49] 34 C.F.R. § 106.41(a) (2010). The 1975 regulations were the last to have received presidential approval. All subsequent administrative interpretations avoided this formality and lacked, as a result, the authority of the 1975 regulations. *See* MELNICK, *supra* note 3 at 43.
[50] 34 C.F.R. § 106.41(b) (2010).
[51] *See* Sex Discrimination in Athletic Programs, 40 Fed. Reg. 52,655, 52,656 (Nov. 5, 1975).

meaningful opportunities – opportunities comparable to those given to male athletes – to compete and win in sports.[52]

While the regulations did not contemplate transgender student-athletes, they did contemplate the possibility that female, or male, students might try out for teams of the other sex. This was deemed permissible if a school operated a team for individuals of one sex but not the other and "athletic opportunities for members of [the excluded] sex ha[d] previously been limited."[53] The regulation carved out an exception for contact sports, identified as "boxing, wrestling, rugby, ice hockey, football, basketball and other sports the purpose or major activity of which involves bodily contact."[54] Given such caveats, students seeking inclusion generally lost under Title IX.[55]

The implementing regulations were followed in 1979 by a Policy Interpretation promulgated by the Department of Health, Education and Welfare that gave schools guidance on how to ensure that sex-segregated athletic teams complied with Title IX.[56] The Policy Interpretation instructed that schools needed to provide male and female students with comparable athletic benefits, opportunities and scholarship aid. With regard to varsity opportunities, the Interpretation outlined three ways by which universities could show compliance with Title IX: (1) Show that male and female students are provided varsity athletic opportunities in numbers substantially proportionate to their numbers in the undergraduate population; (2) Show that where one sex is underrepresented in varsity athletics, the university can demonstrate a history and continuing practice of program expansion which is responsive to the developing interest and abilities of members of that sex; or (3) Show that the interests and abilities of the members of the underrepresented sex have been fully and effectively

---

[52] The regulations likewise made clear that sex-segregated bathrooms and locker rooms were permissible. 34 C.F.R. § 106.33 (2010).
[53] 34 C.F.R. § 106.41(b) (2010).
[54] Id.
[55] Plaintiffs did have somewhat more success under the Equal Protection Clause. See Adams By & Through Adams v. Baker, 919 F. Supp. 1496 (D. Kan. 1996) (female plaintiff challenging exclusion from wrestling team unlikely to succeed under Title IX but likely to succeed on her equal protection claim); Force by Force v. Pierce City R-VI Sch. Dist., 570 F. Supp. 1020 (W.D. Mo. 1983) (using equal protection clause to enjoin school district rule prohibiting girls from participating on high school football team); Barnett v. Texas Wrestling Ass'n., 16 F. Supp. 2d 690 (N.D. Tex. 1998) (defendants were not liable under Title IX for excluding female students from wrestling against boys but might be liable under § 1983 for equal protection violation).
[56] Title IX of the Education Amendments of 1972; a Policy Interpretation; Title IX and Intercollegiate Athletics 44 Fed. Reg. 71,413 (Dec. 11, 1979).

accommodated.[57] Courts have ruled that the implementing regulations and the Policy Interpretation are entitled to judicial deference.[58] Neither, however, provides any guidance for schools on how transgender student-athletes should be assigned to sex-segregated athletic teams.

Transgender girls' access to female sports teams became part of the culture wars during the Obama administration.[59] The Obama administration's position was clear and consistent – Title IX required schools to treat transgender girls in accordance with their gender identity.[60] The Obama administration publicized its position through a series of letters, enforcement actions and guidance documents. In a letter from James A. Ferg-Cadima, Acting Deputy Assistant for Policy, Office for Civil Rights at the Department of Education ("Letter to Emily Prince"), dated January 7, 2015, the OCR explained that while Title IX permits schools to sex-segregate students in certain contexts – for example,

---

[57] *Id.*

[58] *See* Cohen v. Brown Univ., 991 F.2d 888, 895–97 (1st Cir. 1993) (explaining with regard to the implementing regulations that "[t]he degree of deference is particularly high in Title IX cases because Congress explicitly delegated to the agency the task of prescribing standards for athletic programs under Title IX" and providing that the Policy Interpretation is also entitled to "substantial deference" "[b]ecause this document is a considered interpretation of the regulation"); *see also* Biediger v. Quinnipiac Univ., 691 F.3d 85, 96–97 (2d Cir. 2012) (explaining that Title IX's implementing regulation and the subsequent policy interpretation were entitled to a high level of deference). After enacting Title IX, Congress enacted another statute, the Javits Amendment, which instructed the Secretary of Education to publish regulations "implementing the provisions of Title IX … which shall include with respect to intercollegiate activities reasonable provisions considering the nature of the particular sports." Education Amendments of 1974, Pub. L. No. 93-380, § 844, 88 Stat. 484, 612 (1974). Congress also provided in the Javits Amendment that it would review the regulations to determine if they were "inconsistent with the act." *Id.* at 576. Congress did then review the Title IX implementing regulations over six days of hearings and allowed them to go into effect. *See* McCormick *ex rel.* McCormick v. Sch. Dist. of Mamaroneck, 370 F.3d 275, 287 (2d Cir. 2004) (outlining the history of the Javits Amendment and the Title IX implementing regulations).

[59] *See, e.g.*, Kylee Scales, *Indiana Schools, Gov. Pence React to Obama Administration's Directive on Transgender Access to School Bathrooms*, FOX 59 (May 13, 2016, 5:36 PM), https://perma.cc/Q79U-DUTB; David Blank, *Transgender Athletes May Displace Female Competitors*, INDYSTAR (June 5, 2016, 5:04 PM), https://perma.cc/NP8V-299P; Lauren Camera, *Title IX Faces Down the Culture Wars*, U.S. NEWS & WORLD REP. (Nov. 2, 2018, 6:00 AM), https://shorturl.at/jIeP8.

[60] *See* Letter to Emily T. Prince Esq. from James A. Ferg-Cadima, Acting Deputy Assistant Sec'y for Pol'y, C.R. Off., U.S. Educ Dep't (Jan. 7, 2015), https://perma.cc/ZZD6-Q8UA (hereinafter Letter to Emily Prince); Letter to Dear Colleague from Catherine E. Lhamon, Assistant Sec'y for C.R., U.S. Educ Dep't., & Vanita Gupta, Principal Dep. Assistant Att'y Gen. for C.R., U.S. Dep't of Just. (May 13, 2016), www.justice.gov/opa/file/850986/dl [https://perma.cc/GC4V-CSGR] (hereinafter 2016 Dear Colleague Letter).

"locker rooms, shower facilities, housing, athletic teams, and single-sex classes under certain circumstances ... [w]hen a school elects to separate or treat students differently on the basis of sex ... a school generally must treat transgender students consistent with their gender identity."[61]

In 2015, the OCR enforced this view in an action brought against Palatine Township School District in response to a complaint filed by a transgender girl against her high school. The student's school used her preferred name and pronouns, provided her with access to girls' restrooms and allowed her to participate in girls' sports. However, it had denied the student access to the girls' locker rooms and required the student to use a separate facility to change for gym class. The OCR concluded that the school district violated Title IX by denying the student access to the girls' locker room when the privacy of all students could be adequately protected by the installation of privacy curtains to be used by any student who wanted to be shielded from view while changing.[62]

In 2016, the Obama Departments of Justice and Education issued a Dear Colleague Letter ("2016 Dear Colleague Letter") that provided additional guidance about how it understood sex and gender and what it saw as Title IX's nondiscrimination mandate in sex-segregated contexts.[63] According to the Obama administration, gender was sex and was, effectively, the only factor that mattered. Gender trumped, indeed eviscerated, biology as a legal and social category. As the Letter explained: "The Departments treat a student's gender identity as the student's sex for purposes of Title IX and its implementing regulations."[64] Moreover, gender was a matter of self-identification, neither defined by external standards nor determined by experts. "[W]hen a student or the student's parent or guardian, as appropriate, notifies the school administration that the student will assert a gender identity that differs from previous representations or records, the school will begin treating the student consistent with the student's gender identity ... there is no medical diagnosis or treatment requirement that students must meet."[65] With regard to sex-segregated

---

[61] Letter to Emily Prince, *supra* note 60.
[62] Letter to Daniel E. Cates, Twp. High Sch. Dist. 211 from Adele Rapport, Regional Director, Region V, C.R. Off., U.S. Dep't of Educ., OCR Case No. 05-14-1055 (Nov. 2, 2015), www.ed.gov/sites/ed/files/documents/press-releases/township-high-211-letter.pdf.
[63] 2016 Dear Colleague Letter, *supra* note 60 (rescinded in 2017).
[64] *Id.* at 2. The Letter defined "Gender identity" as "an individual's internal sense of gender." *Id.* at 1.
[65] 2016 Dear Colleague Letter, *supra* note 60 at 2.

teams, therefore, transgender students were to be assigned in accordance with their gender.[66]

The Obama administrative agencies did hedge a bit – unable to ignore biology completely. While schools could not treat transgender students differently from those of the same gender identity because of stereotypes or discomfort they could, the 2016 Dear Colleague Letter explained, enact, "tailored requirements based on sound, current, and research-based medical knowledge about the impact of the students' participation on the competitive fairness or physical safety of the sport."[67] Yet the message from the Obama administration was clear: in sex-segregated contexts students must, as a general matter, be categorized by gender.

The Obama-era letters, despite their prescriptive tone and threat to withdraw Title IX funding, did not have the force of law. Having never gone through a formal notice and comment period, they were not entitled the deference accorded to administrative regulations. As the Department of Education's own website explained: "Guidance documents represent the [Department of Education's] current thinking on a topic. They do not create or confer any rights for or on any person and do not impose any requirements beyond those required under applicable law and regulations. Guidance documents lack the force and effect of law."[68] Indeed, under challenge by a district court judge in Texas about the authority of the 2016 Dear Colleague letter, the attorney for the Department of Justice responded that while the government would like schools to comply with its guidelines, they were not forced to, and if schools believed their own different "interpretation of the law is correct they can wait for initiation of an of an enforcement action and then make their argument in context of the enforcement action and they lose nothing."[69] Several states did

---

[66] *Id.* at 3 ("When a school provides sex-segregated activities and facilities, transgender students must be allowed to participate in such activities and access such facilities consistent with their gender identity").

[67] *Id.*

[68] U.S. Dep't of Educ., www2.ed.gov/policy/gen/guid/types-of-guidance-documents.html [https://perma.cc/H7NX-BW2A]. See also Perez v. Mortgage Bankers Ass'n, 575 U.S. 92, 97 (2015) (explaining that interpretive rules are easier to issue because they do not go through a formal notice-and-comment process "[b]ut that convenience comes at a price: Interpretive rules 'do not have the force and effect of law and are not accorded the weight in the adjudicatory process'") (quoting Shalala v. Guernsey Mem'l Hosp., 514 U.S. 87, 99 (1995)).

[69] See Derek Hawkins, *The Short, Troubled Life of Obama's Transgender Student Protections*, WASH. POST (Feb. 23, 2017), https://perma.cc/9T4Y-EBZ9 (describing an interaction between Department of Justice attorney Benjamin Leon Berwick and Judge O'Connor in Texas v. United States, 201 F. Supp. 3d 810 (N.D. Tex. 2016)). Judge O'Connor issued a

just that. In two separate federal lawsuits – one filed in Nebraska and the other in Texas – a total of twenty states challenged the validity of the 2016 Dear Colleague Letter.[70] A federal district court judge in Texas granted a nationwide preliminary injunction barring its enforcement as contrary to law and inappropriately issued without undergoing the notice and comment period.[71]

Upon taking office in 2016, President Trump immediately reversed course and rescinded the Obama guidance. In a Dear Colleague letter of February 22, 2017, the Trump administration criticized the Letter to Emily Prince and the 2016 Dear Colleague Letter for their lack of legal analysis. It was withdrawing the documents, the Trump administration said, "in order to further and more completely consider the legal issues involved."[72] The Letter went on to emphasize that in this context "there must be due regard for the primary role of the States and local school districts in establishing educational policy." Despite this profession of state deference, the Trump administration made its own view of Title IX clear, and the Trump administration, like the Obama administration before it, sought to enforce it.

In one such administrative action, Selina Soule, a high school track and field athlete, along with three other athletes, challenged a Connecticut Interscholastic Athletic Conference (CIAC) policy that required member schools to permit transgender girls, regardless of whether they had begun any form of medical transition, to participate on female sports teams. In an August 2020 Revised Letter of Impending Enforcement Action, the Trump administration OCR opined that assigning transgender students to the team associated with their gender identity rather than their biology was not required by Title IX, but was instead in violation

---

preliminary injunction prohibiting the federal government from enforcing the May 13, 2016, Dear Colleague Letter because it viewed the guidelines as a final agency action that failed to satisfy the notice and comment process of the Administrative Procedures Act. Texas v. United States, 201 F. Supp. 3d 810, 824 (N.D. Tex. 2016).

[70] *See* Nebraska v. United States, No. 4:16-cv-03117 (D. Neb. July 8, 2016); Texas v. United States, No. 7:16-cv-00054-O (N.D. Tex. May 25, 2016). *See also* Texas v. United States, 201 F. Supp. 3d at 824, 828 (granting preliminary injunction enjoining enforcement of the 2016 Dear Colleague Letter to the extent it required transgender access to locker rooms, showers and restrooms consistent with gender identity rather than biology).

[71] Texas v. United States, 201 F. Supp. 3d. The court ended the preliminary injunction when the plaintiffs voluntarily dismissed the lawsuit. Plaintiff's Notice of Voluntary Dismissal, Texas v. United States, No. 7:16-cv-00054 (N.D. Tex. Mar. 3, 2017).

[72] Letter to Dear Colleague from Sandra Battle, Acting Assistant Sec'y for C.R., U.S. Dep't of Educ. & T.E. Wheeler, II, Acting Assistant Att'y Gen. for C.R., U.S. Dep't of Just. (Feb. 22, 2017), https://perma.cc/69D6-4RK3.

of Title IX.[73] Such assignments, the OCR explained, violated Title IX by "denying opportunities and benefits to female student-athletes that were available to male student-athletes, including the opportunity to compete on and against teams comprised of members of one sex."[74] The Letter ended with a threat of further action to either terminate financial assistance to CIAC and the school districts or refer the cases to the US Department of Justice for judicial enforcement.[75] Before the agencies could do so, however, there was a change in executive leadership and policy.[76]

In a second enforcement action, the Trump OCR investigated a complaint filed by Concerned Women for America charging that Franklin Pierce University's policy allowing transgender women to compete on women's sports teams after one year of hormone suppression treatment violated Title IX. The OCR took the position that "[w]here separating students based on sex is permissible – for example, with respect to sex-specific sports teams – such separation must be based on biological sex."[77] In order to settle the case, Franklin Pierce agreed to a

---

[73] Revised Letter to Conn. Interscholastic Athletic Conf., et al. from Kimberly M. Richey, Acting Assistant Sec'y for C.R., U.S. Dep't of Educ., Off. For C.R. (Aug. 31, 2020), www.ed.gov/sites/ed/files/2024-09/01194025-a2.pdf (hereinafter the 2020 Revised Letter of Impending Enforcement).

[74] Id. at 37. The OCR continued that "CIAC also treated male student-athletes whose gender identity does not align with their sex more favorably than other male student-athletes, by affording them the opportunity to compete on and against teams comprised of members of the opposite sex." Id. at 37. "The athletic events in which the female student-athletes competed were coeducational; female student-athletes were denied the opportunity to compete in events that were exclusively female, whereas male student-athletes were able to compete in events that were exclusively male." Id. at 4.

[75] Id. at 48–49.

[76] The plaintiffs in the Soule case also filed suit against the CIAC in federal district court but their complaint was dismissed in April 2021 for lack of justiciability. Second Amended Verified Complaint for Declaratory and Injunctive Relief and Damages, Soule et al. v. Conn. Ass'n of Sch., Inc. et al, No. 3:20-CV-00201 (RNC), 2021 WL 1617206, at *13 (D. Conn. Apr. 25, 2021) (noting that two of the plaintiffs had graduated from high school and there was "no indication that [the remaining plaintiffs would] encounter competition by a transgender student in a CIAC-sponsored event next season"). A panel of the Second Circuit affirmed the dismissal. See Soule et al. v. Conn. Ass'n of Sch., Inc. et al, 57 F.4th 43 (2d Cir. 2022). The Second Circuit, acting en banc, subsequently vacated the dismissal and revived the case. See Soule et al. v. Conn. Ass'n of Sch., Inc. et al., 2023 WL 8656832 (2d Cir. Dec. 15, 2023).

[77] See Letter from Timothy Mattson, Compliance Team Leader, U.S. Dep't of Educ. Off. For C.R. to Kim Mooney, Pres., Franklin Pierce Univ. (Oct. 16, 2020), 4, 6, https://shorturl.at/36pyO (the letter goes on to say that "OCR has concerns that the Policy denies female student-athletes equal athletic benefits and opportunities by permitting transgender athletes to participate in women's intercollegiate athletic teams").

Resolution Agreement by which it withdrew its transgender participation and inclusion policy.[78]

In January 2021, during the waning weeks of Trump's first presidential term, his Department of Education issued its strongest statement to date. In a January 8, 2021, Memorandum ("January 2021 Memorandum"), issued in response to the Supreme Court's decision in *Bostock v. Clayton County*, the Trump Department of Education explained that it would construe the term "'sex' in Title IX to mean biological sex, male or female."[79] It went on to assert that Title IX not only permitted, but required, schools to distinguish students for the purposes of athletic teams "solely based on their biological sex, male or female, and not based on transgender status or homosexuality."[80]

With the election of President Joe Biden in 2020, there was yet another shift in administrative interpretation. Biden had long been a vocal advocate of transgender rights. While on the campaign trail, Biden had pledged to reinstate the "Obama–Biden guidance" on transgender inclusion on his first day in office.[81] Biden did not do so, but he did issue two executive orders making clear his commitment to protect transgender students from misgendering and ordering agencies to ensure that all regulations and guidance documents were consistent with this policy.[82] The Biden administration also withdrew the 2020 Revised Letter of Impending Enforcement Action against the CIAC and marked as "not for reliance" the January 2021 Memorandum.

The Biden administration began to enforce its own view of Title IX. The Biden Department of Education published its first proposed regulations on

---

[78] *See* Resolution Agreement, Franklin Pierce Univ., Case No. 01-20-2023 (Sept. 18, 2020), https://shorturl.at/OnUxm.

[79] Memorandum for Kimberly M. Richey, Acting Assistant Secretary of the Office for Civil Rights, Re: *Bostock v. Clayton Cty.*, 140 S. Ct. 1731 (2020), 4 (Jan. 8, 2021), https://shorturl.at/V1vlm.

[80] *Id.* at 7.

[81] *See* The Biden Plan to Advance LGBTQ+ Equality in America and Around the World, ACADEMIZED (Nov. 19, 2023, 5:52 PM), https://academized.com/blog/lgbtq-policy.

[82] Executive Order on Preventing and Combating Discrimination on the Basis of Gender Identity or Sexual Orientation, Exec. Order No. 13988, 86 Fed. Reg. 7023 (Jan. 20, 2021), www.federalregister.gov/documents/2021/01/25/2021-01761/preventing-and-combating-discrimination-on-the-basis-of-gender-identity-or-sexual-orientation. *See also* Executive Order on Guaranteeing an Educational Environment Free from Discrimination on the Basis of Sex, Including Sexual Orientation or Gender Identity, Exec. Order No. 14021, 86 Fed. Reg. 13803 (Mar. 8, 2021), www.federalregister.gov/documents/2021/03/11/2021-05200/guaranteeing-an-educational-environment-free-from-discrimination-on-the-basis-of-sex-including.

Title IX and invited public comment on them in July 2022. The proposed regulations disavowed as mistaken prior administrative interpretations of Title IX that limited its scope to discrimination based on biological sex. The proposed regulations explained that Title IX's antidiscrimination prohibition encompassed discrimination on the basis of "sex stereotypes, sex characteristics, pregnancy…, sexual orientation, and gender identity."[83] They also sought to clarify that "preventing any person from participating in an education program or activity consistent with their gender identity would subject them to more than de minimis harm on the basis of sex and therefore be prohibited…"[84] Yet on the issue of sex-segregated athletic teams, and how transgender students should be assigned to them, the July 2022 proposed regulations were deliberately silent, with the administration promising a separate regulation on the issue.[85]

The Biden Department of Education issued its proposed rules regarding sports in April 2023.[86] The proposed regulations did not set forth concrete eligibility rules but left open the possibility that different rules might be appropriate for different levels of competition and for different sports. What the proposed regulations did tell schools was the standard under which their eligibility rules would be judged.

First, eligibility rules that limited a transgender student's ability to play on the team consistent with their gender identity needed to serve an important educational objective. Objectives that were sufficiently important, the proposed regulations explained, included, but were not limited to, fairness of competition and prevention of sports-related injury.[87]

---

[83] Nondiscrimination on the Basis of Sex in Education Programs or Activities Receiving Federal Financial Assistance, 87 Fed. Reg. 41390, 41390, 41392 (proposed July 12, 2022) (to be codified at 34 C.F.R pt. 106), www.federalregister.gov/documents/2022/07/12/2022-13734/nondiscrimination-on-the-basis-of-sex-in-education-programs-or-activities-receiving-federal ("The Department … proposes to clarify in this section that, consistent with Bostock and other Supreme Court precedent, Title IX bars all forms of sex discrimination, including discrimination based on sex stereotypes, sex characteristics, pregnancy or related conditions, sexual orientation and gender identity").

[84] Id. at 41535.

[85] Id. The Title IX regulations went into effect on August 1, 2024, but were subsequently withdrawn by the Trump administration. See Biden Administration's Final Title IX Rule Goes into Effect Aug. 1, AM. COUNCIL ON EDUC. (Apr. 22, 2024), https://shorturl.at/FOs9K.

[86] See Nondiscrimination on the Basis of Sex in Education Programs or Activities Receiving Federal Financial Assistance: Sex-Related Eligibility Criteria for Male and Female Athletic Teams, 88 Fed. Reg. 22860 (proposed Apr. 13, 2023) (to be codified at 34 C.F.R. pt. 106), www.federalregister.gov/documents/2023/04/13/2023-07601/nondiscrimination-on-the-basis-of-sex-in-education-programs-or-activities-receiving-federal.

[87] Id. at 22867, 22873.

Maintaining sex stereotypes, conveying disapproval for transgenderism or merely maximizing administrative convenience were not important educational objectives.[88] Moreover, what constituted an important educational objective of sports was deemed different in elementary school – where the focus is primarily on fitness and health – than in high school and college – where competitive fairness becomes a weightier concern.

Second, eligibility criteria that limited a transgender student's ability to play on the team consistent with their gender identity needed to be substantially related to the identified important educational objectives and could not "rely on overly broad generalizations about the talents, capacities, or preferences of male and female students."[89] In other words, the "fit" between the means and ends needed to be tight. The proposed regulations emphasized that criteria must be nuanced and context-specific. Blanket assumptions that transgender girls would always outperform cisgender girls, for example, were not permissible.[90] Criteria needed to be based on evidence that was specific to sport, level of play and participant age.

Finally, the proposed regulations required schools to look to alternatives and minimize harm. Schools were to search for alternative criteria that would serve the same important educational objectives without limiting students' eligibility to participate in sports consistent with their gender identity.[91] To the extent that they adopted eligibility rules that limited transgender students' participation in accordance with their gender identity, schools were required to minimize harm to affected students.[92] The proposed regulations were never finalized. Indeed, the Biden–Harris administration remained silent about them during the 2024 election season.[93]

Upon his election in 2024, President Trump wasted no time reversing course and returning the administrative state to the interpretation of Title IX that existed during his first term. What his interpretation lacks in nuance, it makes up for in clarity and ease of application. On his first day

---

[88] *Id.* at 22872.
[89] *Id.* at 22873.
[90] *Id.*
[91] *Id.* at 22874.
[92] *Id.* at 22877.
[93] *See* Rachel Cohen, *The Trans School Sports Rule the Democrats Didn't Talk About*, Vox (Nov. 15, 2024, 10:00 AM) https://shorturl.at/pOSMD; John E. Johnson, *Update on Title IX and Transgender Athletic Participation*, Nat'l Fed'n of State High Sch. Ass'ns (Dec. 15, 2023) www.nfhs.org/articles/update-on-title-ix-and-transgender-athletic-participation/; Brooke Midgon, *Biden Administration Punts Deadline for Updated Title IX Regulations to March*, The Hill (Dec. 7, 2023), https://shorturl.at/OAHah.

in office, President Trump issued an executive order, asserting it to be the policy of the United States to recognize two sexes and defining boys and girls in terms of reproductive biology at birth.[94] Two weeks later, Trump issued an executive order directly addressing transgender girls' participation in girls' sports. The order, Keeping Men Out of Women's Sports, stated that women and girls were denied equal opportunity in sports when required to compete against biological boys and men and instructed the Secretary of Education to bring Title IX enforcement actions, entailing the possible loss of federal funds, against educational programs that permitted biological males to compete in women's sports.[95]

1.2 State Laws and Policy

In the face of these shifting and unstable interpretations of federal law, states have adopted their own (conflicting) laws regarding transgender girls' participation in girls' sports. A small number of states require that transgender girls be permitted to play on the team associated with their gender identity. A larger number of states prohibit their participation on girls' teams. Indeed, as of October 2025, twenty-seven states have enacted laws excluding transgender girls from girls' sports.[96] The laws typically assign students to sex-segregated athletic teams based on their biological sex at birth and/or their sex as designated in their original birth certificate.

---

[94] *See* Executive Order on Defending Women from Gender Ideology Extremism and Restoring Biological Truth to the Federal Government (Jan. 20, 2025), Exec. Order No. 14168, 90 Fed. Reg. 8615, https://shorturl.at/TB6MC (defining "female" to mean "a person belonging, at conception, to the sex that produces the large reproductive cell," defining "male" to mean "a person belonging, at conception, to the sex that produces the small reproductive cell").

[95] *See* Executive Order on Keeping Men Out of Women's Sports, Exec. Order No. 14201, 90 Fed. Reg. 9279 (Feb. 5, 2025), https://shorturl.at/AEJsc.

[96] *See* Equality Maps: Bans on Transgender Youth Participation in Sports, MOVEMENT ADVANCEMENT PROJECT, www.mapresearch.org/equality-maps/youth/sports_participation_bans. *See also* H.B. 1041 (Ind. 2025); H. File 2416 (Iowa 2022); H.B. 2238 (Kan. 2023); S.B. 83 (Ky. 2022); S.B. 2536 (Miss. 2021); H.B. 112 (Mont. 2021); S.B. 39 (Mo. 2023); H.B. 1205 (N.H. 2024); H.B. 574 (N.C. 2023); H.B. 1249 (N.D. 2023) (k-12) & H.B. 1489 (N.D. 2023) (higher ed.); H.B. 68 (Ohio 2024); S.B. 46 (S.D. 2022); H.B. 391 (Ala. 2021) (k-12) & H.B. 261 (Ala. 2023) (higher ed.); S.B. 1165 (Ariz. 2022); S.B. 354 (Ark. 2023); S.B. 1028 (Fla. 2021); H.B. 500 (Idaho 2020); S.B. 44 (La. 2022); S.B. 2 (Okla. 2022); H.B. 4608 (S.C. 2022); S.B. 0228 (Tenn. 2021) (5th–12th grades) & S.B. 2153 (Tenn. 2022) (higher ed.); H.B. 25 (Tex. 2021); H.B. 3293 (W. Va. 2021); S. File 133 (Wyo. 2023) (7th–12th grades); H.B. 11 (Utah 2022).

On the inclusionary side of the spectrum, California requires that schools permit transgender athletes to compete based solely on their gender identity. The California Education Code provides: "A pupil shall be permitted to participate in sex-segregated school programs and activities, including athletic teams and competitions, and use facilities consistent with his or her gender identity, irrespective of the gender listed on the pupil's records."[97] Massachusetts too provides that students "shall" have the opportunity to participate on the interscholastic or intramural athletic team consistent with their gender identity.[98]

Far more states are on the exclusionary side of the spectrum. Indiana's law, for example, provides: "A male, based on a student's biological sex at birth in accordance with the student's genetics and reproductive biology, may not participate on any athletic team or sport designated" as female or women's. The law applies to athletic teams organized by a public school or those organized by a nonpublic school that competes against a public school.[99]

North Dakota similarly requires that interscholastic or intramural sports teams at the K-12 level must be designated as for "male," "female" or "mixed" sexes and sex is determined by "the biological state of being female or male, based on an individual's nonambiguous sex organs, chromosomes, and endogenous hormone profile at birth."[100] North Dakota has passed a similar law restricting participation in women's sports at the college level.[101]

Texas requires students participating in interscholastic athletic competition sponsored by a school district to compete on sex-segregated athletic teams in accordance with the sex designated on a student's birth certificate "entered at or near the time of the student's birth."[102] Likewise, South Carolina's Save Women's Sports Act requires schools to maintain

---

[97] See Cal. Educ. Code §221.5(f) (West 2015). See also Assemb. B. 1266 (Cal. 2013) (requiring "that a pupil be permitted to participate in sex-segregated school programs and activities, including athletic teams and competitions, and use facilities consistent with his or her gender identity, irrespective of the gender listed on the pupil's records"). See also Unruh Civil Rights Act, Cal. Civ. Code §51 (West 2016) (barring business establishments, including public schools from discriminating on the basis of gender identity, gender expression and sex).

[98] 603 Mass. Code Regs. 26 (2023), www.mass.gov/regulations/603-CMR-2600-access-to-equal-educational-opportunity.

[99] H. Enrolled Act 1041 (Ind. 2022).

[100] H.B. 1249 (N.D. 2023).

[101] H.B. 1489 (N.D. 2023).

[102] H.B. 25 § 33.0834(c)(1) (Tex. 2021).

separate sex-specific athletic teams and provides that students be assigned to such teams based on their official birth certificate filed at or near the time of the student's birth.[103] Florida's Fairness in Women's Sports Act imposes the same requirements.[104]

Schools must comply not only with state laws, but also with the requirements of athletic governing bodies. For elementary and secondary schools these are generally state athletic associations. Sometimes these associational rules simply restate or supplement state laws that already exist. The California Interscholastic Federation policy, for example, provides that "[a]ll students should have the opportunity to participate in CIF activities in a manner that is consistent with their gender identity, irrespective of the gender listed on a student's records."[105] In many places, however, state laws do not exist, and state athletic organizations have filled the void.

A number of state athletic associations have adopted broadly inclusive eligibility rules for girls' sports similar to California's state law. The Washington State Interscholastic Activities Association, for example, provides in its statement of policy regarding gender identity and athletic participation: "All students should have the opportunity to participate in ... athletics and/or activities in a manner that is consistent with their gender identity ... Athletes will participate in programs consistent with their gender identity or the gender most consistently expressed."[106] The rule set forth by the Rhode Island Interscholastic League (RIIL) is similar, though perhaps even stronger in its requirement of inclusion. The RIIL states in its Rules & Regulations that it "has concluded that it would be fundamentally unjust and contrary to applicable state and federal laws, to preclude a student from participation on a gender specific sports team that is consistent with the public gender identity of that student for all other purposes."[107] The rules of the CIAC follow the same approach. The CIAC provides:

> It would be fundamentally unjust and contrary to applicable state and federal law to preclude a student from participation on a gender specific sports team that is consistent with the public gender identity of that student for all

---

[103] H.B. 4608 (S.C. 2022).
[104] S.B. 1028 (Fla. 2021).
[105] *See* Guidelines for Gender Identity Participation, CAL. INTERSCHOLASTIC FED'N, https://shorturl.at/CJ6Mn.
[106] Gender Diverse Youth Sport Inclusivity Toolkit, WASH. INTERSCHOLASTIC ACTIVITIES ASS'N 8, https://shorturl.at/5bC5s.
[107] Rules & Regulations, Art. 3, § 3(B) (2022), R.I. INTERSCHOLASTIC LEAGUE, https://shorturl.at/ROEGk.

other purposes. Therefore, for purposes of sports participation, the CIAC shall defer to the determination of the student and his or her local school regarding gender identification.[108]

Other state associations are more restrictive, either requiring more specific forms of documentation, more extensive forms of medical treatment or satisfaction of biological markers before transgender girls can participate in girls' sports. The Virginia High School League, for example, provides that transgender students may (not must) be permitted to play on the team consistent with their gender identity if any one of three conditions are met: (1) The student "has undergone sex reassignment before puberty"; (2) The student "is verified by appropriate medical documentation as having a consistent identity different than the gender listed on the student's official birth certificate or school registration records"; or (3) The student has undergone "hormonal therapy appropriate for the assigned sex ... administered in a verifiable manner and for a sufficient length of time to minimize gender-related advantages in sports competition."[109] The Missouri State High School Transgender Participation Policy requires one year of documented testosterone suppression treatment before transgender girls are eligible to play on female teams.[110] Until recently, the Wisconsin Interscholastic Athletic Association had a similar policy requiring "one calendar year of medically documented testosterone suppression therapy" for transgender females who wished to participate on a female team.[111] In 2025, however, in response to President Trump's

---

[108] Reference Guide for Transgender Policy, CONN. INTERSCHOLASTIC ATHLETIC CONF., www.transathlete.com/_files/ugd/2bc3fc_a86a597d90a84de690bb2349e0b3cdba.pdf. *See also* 2024-2025 Oregon School Activities Association Handbook, OR. SCH. ACTIVITIES ASS'N 82, www.osaa.org/docs/handbooks/osaahandbook.pdf ("once a transgender student has notified the student's school of their gender identity (boy or girl), the student shall consistently participate as that gender for purposes of eligibility for athletics and activities, provided that if the student has tried out or participated in an activity, the student may not participate during that same season on a team of the other gender"); Vermont Principals' Association Athletic Policies, Policy on Gender Identity, GOOGLE DOCS 4, https://shorturl.at/qpuoO ("The VPA is committed to providing all students with the opportunity to participate in VPA activities in a manner consistent with their gender identity").

[109] Criteria for VHSL Transgender Rule Appeals, VA. HIGH SCH. LEAGUE (May 19, 2021, 4:53 PM), www.vhsl.org/eligibility/.

[110] *See* Dr. Kerwin Urhahn, MSHSAA Executive Director, *2021-2022 Official Handbook, Board Policy on Transgender Participation*, MO. STATE HIGH SCH. ACTIVITIES ASS'N (July 2021) at 136, www.transathlete.com/_files/ugd/2bc3fc_f294075ae2454966b17aba266fccad60.pdf.

[111] Wisconsin Interscholastic Athletic Association Transgender Participation Policy, www.transathlete.com/_files/ugd/2bc3fc_95ec28cdb3ee4df89ee624229b9caa48.pdf.

executive order barring transgender girls from girls' sports, the Wisconsin Interscholastic Athletic Association changed its policy to categorically exclude transgender girls from girls' sports.[112]

At the college level, most four-year colleges are members of the National Collegiate Athletic Association (NCAA) and are governed by its rules.[113] In 2022, the NCAA followed the International Olympic Committee (IOC) in adopting a sport-by-sport approach to transgender inclusion.[114] Participation criteria for transgender student-athletes would be determined by the policy for the national governing body of each sport. In response to NCAA policy, a number of athletic governing bodies moved to revise or enact their own policies for transgender student participation. Generally, these policies distinguish between elite and non-elite athletics, imposing restrictions on transgender females in the former while being more inclusive in the latter. In June 2022 World Aquatics, which sets rules for elite swimming competitions, including the Olympics, adopted a policy that would allow transgender women to compete in women's events "if they have not experienced any part of male puberty ... or before age 12, whichever is later."[115] USA Swimming's

---

[112] Wisconsin Interscholastic Athletic Association ("WIAA") Participation Policy for Transgender Student-Athletes (Feb. 19, 2025), www.wiaawi.org/Portals/0/PDF/Eligibility/WIAAtransgenderpolicy.pdf.

[113] The NCAA is made up of three divisions with over 1,000 member schools. The National Association of Intercollegiate Athletics is significantly smaller, consisting mostly of small, private colleges. There are also separate conferences for junior colleges and community colleges. *See* Comparing Competition Levels in College Sports, FIELDLEVEL (Mar. 18, 2020), https://shorturl.at/BHwiZ.

[114] *See* Participation Policy for Transgender Student-Athletes, NCAA (Jan. 27, 2022), www.ncaa.org/sports/2022/1/27/transgender-participation-policy.aspx.

The 2022 policy replaced the NCAA's 2010 policy, which required one year of testosterone suppression for transgender females who wished to participate on a women's team. *See* 2010 NCAA Policy on Transgender Student-Athlete Participation, NCAA, https://ncaaorg.s3.amazonaws.com/inclusion/lgbtq/INC_TransgenderStudentAthleteParticipationPolicy.pdf. The IOC too deferred to the governing bodies of each sport to determine eligibility rules but set forth a general framework or approach for those governing bodies to use in developing their criteria – a framework that stressed the importance of ensuring that everyone is able to participate in sports "safely and without prejudice." IOC Framework on Fairness, Inclusion and Non-Discrimination on the Basis of Gender Identity and Sex Variations, INT'L OLYMPIC COMM. (Nov. 22, 2021), https://stillmed.olympics.com/media/Documents/Beyond-the-Games/Human-Rights/IOC-Framework-Fairness-Inclusion-Non-discrimination-2021.pdf.

[115] Policy on Eligibility for the Men's and Women's Competition Categories, WORLD AQUATICS (Mar. 24, 2023), https://resources.fina.org/fina/document/2023/03/27/dbc3381c-91e9-4ea4-a743-84c8b06debef/Policy-on-Eligibility-for-the-Men-s-and-Women-s-Competiition-Categrories-Version-on-2023.03.24.pdf.

rules provide that at non-elite levels transgender swimmers may compete in accordance with their gender identity, but, at the elite level, transgender female athletes need to show testosterone levels less than 5 nmol/L for at least thirty-six months.[116] Similarly, USA Volleyball's policy allows transgender female athletes age twelve and under to play on a female team without restriction while imposing testosterone requirements for athletes age thirteen and over.[117] USA Gymnastics' policy is expansive at the non-elite level, allowing transgender athletes to compete in the gender category with which they identify without restriction. At the elite level, USA Gymnastics deferred to the International Gymnastics Federation, which did not, as of October 2025, have a transgender inclusion policy, or to the IOC, which itself sought to defer to the sports' own governing bodies.[118]

1.3 Courts

Courts are, of course, the final arbiters of when eligibility rules for sex-segregated school sports teams are permissible. Their role has become even more critical after the Supreme Court's 2024 decision in *Loper Bright Enterprises v. Raimondo*.[119] In *Loper Bright* the Supreme Court made clear that courts could not simply defer to administrative agency interpretations of vague statutes. What had been termed "Chevron deference," after the Supreme Court's influential decision in *Chevron v. Natural Resources Defense Council*, no longer existed.[120] It was the role of courts, not administrative agencies, to determine the proper interpretation of any

---

[116] *Athlete Inclusion, Competitive Equity, and Eligibility Policy*, USA SWIMMING (Mar. 10, 2023), https://shorturl.at/LAxCg.

[117] USA Volleyball rules provide that athletes aged thirteen to eighteen must have testosterone levels "within normal female reference range (for the age range) for a minimum of 6 months preceding the application to participate." Athletes eighteen and over must have testosterone levels "less than 10 nmol/L for a minimum of 1 year prior to the application to participate." Gender Competition Guidelines (2024–25 Season), USA VOLLEYBALL, https://usavolleyball.org/about/gender-guidelines/.

[118] Policy for Transgender & Non-Binary Athlete Inclusion, USA GYMNASTICS (updated Apr. 2022), https://static.usagym.org/PDFs/About%20USA%20Gymnastics/transgender_policy.pdf.

[119] Loper Bright Enterprises v. Raimondo, 144 S.Ct. 2244 (2024).

[120] *Id.* at 2263 ("The deference that *Chevron* requires of courts reviewing agency action cannot be squared with the APA [Administrative Procedure Act]"). *Chevron* deference referred to the Court's pronouncement in *Chevron, U.S.A., Inc. v. Natural Resources Defense Council, Inc.*, 467 U.S. 837 (1984), that when a statute was silent or ambiguous on an issue a court should defer to administrative agency interpretation.

given statute.[121] Eligibility rules for girls' sports must be consistent with the antidiscrimination demands of Title IX and, to the extent the rules are required by state law, with the Equal Protection Clause of the Fourteenth Amendment.

The most thorough analysis to date of both Title IX and Equal Protection claims comes from the Fourth Circuit in the case of *B.P.J. by Jackson v. West Virginia Board of Education*.[122] The case involved an as applied challenge by a thirteen-year-old transgender girl to West Virginia's "Save Women's Sports Bill," which defined sex in terms of biology at birth and barred all transgender girls and women from women's sports.[123] The district court granted the plaintiff's motion for preliminary injunction, but subsequently dissolved it and granted summary judgment to the state.[124] With regard to the plaintiff's equal protection claim, the district court held the statute survived intermediate scrutiny because "[t]he legislature's definition of 'girl' as being based on 'biological sex' is substantially related to the important government interest of providing equal athletic opportunities for females."[125] The statute survived the plaintiff's Title IX challenge because, according to the district court, requiring transgender students to play on the team associated with their biological sex was precisely the kind of categorization that Title IX permitted.[126]

On appeal, the Fourth Circuit vacated the ruling in favor of the state on plaintiff's equal protection clause. Like the district court, the circuit court concluded that intermediate scrutiny was warranted. The Fourth Circuit explained that the state statute constituted a sex-based classification both because it divided sports teams into those for boys and those for girls, and also because it treated transgender girls (those male at birth) differently than transgender boys (those female at birth). The former were not permitted to play on the team associated with their gender identity while the latter were.[127] The court then asked whether the statute as applied to *B.P.J.* was substantially related to an important government interest. Significantly, the court noted that the state did not have an important

---

[121] *Id.* at 2273 (holding that "courts need not and under the APA may not defer to an agency interpretation of the law simply because a statute is ambiguous").

[122] B.P.J. by Jackson v. W. Virginia State Bd. of Educ., 98 F.4th 542 (4th Cir. 2024), cert granted 2025 WL 1829164 (July 3, 2025).

[123] *Id.*

[124] B.P.J. v. West Virginia State Bd. of Educ., 649 F.Supp.3d 220 (S.D. W. Va. 2023).

[125] *Id.* at 232.

[126] *Id.* at 233.

[127] B.P.J. by Jackson, 98 F.4th at 556.

interest in maintaining biological categories in sports per se. That is, the mere desire to maintain sex-based classifications could not itself constitute an important state interest. Instead the state's interest, in order to be sufficiently important, had to be tied to participant safety and competitive fairness. The defendant was not entitled to summary judgment, the court concluded, because the plaintiff had raised a genuine issue of material fact about whether a transgender girl like the plaintiff, who had not gone through male puberty, nonetheless had a meaningful competitive advantage over cisgender girls.

With regard to the plaintiff's Title IX claim, the Fourth Circuit reversed the trial court entirely. It was the plaintiff who was entitled to summary judgment because she was treated differently on the basis of sex and suffered harm as a result.[128] Yet the court made clear that the scope of its holding was narrow and particularized. Title IX did not always bar the exclusion of transgender girls from girls' sports, but it did bar the exclusion of this transgender girl who had not undergone male puberty.[129]

The Fourth Circuit's Title IX analysis was consistent with that of the district court in the prior case of *A.M. v. Indianapolis Public Schools*.[130] The case involved a challenge by a ten-year-old transgender girl to a 2022 Indianapolis law categorically banning transgender girls from girls' athletic teams.[131] The plaintiff had been living as a girl since she was four years old and was known at school only as a girl. She had played on her public school's girls' softball team in 4th grade, but had been told that because of the new law, she would not be permitted to play on the girls' team in 5th grade. The district court granted A.M.'s motion for preliminary injunction, holding that she was likely to "succeed on the merits of her Title IX claim."[132] Like the Fourth Circuit, the district court in *A.M.* held that the Indiana law impermissibly discriminated on the basis of sex by barring transgender girls but not cisgender girls from participating on the team associated with their gender identity,[133] and by barring transgender girls but not transgender boys from participating on the team associated with their gender identity.[134]

---

[128] *Id.*
[129] *Id.* at 565.
[130] A.M. by E.M. v. Indianapolis Pub. Sch., 617 F. Supp.3d 950 (S.D. Ind. 2022).
[131] *See* Ind. Code Ann. § 20-33-13-4 (West 2022).
[132] *A.M.*, 617 F. Supp.3d at 965–66.
[133] *Id.* at 966.
[134] *Id.*

Congress could, of course, amend Title IX so as to extinguish transgender girls' statutory claims. Indeed, Republican lawmakers are seeking to do just that. In January, 2025, just a week before President Trump's inauguration, the Republican-led House of Representatives voted to amend Title IX to make federal education funding explicitly dependent on school's exclusion of transgender girls from girls' sports.[135] The Act has not, as of early 2025, passed in the Senate.

Yet even if transgender girls' statutory claims were eliminated, their equal protection claims challenging state laws would remain. Several courts, in addition to the Fourth Circuit, have addressed such claims and found them strong. In *Hecox v. Little*, for example, an Idaho district court found the plaintiffs were likely to succeed on the merits of their constitutional challenge to the state's Fairness in Women's Sport Act, which categorically barred transgender girls and women from women's sports.[136] The Ninth Circuit agreed. The circuit court held that classifications based on sex and transgender status triggered intermediate scrutiny. It then agreed with the district court that the plaintiffs were likely to succeed on the merits of their constitutional challenge because the state "failed to adduce any evidence demonstrating that the Act is substantially related to its asserted interests in sex equality and opportunity for women athletes."[137] The categorical ban on transgender girls' participation, without regard to age or level of play, simply was not narrowly tailored enough to the state's interests in promoting fairness in female sports.

The district court of Utah reached a similar conclusion when analyzing a challenge brought under Utah's uniform operation of laws clause, the state constitution's counterpart to the federal Equal Protection Clause.[138] In *Roe v. Utah High School Activities Association*, transgender girls challenged a Utah statute that barred transgender girls from competing in school-related girls' sports.[139] The statute also provided that if

---

[135] *See* Protection of Women and Girls in Sports Act of 2023, H.R. 734, 118th Cong., 1st Sess. (2023), www.congress.gov/bill/118th-congress/house-bill/734/text. As of April 2025, the Act had not been passed by the Senate.

[136] Hecox v. Little, 479 F. Supp. 3d 930 (D. Idaho 2020). The lawsuit was brought by both transgender and cisgender women athletes because the Idaho statute not only barred all transgender girls and women from participating in public school female sports teams, but also included a sex dispute verification process allowing individuals to challenge the sex of athletes participating in female sports.

[137] Hecox v. Little, 104 F.4th 1061, 1068 (9th Cir. 2024), cert granted 2025 WL 1829165 (July 3, 2025).

[138] Roe v. Utah High School Activities Ass'n, 2022 WL 3907182 at *4 (Utah Dist. Ct. Aug. 19, 2022).

[139] *Id.* at *1.

the ban on transgender participation was enjoined "a commission will be established to consider confidentially, for each transgender girl who seeks to compete in school athletics, whether it would [sic] fair to permit that transgender girl to compete on girls' teams."[140] The plaintiffs did not object to this part of the statute. In granting the plaintiffs' motion for preliminary injunction, the court held that the statute, by classifying students based on transgender status, classified them based on sex, thereby warranting heightened scrutiny. The court then concluded that the statute could not withstand heightened scrutiny because the categorical ban was not based on evidence showing "that transgender girls have an automatic physiological advantage over other girls" and was not "the least restrictive method of furthering the law's stated purpose" of protecting fairness of girls' sports.[141] Indeed, as the court noted, a less restrictive alternative was provided for in the statute.

Level of scrutiny is critical for equal protection challenges, and not all courts agree that heightened scrutiny is appropriate. In *D.N. v. DeSantis*, a Florida district court dismissed an equal protection challenge to its Fairness in Women's Sports Act making two critical, and distinctive, holdings.[142] First, the court held that the law was subject to rational review not heightened scrutiny because the Eleventh Circuit, unlike some other circuits, did not treat transgender status as a suspect class and because transgender discrimination was not itself a form of sex discrimination. The court then concluded that the statute survived under this highly deferential standard because it served the state's legitimate interest in excluding "'biological males from girls' sports teams'" and was not motivated by invidious intent.[143] In July 2025, the Supreme Court granted cert in *Hecox* and *B.P.J.* to address the question of whether laws that exclude transgender girls from girls' sports violate the Equal Protection Clause of the Fourteenth Amendment.[144] The Supreme Court heard oral arguments in these cases in January 2026, just as this book was going to press.

1.4 Conclusion

The legal landscape governing transgender girls' eligibility for girls' sports has been unstable over time, inconsistent across place and dizzying in its

---

[140] *Id.*
[141] *Id.* at 7–8.
[142] D.N. by Jessica N. v. DeSantis, 2024 WL 5165857 (S.D. Fla. Dec. 19, 2024).
[143] *Id.* at *14.
[144] West Virginia v. B.P.J., 2025 WL 1829164 (July 3, 2025); Little v. Hecox, 2025 WL 1829165 (July 3, 2025).

complexity. Since 2009, schools have not simply been required to serve multiple masters with different views but masters who are themselves changing views. The legal landscape has been so chaotic, in part because Title IX's antidiscrimination mandate simply does not require particular eligibility rules. It is, instead, at least plausibly consistent with a range of possible eligibility rules for women's sports. The result has been interpretative whiplash at the administrative level.

The equal protection clause provides some check on possible eligibility rules. Yet the equal protection clause, like Title IX, does not require or draw particular eligibility rules, it only narrows the range of the plausible by excluding the impermissible. Moreover, it is judges who must draw this line by deciding which state interests are sufficiently weighty and which costs may appropriately be born. In other words, far from positive law being determinative of the boundaries of women's sports, the drawing of lines and eligibility rules is, and must be, a political determination kept in check by a legal process necessarily imbued with value judgments about the importance of state goals and acceptable costs.

2

The Science

If law alone cannot answer the question of how transgender girls should be assigned to sex-segregated sports teams, perhaps science can help. This chapter explores the scientific connection between sex and sport. It begins by examining the meaning of sex and the criteria used to assign individuals to the male or female category. It ends by exploring the link between sex and sport and identifying the sex-related traits that have the greatest impact on athletic performance.

2.1 Sex

Sex refers to the physical and anatomical features that differ between males and females. Some scholars and scientists focus exclusively on gametes, the cells by which humans reproduce themselves, as the way to define and determine sex. Debra Soh, a neuroscientist, argues, for example, that sex should be defined not by chromosomes, genitals or hormones but by gametes.[1] Evolutionary biologist Carole Hooven explains the reason for this focus in more detail. "What do all males (or females) have in common?" she asks, "[I]t's the relative size of the sex cells or gametes. Males produce small, mobile gametes (sperm), and females produce larger, immobile gametes (eggs)."[2]

Other scholars take a more holistic approach to sex, looking at chromosomes, gonads and gametes, hormones, secondary sex characteristics and genitalia. Bioethicist Alice Dreger, for example, refers to sex as "the conglomeration of anatomical and physiological features that differ between typical females and males."[3] Professors of Women's Studies and Sexuality Rebecca Jordan-Young and Katrina Karkazis, authors of *Testosterone: An*

---

[1] DEBRA SOH, THE END OF GENDER: DEBUNKING THE MYTHS ABOUT SEX AND IDENTITY IN OUR SOCIETY 17 (Threshold ed. 2020).
[2] CAROLE HOOVEN, T: THE STORY OF TESTOSTERONE, THE HORMONE THAT DOMINATES AND DIVIDES US 61 (2021).
[3] Alice Dreger, *Sex Typing for Sport*, 40 HASTINGS CENTER REPORT 22, 22 (2010).

Unauthorized Biography, identify "at least six markers of sex – including chromosomes, gonads, hormones, secondary sex characteristics, [and] external genitalia..."[4] Biologist Sari van Anders takes a similar approach, explaining that "a number of factors make up sex, including genes, reproductive accessories, gonads, hormones, genitals, reproductive potential, secondary sex characteristics and more."[5]

As to each individual factor, as well as to the factors taken as a group, the overwhelming majority of people fall clearly into a female or male category. With regard to chromosomes, people typically have either forty-six XX chromosomes (female) or forty-six XY chromosomes (male). With regard to gametes, people typically have ovaries that produce eggs (females) or testes that produce sperm (males). With regard to hormones, people typically have testosterone levels between 0.5 and 2.4 nmol/L (females) or between 10 and 35 nmol/L (males).[6] With regard to physical features, people typically have breasts and a vagina (females) or they have facial hair and a penis (males).

In recent years, there has been increasing awareness of intersex conditions, also called disorders (or differences) of sexual development. These are conditions that cause an individual to either not fit squarely into either the male or the female category on a particular factor or to be categorized inconsistently across factors. Klinefelter Syndrome, which causes individuals to have XXY chromosomes and testosterone levels that are lower than average for men is an example of the former.[7] So is Turner syndrome in which individuals have one normal X chromosome and a second X chromosome that is missing, partially missing or changed. Complete androgen insensitivity syndrome (AIS) and 5-alpha reductase deficiency (ARD) are examples of the latter. Individuals with complete androgen insensitivity have XY chromosomes and testes. However, because they lack androgen receptors their bodies develop to look more typically female.[8] Individuals with 5-ARD also have XY chromosomes and testes but because of the lack enzyme 5, babies with 5-ARD have genitals that look more female-typical, though

---

[4] Rebecca M. Jordan-Young & Katrina Karkazis, Testosterone: An Unauthorized Biography 128 (2019).
[5] Sari M. van Anders et al., *Biological Sex, Gender, and Public Policy*, 4 Policy Insights Behav. Brain Sci. 194, 194–95 (2017).
[6] *See Testosterone Information*, Mount Sinai: Health Library, www.mountsinai.org/health-library/tests/testosterone.
[7] Dreger, *supra* note 3 at 23.
[8] *Id.* at 23.

in adolescence they go through a male-typical puberty. As Dreger explains, "[t]he child undergoes a male-typical puberty: the child's muscles, hair, and voice become those typical of males, and the phallus, once more like a clitoris, grows larger, to look more like a penis."[9] There are many more intersex conditions, indeed current counts are of around forty such conditions.[10]

Estimates of the number of individuals born with intersex conditions are imprecise both for definitional and record-keeping reasons. The United Nations cites estimates of 1.7 percent of the population as having intersex conditions.[11] Soh puts the number lower at about 1 percent.[12] This is consistent with the estimates of Law Professor Doriane Lambelet Coleman who contends that

> [a]lthough there is some dispute at the margins, it is generally accepted that anomalies arise in one per 1,500 births; in other words, more than 99% of the time, an individual's biological sex traits are fully concordant: their genetic sex (XX or XY), gonad sex (hormonal activity), and phenotypic sex (external genitalia) are all either typically male or typically female, and the individual is identified accordingly at birth.[13]

Some scholars point to the existence of intersex conditions as evidence that there are more than two sexes. In a widely read article from 1993, sexologist Anne Fausto-Sterling, for example, argued that society should recognize five sexes. She referred to the five sexes as male, female, herms, "who possess one testis and one ovary," merms, "who have testes and some aspect of the female genitalia but no ovaries," and ferms, "who have ovaries and some aspects of the male genitalia but lack testes."[14] In a follow-up article seven years later, Fausto-Sterling said her argument for a five-sex

---

[9] *Id.*

[10] HELEN JOYCE, TRANS: WHEN IDEOLOGY MEETS REALITY 13 (2021) (explaining that intersex or disorders of sex development (DSD) is "an umbrella term for around forty different developmental conditions of the genitalia and gonads").

[11] *Intersex People: OHCHR and the Human Rights of LGBTI People*, UNITED NATIONS, www.ohchr.org/en/sexual-orientation-and-gender-identity/intersex-people#:~:text=Experts%20estimate%20that%20up%20to,of%20intersex%20human%20rights%20defenders.

[12] SOH, *supra* note 1 at 25.

[13] Doriane Lambelet Coleman, *Sex in Sport*, 80 LAW & CONTEMP. PROBS. 63, 82–83 (2017). *See also* Dillon E. King, *The Inclusion of Sex and Gender beyond the Binary in Toxicology*, 4 FRONT. TOXICOL. (2022) (estimating that intersex individuals comprise 1–2 percent of the US population if one includes such conditions as "Klinefelter syndrome, Turner syndrome, and late-onset adrenal hyperplasia," and around 0.02 percent of the population if these conditions are excluded).

[14] Anne Fausto-Sterling, *The Five Sexes*, 33 THE SCIENCES 20, 21 (1993).

system was meant to be provocative and was made with "tongue firmly in cheek."[15] Yet her rejection of the idea that human beings are dimorphic remained strong and her commitment to the view of sex as on a spectrum remained intact.[16] Alice Dreger similarly argues that the sexual binary is a social construct imposed on a more complicated reality. According to Dreger, "[n]ature doesn't draw the line for us between male and female, or between male and intersex and female and intersex; we actually draw that line on nature ... these categories that we thought of as stable anatomical categories, that mapped very simply to stable identity categories are a lot more fuzzy than we thought."[17]

Others argue that the existence of intersex conditions does not change the binary nature of sex. Scholars like Soh, Hooven and Joyce emphasize that human reproduction results from two gametes: sperm which are produced by males and eggs which are produced by females, and because there are only two gametes, human sex is by definition binary. Soh explains: "There are no intermediate types of gametes between eggs and sperm cells. Sex is therefore binary. It is not a spectrum."[18] For Hooven, the analysis is similarly clear-cut. "The facts," she explains, "are that there are ... two sexes ... there are male and female, and those sexes are designated by the kinds of gametes we produce."[19] Joyce expands the point beyond humans. "Sexual dimorphism," she explains, "first appeared on Earth 1.2 billion years ago. Mammals – animals like humans that grow their young inside them, rather than laying eggs – date back 210 million years. In all that time, no mammal has ever changed sex."[20]

Yet even if one defines sex by looking at a range of factors beyond gametes alone, rejecting sexual dimorphism makes sense only if one ignores the (in)frequency of intersex conditions. Coleman makes this point

---

[15] Anne Fausto-Sterling, *The Five Sexes, Revisited*, 40 THE SCIENCES 18, 19 (2000).
[16] *Id.* at 22.
[17] Alice Dreger, *Is Anatomy Destiny?*, TEDxNORTHWESTERNU (Dec. 2010), www.ted.com/talks/alice_dreger_is_anatomy_destiny.
[18] SOH, *supra* note 1 at 17. *Cf.* SOH, *supra* note 1 at 25 (Soh recognizes that individuals with the condition ovotestis do possess both ovarian and testicular tissue, but she explains that "[i]n most cases, however, only one type of tissue is functional; their ovaries will produce eggs, but their testes are unable to produce sperm. This condition is extremely rare, occurring in 1 in 20,000 births").
[19] Carole K. Hooven, *Academic Freedom is Social Justice: Sex, Gender, and Cancel Culture on Campus*, 52 ARCH. SEX. BEHAV. 35, 35, 37 (2023).
[20] JOYCE, *supra* note 10 at 4, 13 (Joyce goes on to argue that "for humans, as for all mammals, individuals are of one sex or the other, and that sex is immutable and determined at conception. The existence of 'intersex' conditions or disorders of sex development (DSDs) ... does not alter this").

forcefully. She explains that the view of sex as fluid or falling on a spectrum "is most persuasive when only difference not incidence is plotted, and when we ignore that this incidence is not just noise. That is, if one imagines three people, one sex-typical female, one intersex person, and one sex-typical male. The rendering is persuasive. Once incidence is factored in, however, the impression that sex is binary is difficult to ignore."[21] In other words, to use a common analogy: the fact that a small number of people are born without ten fingers does not change the fact that humans are a ten fingered species; similarly, the fact that a few people are born with atypical sex characteristics does not change the fact that humans are sexually dimorphic.[22]

While intersex people may themselves, at times, be difficult to categorize into binary sex categories and may even problematize traditional thinking about sex as binary, transgendered individuals are not intersexed. Transgenderism refers to a mismatch between an individual's gender and their sex, not to ambiguity or inconsistency within or among one's identifying sex traits. As the American Psychological Association explains: "Transgender is an umbrella term for persons whose gender identity, gender expression or behavior does not conform to that typically associated with the sex to which they were assigned at birth."[23]

The term transgender is expansive and flexible. "[B]eing transgender is not dependent upon physical appearance or medical procedures. A person can call themselves transgender the moment they realize that their gender identity is different than the sex they were assigned at birth."[24] Indeed, as Transgender Archives founder Cristan Williams explains, the term describes "a range of gender-variant identities and communities."[25] According to the American Psychological Association,

---

[21] Coleman, *supra* note 13 at 115.

[22] JOYCE, *supra* note 10 at 65 ("As with any part of the body, reproductive organs may develop in anomalous ways, just as some people are born with extra fingers or toes, or missing eyes or legs, but humans are still ten-fingered and ten-toed, binocular and bipedal. For there to be even three sexes there would have to be a third gamete, and there is not"); SOH, *supra* note 1 at 26 ("An analogy that helps illustrate this point [that sex is binary] is the fact that most of us have ten fingers. Some people have fewer or more than ten digits on their hands, but this hasn't led to a reconceptualization of how many fingers human beings have").

[23] *Understanding Transgender People, Gender Identity and Gender Expression*, AM. PSYCH. ASS'N (July 8, 2024), https://shorturl.at/dEx7W.

[24] *Glossary of Terms: Transgender*, GLAAD MEDIA REFERENCE GUIDE 11TH ED. (2022), https://glaad.org/reference/trans-terms.

[25] Erin Blakemore, *How Historians are Documenting the Lives of Transgender People*, NATIONAL GEOGRAPHIC (June 24, 2022), https://tinyurl.com/2s3j5hwp (noting that scholars trace the origins of the term to the 1960s).

the term encompasses people who are transsexual (those who wish to alter their bodies to make them congruent with their gender identities), those who cross-dress (wear clothing stereotypically worn by a different gender), drag queens ("men who dress as women for the purpose of entertaining others"), those who are genderqueer ("people who identify their gender as falling outside the binary constructs of 'male' and 'female'"), as well as those who are androgynous, multigendered, gender nonconforming, third gender and two-spirit people.[26]

The term is not a medical diagnosis, though it has been associated with a variety of conditions over the years. Published in 1980, the Diagnostic and Statistical Manual of Mental Disorders (DSM)-III first included the term transsexualism under Gender Identity Disorders. The DSM-III defined transsexualism as "a persistent sense of discomfort and inappropriateness about one's anatomic sex and a persistent wish to be rid of one's genitals and to live as a member of the other sex."[27] The diagnosis was only appropriate if the "disturbance ... is not associated with physical intersex or genetic abnormality."[28] The DSM-IV, published in 1994, replaced transsexualism with the term gender identity disorder, which it similarly defined as "persistent discomfort about one's assigned sex or a sense of inappropriateness in the gender role of that sex" not attributable to a physical intersex condition.[29] The DSM-V, released in 2013, replaced gender identity disorder with "gender dysphoria," which it explained as "[a] marked incongruence between one's experienced/expressed gender and assigned gender, of at least 6 months duration."[30] The DSM-V further made clear that it was gender dysphoria, or distress, that was the clinical problem, not gender nonconformity per se.[31] Transgendered, the DSM-V explained, was not itself a diagnostic category, but referred to "the broad spectrum of individuals who transiently or persistently identify with a gender different from their natal gender."[32]

---

[26] *Answers to Your Questions about Transgender People, Gender Identity, and Gender Expression*, AM. PSYCH. ASS'N (2014), www.apa.org/topics/lgbtq/transgender.pdf.
[27] AMERICAN PSYCHIATRIC ASSOCIATION, DIAGNOSTIC AND STATISTICAL MANUAL OF MENTAL DISORDERS 262 (3d ed. 1980), https://shorturl.at/a5BaX.
[28] *Id.*
[29] AMERICAN PSYCHIATRIC ASSOCIATION, DIAGNOSTIC AND STATISTICAL MANUAL OF MENTAL DISORDERS 533 (4th ed. 1994).
[30] AMERICAN PSYCHIATRIC ASSOCIATION, DIAGNOSTIC AND STATISTICAL MANUAL OF MENTAL DISORDERS 452 (5th ed. 2013), https://shorturl.at/FIoPzhttps://shorturl.at/MoUJl.
[31] *Id.* at 451. *See also Gender Dysphoria Diagnosis*, AM. PSYCH. ASS'N (Nov. 2017).
[32] AMERICAN PSYCHIATRIC ASSOCIATION, *supra* note 30 at 451.

Transgender girls, unless they have a distinct disorder of sexual development, are not intersexed – their sexual characteristics are male. They are transgendered because their biological markers differ from how they experience their gender identity. Of course, with medical intervention, transgender girls and women may change some of the biological markers associated with sex – namely their hormones and their bodies – to be more consistent with the female category with which they identify. The next section explores the effect that sex, or more accurately, specific sex markers, have on athletic performance.

2.2 Sex and Athletic Performance

The performance gap between male and female athletes becomes both significant and stable post puberty. After that point, male athletes outperform female athletes in most contests. Data on the timing and breadth of the gap is extensive and uncontested. There is also considerable agreement about the reasons why it exists.

Before puberty, males do not have a significant advantage over females in competitive sports.[33] It is at puberty that the sex-based performance gap arises. David Handelsman has studied age-based sex differences in athletic performance in order to identify "the timing of the gender divergence in athletic performance."[34] Looking at US Age Group Swimming time standards, he found that the sex differences in swimming in the 10 and under category were 1 percent or below in all strokes except the individual medley where the sex gap was under 2 percent. The sex gap increased slightly for the 11–12-year-old category to between 1 and 3 percent. The gap jumped significantly, however, for the 13–14-year-old age category to between 5 and 7 percent, then jumped again for the 15–16-year-old category to between 7 and 9 percent and again for the 17–18-year-old category to between 9 and 11 percent.[35] Looking at world records in track and field events, he found similar results. For the 10 and under category for running events there was a 3 percent sex gap. By age thirteen, the sex gap increased to 7 percent, and then leveled off at around 10 percent at age

---

[33] See David J. Handelsman et al., *Circulating Testosterone as the Hormonal Basis of Sex Differences in Athletic Performance*, 39 ENDOCRINE REVIEWS 803, 803, 805, 812 (2018); David J. Handelsman, *Sex Difference in Athletic Performance Emerge Coinciding with the Onset of Male Puberty*, 87 CLINICAL ENDOCRINOLOGY 68, 68–72 (2017).
[34] Handelsman, *supra* note 33 at 68.
[35] *Id.* at 69.

fifteen. In jumping events, the sex gap at age ten was just under 6 percent. It increased significantly to 15 percent at age fourteen and then leveled off around 19 percent around age sixteen years of age.[36] Handelsman also looked at data regarding hand-grip strength of nonathletes to examine sex divergence as a feature of normal male puberty rather than of athletic performance. He found marginal strength advantages for boys prior to age thirteen with significant increases in the gap between ages thirteen to nineteen.[37] Handelsman concluded that "the gender divergence in athletic performance begins at the age of 12–13 years and reaches adult plateau in the late teenage years."[38]

Among the world's very best athletes, the sex gap is approximately 10 percent and stable.[39] Indeed, while the gap for elite athletes narrowed in the decade or so after the passage of Title IX in 1972 due to enhanced training and competition for women, in recent decades the gap has remained steady and persistent.[40] In an exhaustive study, Valerie Thibault and colleagues compared results from eighty-two Olympic events where women's and men's contests were the same. The events spanned track, swimming, speed skating, track cycling and weightlifting. The authors compared men's and women's world records from their initiation. They also compared the top ten male and female performances each year. They found that across events, and with small variation, the gender performance gap became stable and consistent around 1983. In running events, for example, they found that the sex gap in world records decreased from 30 percent in 1922 to 10.7 percent in 1984. For the ten best performances the stability date was just before 1984 and the ten best performances' sex gap shrunk from 25.3 percent to 11.2 percent.[41] In swimming the sex gap has been stable even longer. Thibault found that in swimming, world record sex gaps decreased from 22 percent in 1916 to 8.9 percent just before 1980. For the ten best performances, stability in the gender gap was achieved in 1981, dropping from 13.4 percent in 1963 to 10.16 percent.[42] The results in

---

[36] *Id.* at 70.
[37] *Id.* at 71.
[38] *Id.* at 72.
[39] *See* Doriane Lambelet Coleman et al., *Re-Affirming the Value of the Sports Exception to Title IX's General Non-Discrimination Rule*, 27 Duke J. Gender L. & Pol'y 69, 69 (2020); Hooven, *supra* note 2 at 71.
[40] Hooven, *supra* note 2 at 71–72.
[41] Valérie Thibault et al., *Women and Men in Sport Performance: The Gender Gap Has Not Evolved since 1983*, 9 J. Sports Sci. Med. 214, 214, 217 (2010).
[42] *Id.* at 218.

jumping, cycling and speed skating events were comparable with stabilization in the sex gap achieved in the 1980s or 1990s following a period during which the gap narrowed. In weightlifting, by contrast, the sex gap has remained stable at 36.8 percent since women officially started competing in 1998.[43]

What these gaps mean is not only that the very best male athlete will beat the very best female athlete, but that the very best female athlete will be beaten by many elite and not-so-elite male athletes. According to sports scientist Ross Tucker: "[m]ost of the women's world records [in track], even doped, lie outside the top 500 times run by men."[44] For example, he explains, Paula Radcliff's marathon world record "is beaten by between 250 and 300 men per year."[45] "In 2019, about twenty-five hundred men, almost one-third of the total number of men competing worldwide in the IAAF [International Association of Athletics Federations] 100-meter event, beat the fastest women's time."[46] As Coleman has pointed out, "[t]he women's 100, 400, and 800 meters records … are beaten by literally hundreds of men each year, including by many high school boys."[47]

Indeed, Coleman and Wickliffe Shreve have extensively documented how often the very best female athletes in the world would be beaten not only by men but by boys – that is males under the age of eighteen. They draw upon data from the IAAF and the numbers are striking. Just in 2017, Coleman and Shreve explain, "Olympic, World, and U.S. Champion Tori Bowie's 100 meters lifetime best of 10.78 was beaten 15,000 times by men and boys."[48] They explain that Olympic, world and US Champion Allyson Felix's 400-meter lifetime best was similarly outperformed by more than 15,000 men and boys around the world in 2017. As Coleman and Shreve show, the very best women's result in the 100 meters in 2017 was beaten by 2,474 men and by 124 boys in that year. The results at longer distances are less dramatic but still significant. The best women's result in the 5,000 meters in 2017 was beaten in that year by 684 men and by 10 boys.[49]

---

[43] *Id.* at 217–19.
[44] Ross Tucker, *The Caster Semenya Debate*, THE SCIENCE OF SPORT (July 16, 2016), https://perma.cc/5A8Z-7W56 (website archived).
[45] *Id.*
[46] HOOVEN, *supra* note 2 at 106.
[47] Coleman, *supra* note 13 at 89.
[48] Doriane Lambelet Coleman & Wickliffe Shreve, *Comparing Athletic Performances: The Best Elite Women to Boys and Men*, DUKE CENTER FOR SPORTS LAW & POLICY, https://shorturl.at/tsQZG.
[49] *Id. See also* Coleman et al., *supra* note 39 at 89–90.

Although the sex gap is most transparent in sports with clear records, the performance gap, and its breadth, holds across sports. In 2017, for example, the US women's soccer team was defeated in a scrimmage by a team of high-school-age boys.[50] In 1998, Serena and Venus Williams issued a challenge saying that either of them could beat any male player ranked 200 or below in the world. Each was handily defeated by Karsten Braasch, then ranked 203 in the world.[51]

The sex-based performance gap exists not only among the most elite athletes, but also those of more modest and ordinary abilities. Coleman, for example, compares the 2019 California Regional high jump results for high school boys and girls. In every region, the top boy outperformed the top girl and the percentage differentials ranged from 11 to 20 percent.[52] The same is true across events. In the 2023 outdoor track and field season in California the fastest high school boys in the North Coast ran the 100m in 10.31s and the 800m in 1:53.25s. The fastest high school girls in the same region ran the 100m in 11.87s and the 800m in 2:10.03s.[53] The results in swimming are similar. The records from Southern California swimming for fifteen to sixteen-year-old boys in the 50Y freestyle and 500Y freestyle were 19.96s and 4:18.91s. The fastest girls' times in the same events were 22.24s and 4:29.38s.[54]

There is widespread agreement about the physical differences most responsible for this performance gap between post-pubertal males and females. Men have larger and stronger bones, greater muscle mass, lower body fat, higher aerobic capacity and higher circulating hemoglobin, which gives advantages in aerobic capacity.[55] Men are also typically taller and heavier than women.[56] These physical differences give men advantages in contests that require strength, speed and endurance – in other words, most sports.[57]

[50] Roger Gonzalez, *FC Dallas Under-15 Boys Squad Beat the U.S. Women's National Team in a Scrimmage*, CBS SPORTS (Apr. 4, 2017, 3:33 PM), https://shorturl.at/rnMOV.
[51] JOYCE, *supra* note 10.
[52] Coleman et al., *supra* note 39 at 91–92; for additional statistics see alltime-athletics.com; Athletic.net.
[53] *North Coast High School 2023 Outdoor Track and Field*, ATHLETIC.NET, www.athletic.net/TrackAndField/State/Archive.aspx?State=134981.
[54] *SCS Records – 15–16 Boys*, S. CAL. SWIMMING, www.socalswim.org/records/boys-15-16; *SCS Records – 15–16 Girls*, www.socalswim.org/records/girls-15-16.
[55] *See* Handelsman et al., *supra* note 33 at 803, 812; Thibault et al., *supra* note 41 at 214.
[56] Handelsman et al., *supra* note 33 at 805; Thibault et al., *supra* note 41 at 214.
[57] Women do seem to have an advantage in ultra long distance swimming and running competitions where higher levels of body fat prove advantageous. *See* Christine Ro, *The Sports Where Women Outperform Men*, BBC (Aug. 1, 2024), www.bbc.com/future/article/20240731-the-sports-where-women-outperform-men.

There is also agreement about the cause of these physical differences – the dramatic increase in testosterone that males experience post puberty.[58] Hooven explains how this process works. First, "T influences stem cells ... to take the muscle route, and it actively discourages them from turning into fat."[59] Males' higher T "enlarges [their] muscle fibers, resulting in stronger, larger muscles."[60] Second, higher T levels and the increased muscle it produces, lead to larger and stronger bones. Hooven explains: "In puberty, bone architecture is especially sensitive to mechanical load and develops in response to it. And the muscles of pubertal boys apply greater load to the developing bones than do those of girls ... causing them to respond by increasing mineral density and diameter."[61] These effects are permanent and are not lost even if T is reduced later in life. Third, T at puberty increases males' hemoglobin levels. Hemoglobin, Hooven explains, "is a protein inside red blood cells that carries oxygen from the lungs to working muscles, fueling their action and increasing endurance."[62] This effect of testosterone, Hooven notes, is not permanent and would be altered by changing one's testosterone levels.[63]

In recent years, there has been debate on two questions relevant to sex categorization in sports. First, how much overlap, if any, exists between the testosterone levels of women and men. Second, how well and how closely does testosterone affect and predict athletic performance. The debate is important because if testosterone levels are nonoverlapping between men and women and are responsible for group-based advantages for men over women, then testosterone level may be a sensible way to assign transgender athletes to sex-segregated teams. If testosterone levels overlap for women and men or do not cause systematic and predictable sex-based advantages, then testosterone levels make less sense as an assignment tool.

On the first point, the vast majority of scientific research supports the conclusion that testosterone levels are nonoverlapping between men and

---

[58] *See* Handelsman et al., *supra* note 33 at 812 (explaining that "[t]he striking post pubertal increase in male circulating testosterone provides a major, ongoing, cumulative, and durable advantage in sporting contests by creating greater muscle mass and strength. These sex differences render women unable to compete effectively against men, especially (but not only) in power sports").

[59] HOOVEN, *supra* note 2 at 119.

[60] *Id.*

[61] *Id.* at 121.

[62] *Id.*

[63] *Id.* at 128 (explaining "When evaluated after a year of T-suppressing medication, along with increasing estrogen, many of the sports-related benefits of high T decline significantly. For example, hemoglobin plummets to female levels. But bone size (including height, of course) doesn't budge, and much of T induced bone strength is also retained").

women. Endocrinologist David Handelsman conducted a meta-analysis of studies of healthy women and men to determine male and female reference ranges for circulating testosterone. Handelsman explains that "[p]rior to puberty, levels of circulating testosterone ... are the same in boys and girls. They remain lower than 2 nmol/L in women of all ages. However, from the onset of male puberty the testes secrete 20 times more testosterone resulting in circulating testosterone levels that are 15 times greater in healthy young men than in age-similar women."[64] He concludes, based on the studies, that "circulating testosterone in adults has a strikingly nonoverlapping bimodal distribution with wide and complete separation between men and women."[65] Even the most vocal critics of this conclusion, Rebecca Jordan-Young and Katrina Karkazis, recognize that "[i]n most studies, men's T levels are about 10 times those of women, and the highest levels seen in women are well below the lowest levels seen in healthy men."[66]

Nonetheless, Professors Jordan-Young and Karkazis argue that testosterone levels of women and men are not bimodal. Indeed, they assert that they have talked with scientists "in a range of fields including endocrinologists, the longtime head of a national anti-doping lab, a high-profile sports scientist working in professional sports, and scientists who study elite amateurs. All of them matter-of-factly agreed that men's and women's levels overlap."[67] Professor Van Anders similarly asserts that men's testosterone "[l]evels reach as low as those in women and overlap between women and men more than presumed."[68]

Yet disagreement about the underlying science may be less real than it first appears. Jordan-Young and Karkazis, for example, rely on a study by Marie-Louise Healy and colleagues which studied hormone profiles of 693 elite athletes. Their study found "a complete overlap between men and women" in testosterone values.[69] More specifically they found that

---

[64] Handelsman et al., *supra* note 33 at 806.

[65] *Id. See also* Coleman, *supra* note 13 at 75 (referring to the "bimodal and non-overlapping production of testosterone"). HOOVEN, *supra* note 2 at 114 (explaining that "In people without DSDs, serious disorders of their endocrine glands, or other rare conditions that have a large impact on T levels, men's T levels are ten to twenty times higher than those of women").

[66] Katrina Karkazis & Rebecca Jordan-Young, *Debating a Testosterone "Sex Gap,"* 348 SCIENCE 858, 858, 859 (2015).

[67] JORDAN-YOUNG & KARKAZIS, *supra* note 4 at 184–85.

[68] Van Anders et al., *supra* note 5 at 194, 197.

[69] JORDAN-YOUNG & KARKAZIS, *supra* note 4 at 182 (citing Marie-Louise Healy et al., *Endocrine Profiles in 693 Elite Athletes in the Postcompetition Setting*, 81 CLINICAL ENDOCRINOLOGY 294, 294–95 (2014)).

"[a]mong women, 13.7 percent had T above the typical female range, and 4.7 percent were within the typical male range. Likewise, 16.5 percent of the elite male athletes had T below the typical male range, and 1.8 percent of them had T low enough to be classified as within the typical female range."[70] Yet the authors themselves acknowledge that their sample likely included in the female category those with differences of sex development that elevate testosterone levels beyond the normal female range. According to the authors, "it seems quite possible that one or more of [the women with elevated testosterone levels] had the androgen insensitivity syndrome (AIS)" and others "may well have had the polycystic ovary syndrome or a more rare form of hyperandrogenism."[71] These athletes would not, as a result, have been included as females in the studies included in Handelsman's meta-analysis.

Those with AIS are born with a Y chromosome and testes. They also have testosterone levels in the blood in the male range, though, because their bodies are unable to absorb it into their cells, they are not thought to have a significant advantage in sports over females with testosterone levels in the normal female range.[72] Those with 5-ARD also have a Y chromosome but because of a genetic mutation that affects the development of male genitalia, 5-ARD babies are often assigned female at birth. Those with 5-ARD have testes and testosterone levels in the male range.[73] Perhaps not surprisingly, those with 5-ARD have been found to be "overrepresented in elite female sports by 140 times, compared to the prevalence in the general population."[74] Those with polycystic ovarian syndrome (PCOS) are born with two XX chromosomes but have a disorder of the ovaries that leads to production of testosterone at the high end or above the normal female level, though below the low end of the normal male range.[75] Those with PCOS have also been found to be overrepresented in elite women's sports

---

[70] JORDAN-YOUNG & KARKAZIS, *supra* note 4 at 182 (citing Healy et al., *supra* note 69 at 295).

[71] JORDAN-YOUNG & KARKAZIS, *supra* note 4 at 302.

[72] *See* Joanna Harper, *A Brief History of Intersex Athletes in Sport*, LETSRUN.COM (Sept. 19, 2014), www.letsrun.com/news/2014/09/brief-history-intersex-athletes-sport/. *See also* Bibhas Kar et al., *Complete Androgen Insensitivity Syndrome in Three Generations of Indian Pedigree*, 66 J. OBSTET. GYNECOL. INDIA 358, 358 (2016) ("Women with complete androgen insensitivity syndrome who have intact gonads have the endocrine profile of a hormone-resistant state. Serum testosterone concentrations are either within or above the normal range for men…").

[73] *See* Harper, *supra* note 72; *see also* HOOVEN, *supra* note 2 at 114–15, 125.

[74] HOOVEN, *supra* note 2 at 125.

[75] *Id.* at 114.

though less so than those athletes with 5-ARD. Indeed, "in one study of ninety female Swedish Olympians, 37 percent had PCOS, approximately three times the general population rate for the same age group."[76]

Van Anders relies for support on an article by Professor of Psychology Francisco Sanchez and his colleagues, the purpose of which was to assess the 2011 International Olympic Committee (IOC) regulations which set testosterone limits for participation in female sports.[77] Although the authors do say that "some women will cross the [men's] threshold"[78] for testosterone, it is clear that the authors are talking here about individuals with XY chromosomes who identify as female but have testosterone levels in the male range. The authors explain that "XY women who have an androgen insensitivity syndrome and who may or may not have intact testicles will be allowed to compete with women even though they developed characteristics that are usually present in men but not women."[79] They likewise explain that the IOC policy may result in the exclusion of an XY woman "from competing against female athletes if her testosterone levels are within the male range and she is not found to have a condition that prevents her from utilizing androgens."[80] Indeed, rather than supporting Van Anders's assertion that testosterone levels are not bimodal, the Sanchez paper itself asserts, apparently using a different definition of women and men than that used in other parts of the paper: "[T]here is a trait which is known to influence one's athletic performance and which happens to be sexually dimorphic: androgens. Although women produce androgens – mainly secreted by their adrenal glands – their androgen levels are markedly lower than the level in men."[81]

Disagreement about whether men's and women's testosterone levels overlap may then really be a political disagreement rather than a scientific

---

[76] *Id.* at 125.
[77] Francisco J. Sánchez et al., *The New Policy on Hyperandrogenism in Elite Female Athletes Is Not about "Sex Testing,"* 50 J. SEX RSCH. 112, 112 (2013).
[78] *Id.* at 113.
[79] *Id.* at 114.
[80] *Id.*
[81] *Id.* at 113. Van Anders also relies on a study that involved measuring salivary testosterone concentrations of 550 University of Chicago MBA students to study the effects of testosterone on financial risk-taking. The study found overlap of the testosterone distributions of men and women, though the authors did not indicate whether participants were tested for or asked about DSDs, so it is unclear whether individuals with XY chromosomes were included in the women's category. *See* Paola Sapienza et al., *Gender Differences in Financial Risk Aversion and Career Choices Are Affected by Testosterone,* 106 PROC. NAT'L ACAD. SCIS. 15268, 15268 (2009).

one. It may reflect a difference of opinion about which individuals should be included in the category of women in the first place. In other words, political differences about how to define a woman, lead then to differences in the results of what "women's" testosterone levels look like. Jordan-Young and Karkazis are transparent about the importance of this political choice in the way testosterone levels are coded. They explain that women's and men's testosterone levels "overlap more or less depending on how you choose the women and men in the sample." They go on to explain: "The decision about whom to include as research subjects isn't an arcane methodological issue, but a social and ethical one concerning how we understand and frame human diversity."[82] Van Anders too is clear about her political choice, explaining: "transgender women are women; attributing men's biology or behavior to transgender women is wrong as science and as a basis for policy."[83]

These political differences are surely important, indeed they are at the heart of the debate about transgender girls' and women's inclusion in female sports. Importantly though, these disagreements about how to categorize individuals with various differences of sex development or with gender dysphoria do not mean there is actual disagreement about the testosterone levels of males and females who do not have such conditions.

The second issue of contention deals with the connection between athletic performance and testosterone levels. If there is no causal connection, as Jordan-Young and Karkazis as well as Van Anders argue, then using testosterone levels to draw eligibility lines for female sports in order to tighten competition and exclude outliers does not make sense. According to Jordan-Young and Karkazis, "It may seem logical to infer ... that a person with more T will have greater athletic ability than one with less T, but this kind of prediction doesn't pan out."[84] As Van Anders elaborates:

> At elite levels of athletic competition, some men and women have low levels of testosterone, much lower than population averages. And some women competing in elite athletics have no functioning testosterone ... yet they build muscle, compete, and win. Similarly, men with low testosterone levels compete against other men, and win ... If testosterone accounted for athletic performance, none of this could be the case.[85]

---

[82] JORDAN-YOUNG & KARKAZIS, *supra* note 4 at 184.
[83] Van Anders et al., *supra* note 5 at 198.
[84] JORDAN-YOUNG & KARKAZIS, *supra* note 4 at 161.
[85] Van Anders et al., *supra* note 5 at 197.

These views seem to stand in stark contrast to those of Coleman and Handelsman. According to Coleman, "there is no scientific doubt that testosterone is the reason that men as a group perform better than women in sports."[86] According to Handelsman, the "order-of-magnitude difference in circulating testosterone concentrations is the key factor in the sex difference in athletic performance…"[87]

Yet the differences on this point too may be narrower than first appears. There is in fact agreement that testosterone levels do not affect within-sex athletic performance in a predictable and linear way. It is not the case, for example, that men with higher testosterone levels perform better than men with lower testosterone levels. This lack of in-group causation is what Jordan-Young and Karkazis and Van Anders focus on, and it is not a point of larger dispute.

The disagreement is, instead, about whether testosterone levels lead to predictable and consistent performance differences across sex groups. Jordan-Young and Karkazis argue that the fact that testosterone levels do not predict within group performance is meaningful and that those looking for a causal connection between testosterone and performance differences across groups wrongly ignore the numerous other differences between women and men that can cause group disparity. The authors explain that "when confronted with the lack of evidence that T is related to inter-individual differences in performance, supporters of the regulations [tying eligibility to compete in female sports to testosterone levels] often fall back on the female–male difference in athletic performance."[88] But, they argue, "it is precisely because there are so many other differences between women and men athletes, both physiological and social, that many scientists don't consider male–female comparison a useful form of evidence for understanding how T affects athletic performances. Female-male comparisons are too confounded, so only within-sex analyses can give clear enough information about the specific role of T."[89]

Hooven, by contrast, argues that when studying the effects of testosterone, the difference between within-group and cross-group effects is critical. Indeed, she argues that "the conclusion that T levels don't explain differences between the sexes is the result of a subtle bait and switch."[90]

---

[86] Coleman, *supra* note 13 at 75.
[87] Handelsman et al., *supra* note 33 at 811.
[88] JORDAN-YOUNG & KARKAZIS, *supra* note 4 at 196.
[89] *Id.* at 197.
[90] HOOVEN, *supra* note 2 at 109.

According to Hooven, "all the evidence points to the same conclusion: a male level of T in puberty and adulthood ... is the master key for superior performance in most sports."[91]

2.3 Conclusion

Science has a great deal to say about what factors make people male or female and about how these factors affect athletic performance. There remain important points of disagreement, however, even if there were perfect agreement within the scientific community on the answers to these questions, science could not tell us how transgender girls and women should be categorized for sport. Whether transgender girls should be included in girls' sports depends ultimately on the social meaning and purpose of sports. These are distinctly social, not scientific questions. The female sports category might, for example, be understood as an ability category drawn to tighten competition for those who would lose to men in direct competition. Alternatively, it might be understood as an anti-subordination category drawn to undermine particular social hierarchies. Once choices are made, science can help determine where and how eligibility lines should be drawn, but science alone cannot answer these foundational questions. As Alice Dreger has insightfully pointed out, when it comes to determining the eligibility boundaries for female sports, "[t]he fundamental problem is that the science of sport has outpaced the philosophy of sport."[92] The next three chapters work to fill this void.

---

[91] *Id.*

[92] Alice Dreger, *Science Is Forcing Sports to Re-examine Their Core Principles*, N.Y. TIMES (Sep. 12, 2009) (explaining: "[S]ports officials certainly need to tap expert scientists to come up with a clear rulebook for sex verification and a more rational policy on waivers for testosterone. But what we will need first is for sports leaders to come to some consensus on the question: what is sport really about?").

3

The Argument for Inclusion

To date, the loudest voices in the fight over girls' sports have been the most extreme. On one side are those who argue that transgender girls are girls and must always be treated as such.[1] On the other side are those who argue that sex is determined at birth and can never be changed.[2] The arguments are absolutist both in the sense that they call for categorical inclusion (or exclusion) of transgender girls in girls' sports and in the sense that they hold across contexts and outside of sports.

This chapter, and the next, focus on the arguments for inclusion and exclusion that have been dominating the public and political discourse about transgender girls and girls' sports. They describe the arguments, identify the explicit, and sometimes implicit, empirical and normative beliefs that motivate them, and explain why an absolutist approach – whether for inclusion or exclusion – is an unduly simplistic response to a complex problem.

---

[1] *See* Jack Turban, *Trans Girls Belong on Girls' Sports Teams*, SCI. AM. (Mar. 16, 2021), www.scientificamerican.com/article/trans-girls-belong-on-girls-sports-teams/; *see also* Chase Strangio & Gabriel Arkles, *Four Myths about Trans Athletes, Debunked*, ACLU NEWS & COMMENT. (Apr. 30, 2020), www.aclu.org/news/lgbtq-rights/four-myths-about-trans-athletes-debunked; Brenda Alvarez, *Fair Play for Trans Girls and Women in School Sports*, NEA TODAY (June 21, 2021), https://shorturl.at/8xJME.

[2] This view is most evident in the wave of US legislative actions, some successful and some not, seeking to bar transgender girls from participating in girls' sports. In 2021, Texas enacted a law providing that only individuals designated female at birth may compete on girls' athletic teams. H.B. 25, 87th Leg., 3d Spec. Sess. (Tex. 2022). Also in 2021, Florida passed a law providing that sex for athletic participation in public schools will be established by "official birth certificate" fixed at or near birth. S.B. 1028, Leg., 2021 Sess. (Fla. 2021). In 2022, Republican lawmakers in Indiana overrode a veto by the Republican governor to pass a law prohibiting transgender girls from participating in girls' sports. The law provides: "A male, based on a student's biological sex at birth may not participate on an athletic team or sport designated under this section as being a female, women's or girls' athletic team or sport." H.B. 1041, 122nd Gen. Assemb., 2d Reg. Sess. (Ind. 2022). *See generally* Katie Barnes, *Alabama to Wyoming: State Policies on Transgender Athlete Participation*, ESPN (June 7, 2022), https://shorturl.at/SNxzW.

For transgender advocacy groups the argument for inclusion is at its core an argument against misgendering. Inclusion is necessary to recognize transgender girls and women for who they really are – girls and women. The American Civil Liberties Union (ACLU), for example, proclaims as "FACT: Trans girls are girls."[3] The organization goes on to debunk the "myth" that "[s]ex is binary, apparent at birth, and identifiable through singular biological characteristics," and to explain that "[u]pholding trans athletes' rights requires rooting out the inaccurate beliefs underlying harmful policies sweeping through state legislatures."[4] The Human Rights Campaign similarly cautions that "[c]ontrasting transgender people with 'real' or 'biological' men and women is a false comparison."[5] And in an open letter supporting trans women and girls spearheaded by GLAAD, nearly 500 leaders in advocacy, business, entertainment, media and politics, proclaimed "with clarity and strength that transgender women are women and that transgender girls are girls" and went on to note that "anti-trans sports bans are as unnecessary as they are harmful."[6]

What drives the argument against misgendering is a concern about pain, an opposition to social oppression and a commitment to biological erasure as a way to end both. Indeed, in an interesting and often blurry way, the arguments for inclusion combine a focus on subjective injury with assertions about objective social priorities. The subjective injury arguments focus on pain in an individual and absolute sense – exclusion causes such intense pain to transgender individuals that the pain itself becomes a legal injury warranting redress. The subjective injury arguments also focus on broader social utility – transgender inclusion minimizes social pain and maximizes social happiness. By contrast, the objective arguments focus, not on pain, but on the social injustice of the cisgender normativity underlying transgender exclusion from sports. At times, the objective arguments seem perfectionist – challenging cisgender normativity is uniquely important because it undermines human flourishing. At other times, the objective arguments seem grounded in a hierarchy of oppression – challenging cisgender normativity is simply more important than challenging other forms of oppression. Critical to

---

[3] Strangio & Arkles, *supra* note 1.
[4] *Id.*
[5] *HRC's Brief Guide to Getting Transgender Coverage Right*, HUMAN RIGHTS CAMPAIGN, www.hrc.org/resources/hrcs-brief-guide-to-reporting-on-transgender-individuals.
[6] *Open Letter Supporting Trans Women and Girls*, THE GAY AND LESBIAN ALLIANCE AGAINST DEFAMATION (GLAAD) (Mar. 31, 2021), https://glaad.org/tdovletter/.

the objective arguments is the rejection of biological sex as a meaningful social category.

3.1 Subjective Claims

Arguments against misgendering emphasize the intense subjective discomfort experienced by transgender students who are not treated in accordance with their gender identity. Such pain is used both to establish an injury and to justify a legal right of protection. In other words, advocates emphasize the intensity of the pain experienced by transgender students who are misgendered and contend that transgender youth have a legal right to protection from such pain.

Descriptions of pain are pervasive. According to the ACLU: "Excluding trans people from any space or activity is harmful, particularly for trans youth. A trans high school student, for example, may experience detrimental effects to their physical and emotional wellbeing when they are pushed out of affirming spaces and communities."[7] Athlete Ally, an advocacy organization for LGBTQ athletes, describes the pain experienced by transgender youth who are misgendered even more starkly: "Transgender and nonbinary youth who have access to a gender-affirming space at school, like a sports team, are 25% less likely to report a suicide attempt within a year."[8] Athlete Ally is, moreover, explicit about the primacy it accords to pain. The group argues that transgender women must be included in women's sports, regardless of whether they have biological advantages, because of the pain that exclusion causes them. In its Statement on the Future of Women's Sports, the group proclaims that "most important[ ] ... is the fact that transgender inclusion in sport is fundamentally an ideological, rather than a scientific, issue. People may turn to certain forms of scientific knowledge to understand the nuances of athletic performance, but what is at stake is not a scientific matter but the health and wellbeing of trans people."[9]

The pain advocates for inclusion describe is psychological. It comes not only from the inability to express one's authentic identity, but from the stigma, humiliation and feeling of degradation that misgendering imposes. Being treated as not a "normal" or "real" girl or boy results in

---

[7] Strangio & Arkles, *supra* note 1.
[8] *The Future of Women's Sports Includes Transgender Women and Girls*, ATHLETE ALLY, https://shorturl.at/10ZrR.
[9] *Id.*

psychic injury. As lawyers and advocates Harper Jean Tobin and Jennifer Levi explain:

> Denying equal access to school facilities for transgender students effectively singles them out, apart from all others in the community, with a stigmatizing message that a transgender boy is not a normal or real boy, or a transgender girl is not a normal or real girl... This is precisely the kind of "badge of inferiority" that antidiscrimination laws, such as Title IX, forbid.[10]

The pain advocates describe is physical. Tobin and Levi, for example, explain that "[f]or transgender youth for whom social role transition is recommended, 'life in their assigned gender is very distressing and the relief they get from switching their gender presentation [is] very palpable.'"[11] Legal scholars Scott Skinner-Thompson and Ilona Turner agree. They urge that allowing transgender students to participate in accordance with their gender identity "best advances the well-being of already vulnerable transgender youth by helping to incorporate and include such students in activities that are critical to physical, social, mental, emotional development, and health."[12] For the plaintiffs in *Hecox v. Little*, physical pain was central to their challenge to Idaho's law barring transgender women from women's sports teams. "[F]orcing a girl who is transgender out of spaces designated for girls is extremely harmful and can result in serious health consequences,"[13] they asserted, before elaborating that "[e]xcluding girls who are transgender and intersex from athletics alongside their peers increases shame and stigma and contributes to negative physical and emotional health outcomes for those who are excluded."[14]

---

[10] Harper Jean Tobin & Jennifer Levi, *Securing Equal Access to Sex-Segregated Facilities for Transgender Students*, 28 WIS. J.L. GENDER & SOC'Y 301, 309 (2013). *See also* Erin E. Buzuvis, *"As Who They Really Are": Expanding Opportunities for Transgender Athletes to Participate in Youth and Scholastic Sports*, 34 LAW & INEQ. 341, 353–54 (2016) ("[P]olicies that permit gender-consonant participation are 'critically important' to transgender individuals for a host of reasons, including promoting emotional, psychological, physical, and academic benefits").

[11] Tobin & Levi, *supra* note 10 at 302 (quoting Edgardo Menvielle, *A Comprehensive Program for Children with Gender Variant Behaviors and Gender Identity Disorders*, 59 J. HOMOSEXUALITY 357, 361 (2012)).

[12] Scott Skinner-Thompson & Ilona M. Turner, *Title IX's Protections for Transgender Student Athletes*, 28 WIS. J.L. GENDER & SOC'Y 271, 272 (2013).

[13] Complaint for Declaratory and Injunctive Relief at 35, Hecox, 479 F. Supp. 3d 930 (D. Idaho 2020) (No. 1:20-cv-00184-DCN).

[14] *Id.* at 43.

At times, the pain described seems almost spiritual. Legal scholar Erin Buzuvis, for example, describes a fictional high school student, Jaime, who is a transgender girl. In arguing that Jaime should have the right to join a girls' sports team, Buzuvis focuses on Jaime's feelings of identity and authenticity. "[I]t just feels wrong to Jaime," Buzuvis explains, "to consider joining the boys' team, when in her heart she does not feel like a boy."[15]

Yet, as a practical matter, subjective pain alone rarely constitutes a legal injury or justifies a legal right. Instead, legal injuries, from which people are entitled to protection and redress, are almost always defined objectively rather than subjectively. It is not enough that a plaintiff suffered injury. Liability typically requires that the defendant's conduct violate some objective standard of care.

Consider, for example, sexual harassment law. It is not enough that the plaintiff experienced severe emotional distress or even that she or he were unable to perform her or his work as a result of the challenged conduct. Liability requires that a reasonable person would find the conduct to be severe or pervasive enough to alter the workplace.[16] In the First Amendment context, too, it is not enough that the speaker felt silenced by a particular speech restriction. In deciding whether a speech restriction has gone too far, a court must decide whether as an objective matter the speaker has not been left with adequate alternative avenues of speech.[17] The speaker's claim that restrictions left inadequate alternatives for communication is not enough.[18] Similarly, in the Fourth Amendment context, it is not enough that one feels her or his privacy has been invaded. The

---

[15] Erin Buzuvis, *Including Transgender Athletes in Sex-Segregated Sport*, in SEXUAL ORIENTATION AND GENDER ORIENTATION AT SPORTS: ESSAYS FROM ACTIVISTS, COACHES, AND SCHOLARS 23, 24 (George B. Cunningham ed., 2012).

[16] *See Harris v. Forklift Systems, Inc.*, 510 U.S. 17, 21 (1993) ("Conduct that is not severe or pervasive enough to create an objectively hostile or abusive work environment – an environment that a reasonable person would find hostile or abusive – is beyond Title VI's purview").

[17] *See* MARK G. KELMAN, WHAT IS IN A NAME? TAXATION AND REGULATION ACROSS CONSTITUTIONAL DOMAINS 58 (2019) (explaining that "[w]hen the state defends such a speech restriction, it must convince the court that it is objectively the case that the speaker has been left adequate 'alternative channels of communication.'").

[18] *See, e.g., City of Renton v. Playtime Theaters, Inc.*, 475 U.S. 41, 54 (1986) (explaining that: "In our view, the First Amendment requires only that Renton refrain from effectively denying respondents a reasonable opportunity to open and operate an adult theater within the city"); *McCullan v. Coakley*, 134 S. Ct. 2518, 2535 (2014) (finding that the buffer zones at issue "impose serious burdens on petitioners' speech… [T]he zones carve out a significant portion of the adjacent public sidewalks, pushing petitioners well back from the clinics' entrances and driveways").

right to protection is only triggered if one's feelings of intrusion are considered objectively reasonable.[19]

There are sound reasons – both empirical and normative – for the law's focus on objective rather than purely subjective measures of deprivation. As an empirical matter, individual reports of subjective pain are unstable over time and context. Which moment or context is the most accurate to measure? When is one's pain report most authentic and true? As a normative matter, if one cares about subjective pain as an indicator of social oppression, what if objective oppression and subjective pain are highly imperfect correlates? What if, in fact, reports of subjective pain are inversely correlated to objective oppression?

Measuring subjective pain is difficult not only because it is hard to know exactly what one is measuring and hard to compare measurements across individuals,[20] but also because even measurements for a single person change over time and are susceptible to small environmental changes. Indeed, when individuals are asked to assess their overall well-being multiple times over the course of a couple of weeks or even over the course of a single hour, studies find only moderate levels of reliability,[21] and susceptibility to small environmental changes – such as finding a dime or the current weather.[22]

---

[19] *See, e.g.*, *Kyllo v. United States*, 533 U.S. 27, 33 (2001) (explaining that "a Fourth Amendment search occurs when the government violates a subjective expectation of privacy that society recognizes as reasonable"); *Smith v. Maryland*, 442 U.S. 735, 740 (1979) (explaining that application of the Fourth Amendment depends on two questions: "The first is whether the individual, by his conduct, has 'exhibited an actual (subjective) expectation of privacy[]' ... The second question is whether ... the individual's expectation, viewed objectively, is 'justifiable'" (first quoting *Katz v. United States*, 389 U.S. 347, 361 (1967) (Doublas, J., concurring), then quoting *Katz*, 389 U.S. at 353)).

[20] *See, e.g.*, Adam J. Kolber, *Pain Detection and the Privacy of Subjective Experience*, 33 Am. J. L. & Med. 433, 446–47 (2017) (describing the challenges of measuring pain and comparing measurements across individuals); Amartya Sen, Interpersonal Comparisons of Welfare, in Choice, Welfare and Measurement (1982). *See also* Robin L. West, *Taking Preferences Seriously*, 64 Tul. L. Rev. 659, 680–87 (1990) (arguing that empathy and "sympathetic understanding" makes it possible for individuals to both understand others' pain and compare pain across individuals, but recognizing that "[i]t is not impossible to sympathize with those least like ourselves, but it is harder").

[21] *See* Alan B. Krueger & David A. Schkade, *The Reliability of Subjective Well-Being Measures*, 92 J. Pub. Econ. 1833, 1835 (2008) (finding "serial correlation of about .60" when study participants were asked to assess their subjective well-being on occasions two weeks apart); Richard Kammann & Ross Flett, *Affectometer 2: A Scale to Measure Current Level of General Happiness*, 35 Australian J. Psych., 25965 (1983) (finding reliability of 0.50–0.55 when individuals were asked about their well-being twice within the same day).

[22] *See* Krueger and Schkade, *supra* note 21, at 1836; *see also* Michael Eid & Ed Diener, *Global Judgments of Subjective Well-Being: Situational Variability and Long-Term Stability*, 65 Soc. Indicators Rsch. at 245 (2004).

Unsurprisingly, then, individuals are easily primed, making reports of subjective well-being susceptible to whatever emotions were triggered in them first.[23] For example, when students were asked about their happiness with their dating lives before being asked about their overall happiness, their answer to the former question impacted their answer to the latter.[24] Positive (or negative) feelings on the specific question primed the students to feel similarly in response to the general question.

Sociologists Christopher Uggen and Chika Shinohara suggest that priming may also work from the general to the more specific. In other words, priming individuals to a particular type of rights violation or abuse in the world generally may make individuals more likely to see and feel such violations in their own lives. They found that female workers in both America and Japan who entered the workforce during periods of legal change and heightened salience regarding sexual harassment reported higher lifetime rates of sexual harassment than did workers who entered the workforce either prior to or after the period of legal change.[25]

A similar kind of priming may be occurring on college campuses. As colleges focus more openly, explicitly and persistently on anti-Blackness and white supremacy – through, for example, training on unconscious bias, microaggressions and antiracism – students may become primed to experience particular events or interactions as more racialized, more harmful and more painful than they otherwise would. Consider two cases that received considerable attention during the 2020–21 school year. In September 2020, a University of Southern California (USC) business school professor, Greg Patton, was teaching a class on "filler words" in his course on communication for management when he referred to a filler word used in China that sounds somewhat similar to a racial epithet in English.[26] The experience caused extreme pain to some students. A group of students identifying themselves as "Black M.B.A. Candidates c/o 2022" wrote a letter to the school's dean explaining that they were "offended"

---

[23] The phenomenon behind the priming is that "information activated in one context will become more accessible and therefore more likely to be used in subsequent judgment to which it is relevant." See Fritz Strack et al., *Priming and Communication: Social Determinants of Information Use in Judgments of Life Satisfaction*, 18 EUROPEAN J. SOC. PSYCH. 429, 435 (1988).

[24] *Id.* at 434–35.

[25] Christopher Uggen & Chika Shinohara, *Sexual Harassment Comes of Age: A Comparative Analysis of the United States and Japan*, 50 SOCIO. Q. 201, 220–23 (2009).

[26] *See* Colleen Flaherty, *Failure to Communicate: Professor Suspended for Saying a Chinese Word that Sounds like a Racial Slur in English*, INSIDE HIGHER ED. (Sept. 8, 2020), https://perma.cc/KZ5Z-DFV3.

and "appalled" and that their "mental health ha[d] been affected" by the incident.[27] Professor Patton had used the same example in his class for years, with no prior complaint.[28]

In December 2020, Professor Jason Kilborn of the University of Illinois Chicago School of Law gave an examination in his Civil Procedure II class that contained a hypothetical involving racial harassment in which he included an epithet for African Americans in redacted form, using only the first letter of the word followed by several spaces.[29] Seeing the word, even in redacted form, caused some students extreme pain. According to a letter sent from the Black Law Students Association, one student experienced "heart palpitations" upon reading the word, another was so "flustered" by seeing the word on the exam that she "had to take several moments to gather [herself] prior to proceeding with the exam" and then "had to seek counsel immediately after the exam to calm myself."[30] Professor Kilborn had used the same question for years without prior complaint.[31] What was different in fall 2020 – following the summer in which George Floyd was brutally killed by police and Black Lives Matter protests swept the country – was the salience of racism and racial oppression in the minds of the students in both Patton's and Kilborn's classes.[32]

Framing also affects individual reports of subjective well-being. Who one compares oneself to helps determine whether one feels good or bad

---

[27] *See* Tom Bartlett, *How One Word Led to an Uproar*, CHRON. HIGHER ED. (Sept. 14, 2020), https://perma.cc/TF3Z-64CR (citing E-mail from Black M.B.A. Candidates c/o 2022 to Geoffrey Garret, Dean, Univ. of S. Cal. Marshall Sch. Of Bus. (Aug. 21, 2020, 7:00 AM), https://perma.cc/KU5Z-QUYU).

[28] *Id.*

[29] *See* Kathryn Rubino, *Law School N-Word Controversy Is More Complicated Than It Appears at First Glance*, ABOVE THE LAW (Jan. 13, 2021, 4:53 PM), https://perma.cc/DA2X-KJPG.

[30] UIC JMLS Black Law Student Association (@uic_jmls_blsa), TWITTER (Dec. 30, 2020, 9:34 AM), https://perma.cc/2QL2-TZ3E.

[31] Andrew Koppelman, *Is This Law Professor Really a Homicidal Threat? The Punitive Overreactions of University Administrators Grow Ever More Demented*, CHRON OF HIGHER ED. (Jan. 19, 2021), https://perma.cc/KVV9-ZKS3.

[32] Indeed, in their letter to the dean, USC's Black M.B.A. Candidates c/o 2022 referenced both "the murders of George Floyd and Breonna Taylor and the recent and continued collective protests and social awakening across the nation," as well as the diversity training provided to them by USC. *See* Bartlett, *supra* note 27. For a discussion of the effects of enduring perceptions of victimhood, *see* Rahav Gabay et al., *The Tendency for Interpersonal Victimhood: The Personality Construct and its Consequences*, 165 PERSONALITY & INDIVIDUAL DIFFERENCES 1 (2020); Scott Barry Kaufman, *Unraveling the Mindset of Victimhood: Focusing on Grievances Can be Debilitating; Social Science Points to a Better Way*, SCI. AM. (June 29, 2020), https://perma.cc/47KM-6BSV.

about one's current state. Theories of "relative deprivation" were used as early as the 1960s to explain why socially disadvantaged groups sometimes express higher levels of satisfaction than would be expected given their objective disadvantage.[33] The basic insight behind relative deprivation theory is that feelings of satisfaction or dissatisfaction "depend upon comparative context."[34] Members of disadvantaged groups feel less disadvantaged when they compare themselves primarily to those within their group as opposed to those of more privileged groups.[35] As a result, women in highly sex-segregated jobs have been found to have pay and job satisfaction similar to or higher than those of male workers despite lower levels of pay and authority.[36] Women in sex-segregated fields feel happier simply because they are comparing themselves with other women who are also underpaid and underplaced.[37]

Subjective well-being reports are not simply unstable and unpredictable, they are sometimes irrational. In a series of experiments, Daniel Kahneman and colleagues found that individuals under certain circumstances actually preferred more pain over a longer duration than less pain over a shorter duration. In one study, subjects were exposed to two painful experiences – first their hand was immersed in painfully cold water for sixty seconds, and second their hand was immersed in the same painfully cold water for sixty seconds followed by immersion for another thirty seconds in water that was gradually warmed to a still cold but less painful temperature. Subjects preferred the longer trial, even though it involved more overall pain, than the shorter trial.[38] They experienced the more painful experiences as less painful. Kahneman and his colleagues found similar results in a clinical setting when they studied patients'

---

[33] *See, e.g.*, Ronald P. Abeles, *Relative Deprivation, Rising Expectations, and Black Militancy*, 32 J. Soc. Issues 119 (1976); ANGUS CAMPBELL ET AL., THE QUALITY OF AMERICAN LIFE (1976); FAYE J. CROSBY, RELATIVE DEPRIVATION AND WORKING WOMEN (1982).

[34] *See* Karyn A. Loscocco & Glenna Spitze, *The Organizational Context of Women's and Men's Pay Satisfaction*, 72 Soc. Sci. Q. 3, 5 (1991).

[35] *Id.* at 5–6.

[36] *Id.* at 3–5, 12. *See* Linda A. Jackson, *Relative Deprivation and the Gender Wage Gap*, 45 J. Soc. Issues 117, 119–20 (1989) (describing research showing women to be as satisfied with their jobs and pay as men, despite earning less than men).

[37] *See* Jackson, *supra* note 36; Loscocco & Spikes, *supra* note 34 (finding women are satisfied with lower wages when they do the same work as men and do not compare their pay with male coworkers, but are less satisfied when they do compare their pay with higher paid men).

[38] *See* Daniel Kahneman et al., *When More Pain Is Preferred to Less: Adding a Better End*, 4 PSYCH. SCI. 401, 403 (1993).

memories of a painful medical procedure. They found that individuals who went through a colonoscopy procedure during which there was a short and nonpainful interval added to the end of the procedure reported the entire experience as less painful than did those who underwent the procedure without the added interval.[39] Individuals, Kahneman and his colleagues hypothesized, focused predominantly on the worst and the final moments of a particular episode – making reports not only inaccurate, but also irrational at times.

These empirical problems suggest a normative one. To the extent that subjective pain is being used as a proxy for objective oppression, it may not be a very good one. Indeed, subjective pain may at times be inversely correlated with objective oppression.

Amartya Sen has made this point quite vividly. In his book *Commodities and Capabilities*, he looks at the results of a 1944 survey conducted by the All-Indian Institute of Hygiene and Public Health in Singur, India.[40] The survey asked individuals about their health and found that while 48.5 percent of the widowers stated they were either "ill" or in "indifferent" health, only 2.5 percent of widows so reported.[41] Moreover, when individuals were asked if they were simply in "indifferent" health, 45.6 percent of the widowers answered affirmatively while 0 percent of the widows did so.[42] As Sen notes, these findings are striking because females in India have worse objective levels of health when one looks at nutrition levels and access to medical care.[43] Sen argues that the self-reports may be off as true measures of well-being because they may be affected by the social status of the individual.[44] Men, as the heads of households, may magnify their needs and ailments, while women, because of their lower social status, may underplay or diminish their own.[45] Social status may affect expectations and one's expectations may then affect one's report of well-being. This indicates that self-reports may not reflect measurements of the kind of well-being we really care about, which, for Sen, is better reflected by individual capabilities.[46]

---

[39] *See* Donald A. Redelmeier et al., *Memories of Colonoscopy: A Randomized Trial*, 105 PAIN 187, 192 (2003).
[40] AMARTYA SEN, COMMODITIES AND CAPABILITIES app. B at 82 (1985).
[41] *Id.* at 82.
[42] *Id.* at 82–83.
[43] *Id.* at 82–104.
[44] *Id.* at 81–82.
[45] *Id.* at 81–82.
[46] *Id.* at 82.

These challenges with measuring and interpreting subjective pain reports make pain a weak and unstable basis for individual rights. Women in the United States may have been happier when the job market was more segregated. They may have felt less bothered by sexual harassment before they were aware of a legal cause of action to prevent it – but women were not necessarily better off. Black students may have experienced less pain in the classroom before microaggression and antiracism training became commonplace – but they may not have been better off.

But there is another problem as well. If pain matters for the creation of legal rights, then whose pain counts? Excluding transgender girls from female sports teams causes pain, yet their inclusion causes pain as well. If pain matters for legal rights, then how should such tradeoffs be made?

Legal rights are, as scholar Wesley Newcomb Hohfeld explained over a century ago, relational – they impact both the right holder and those whose behavior is limited or constrained as a result.[47] Hohfeld explained that the term "right" is used in different ways but that it is always relational – giving to one person and taking away from another. To use Hohfeld's terminology, a person with a "right" against another person – such as is created by a binding contract – imposes a duty upon that person to act in a particular way. A person with a "privilege" – such as is created by a law protecting certain behavior – may act in a certain way without liability to others who have "no-right" to prevent the conduct.[48] In the context of school sports, if Title IX prohibits misgendering of transgender athletes, then transgender girls will have the "privilege" to play on cisgender girls' teams and cisgender girls will have no "right" to stop them. The relational nature of rights provides a theory for the stark reality that protecting one party or group ends up harming or restricting another.[49] Such is certainly the case in sports.

Transgender girls' inclusion may eliminate their pain, but it does so at the cost of imposing pain on those cisgender girls who oppose inclusion. Consider, for example, the pain expressed by the cisgender plaintiffs in the *Soule* case. The plaintiffs, who were challenging the Connecticut

---

[47] *See* Wesley Newcomb Hohfeld, *Some Fundamental Legal Conceptions as Applied in Judicial Reasoning*, 23 YALE L.J. 16 (1913).

[48] *Id.* at 30 (describing four legal relationships in a table of "Jural Correlatives," the relationships are: right–duty, privilege–no right, power–liability, immunity–disability), *see* Curtis Nyquist, *Teaching Wesley Hohfeld's Theory of Legal Relations*, 52 J. LEGAL EDUC. 238, 239–40 (2002) (providing an overview of Hohfeld's theory and use of terms).

[49] As Mark Kelman bluntly explains: "Remedying the complaining party's felt injury inevitably worsens the position of some other party or parties." KELMAN, *supra* note 17, at 65.

policy allowing transgender girls to play on cisgender girls' high school sports teams, described feeling hopeless, dispirited and depressed as a result of having to compete against students who were biologically male.[50] They experienced pain stemming from lost opportunities to play and lost opportunities to win.[51] According to the plaintiffs: "[W]hen an athlete who is genetically and physiologically male is competing in the girls' division, [p]laintiffs and other girls are forced to step to the starting line thinking, 'I can't win.' 'I'm just a girl.'"[52] They explain that for the plaintiffs "and many other female athletes, they also feel stress, anxiety, intimidation, and emotional and psychological distress from being forced to compete against males with inherent physiological advantages in the girls' category."[53] The plaintiffs describe feeling both physically sick and depressed as a result of having to compete against transgender girls.[54]

For pain to have power in determining rights one must decide whose pain matters and what pain counts. As law professor Mark Kelman notes in his book, *What is in a Name?*, there are, in effect, two options: One can argue that one side's pain is worse, in the sense of being more intense, or, one can argue that one side's pain is more valid, in the sense of being more worthy of attention.[55] Those arguing for inclusion have asserted both.

Those seeking inclusion argue that the pain caused by transgender girls' exclusion is worse than the pain caused by their inclusion. They downplay the pain experienced by cisgender girls by noting that few will be excluded as a result of transgender girls' participation. As Skinner-Thompson and Turner, for example, explain: "There is no evidence or indication that the number of transgender girls desiring to participate in a given sport could be significant enough to deny cisgender girls meaningful athletic opportunities."[56] Of course, if spots are limited, then inclusion by any transgender girl will exclude participation by a cisgender girl. Inclusion will only maximize social happiness if transgender girls will experience more pain

---

[50] *See* Second Amended Verified Complaint for Declaratory and Injunctive Relief and Damages, Soule v. Connecticut Ass'n of Schs., 34–35 No 3:20-CV-00201 (RNC), 2021 WL 1617206 (D. Conn. Apr. 25, 2021).
[51] *Id.* at 34–35.
[52] *Id.* at 34.
[53] *Id.* at 35. *See also* Kelsey Bolar, *8th Place: A High School Girl's Life after Transgender Students Join Her Sport*, DAILY SIGNAL (May 6, 2019), https://perma.cc/LX4T-633Z (describing several cisgender girls' feelings that competing against transgender girls in sports is unfair).
[54] Second Amended Verified Complaint, *supra* note 50, at 35.
[55] *See* KELMAN, *supra* note 17, at 67.
[56] See Skinner-Thompson & Turner, *supra* note 12, at 279.

and loss upon being excluded than will cisgender girls. Those arguing for inclusion argue this as well.

Those arguing for inclusion contend that transgender girls lose more from exclusion and suffer more pain as a result than do cisgender girls because transgender girls are more socially marginalized. Buzuvis, for example, argues that what cisgender girls lose as a result of exclusion is not as important as what transgender girls gain from inclusion. Sports participation is associated with a wide range of physical, psychological and social benefits for participants. While these benefits are important for all individuals, they are particularly salient, Buzuvis contends, for the "especially vulnerable population" of transgender youth.[57] Skinner-Thompson and Turner agree, explaining that "[t]hese social, mental, and physical benefits of interscholastic sports participation are even more necessary for vulnerable groups such as transgender students."[58]

But who really knows? Intersubject pain comparisons are difficult and fraught.[59] How can we measure the subjective pain experienced by the transgender girl who wants to play on a girls' team and is excluded because of her too-masculine body? Similarly, how can we measure the subjective pain experienced by the cisgender girl who does not make a competitive team or fails to win a competitive event because of the participation of a transgender girl? It is at least possible that cisgender girls will feel more pain as a result of transgender inclusion than transgender girls will feel as a result of exclusion simply because cisgender girls may feel more of a sense of entitlement to their preferred outcome than do transgender girls.[60]

Moreover, if rights are to be allocated to maximize overall happiness, then there is no reason to count only the pain of those student-athletes who are most directly affected. Parents, spectators, those who care about transgender rights and those who care about sports may all experience pain depending upon whether transgender girls are included or excluded. Given how divided the country is currently on transgender inclusion, it is not at all clear which position would maximize overall happiness.

---

[57] Erin E. Buzuvis, *Transgender Student-Athletes and Sex-Segregated Sport: Developing Policies of Inclusion for Interscholastic Athletics*, 21 SETON HALL J. SPORTS & ENT. L. 1, 48 (2011) (quoting Arnold Grossman & Anthony R. D'Augelli, *Transgender Youth: Invisible and Vulnerable*, 51 J. HOMOSEXUALITY 111, 112–13 (2006)).

[58] Skinner-Thompson & Turner, *supra* note 12, at 298.

[59] SEN, *supra* note 20.

[60] SEN, *supra* note 40.

It would be cleaner and easier to simply disregard the pain caused by transgender inclusion altogether. Indeed, those arguing for transgender inclusion sometimes do just that, arguing that the pain felt by those who object to inclusion flows from bias and animus and hence is invalid or illegitimate. Tobin and Levi, for example, argue that cisgender girls' discomfort "cannot constitute a legitimate, nondiscriminatory motive for adverse treatment" because the feelings are "a manifestation of bias."[61] "While some non-transgender students or staff may feel genuine discomfort with the presence of a transgender person of the same self-identified and lived gender, these feelings of discomfort," they explain, "are rooted in unfortunate cultural bias and stereotypes regarding transgender people."[62] As such, they conclude, these feelings of discomfort "cannot constitute a legitimate, nondiscriminatory motive for adverse treatment."[63] The Obama administration adopted a similarly dismissive view of cisgender pain in its Dear Colleague Letter, explaining that: "A school's Title IX obligation ... requires schools to provide transgender students equal access to educational programs and activities even in circumstances in which other students, parents, or community members raise objections or concerns... [T]he desire to accommodate others' discomfort cannot justify a policy that singles out and disadvantages a particular class of students."[64]

Similar arguments about the illegitimacy of cisgender discomfort with transgender access have been made in the context of bathrooms. Nathan Heffernan, for example, argues that the efforts to exclude transgender boy Gavin Grimm from using the boys bathroom at his high school were not driven by privacy concerns, but instead by unfounded fear and bias.[65] Ayana Osada calls fears about transgender bathroom use "unfounded" and invalid.[66] Sheila Cavanaugh, in her book, *Queering Bathrooms*, describes a transgender woman who recounts her own fear of using men's

---

[61] Tobin & Levi, *supra* note 10, at 317–18.
[62] *Id.* at 317.
[63] *Id.* at 317–18.
[64] Letter from Catherine E. Lhamon, Assistant Sec'y for C.R., U.S. Dep't of Educ., & Vanita Gupta, Principal Dep. Assistant Att'y Gen. for C.R., U.S. Dep't of Just. to Dear Colleague (May 13, 2016), https://perma.cc/GC4V-CSGR (hereinafter 2016 Dear Colleague Letter).
[65] Nathan Hefferman, Comment, *Potty Politics: G.C. ex rel. Grimm v. Gloucester County School Board, Title IX, and the Challenges Faced by Transgender Students under the Trump Administration and Beyond*, 32 WIS. J. L. GENDER & SOC'Y 215, 230–31 (2017).
[66] Ayana Osada, Note, Obergefell *Liberates Bathrooms*, 62 N.Y.L. SCH. L. REV. 303, 316 (2017–18).

bathrooms yet attributes cisgender women's discomfort at seeing her in female restrooms to hatred rather than fear.[67]

Even if one finds such arguments in the bathroom context convincing – that is, even if one believes that there can be no legitimate reason to oppose transgender women's access to female restrooms – athletics may still require a different analysis. It may be too simple and unduly dismissive to attribute the pain expressed by cisgender girls exclusively to anti-trans bias. Certainly, the cisgender girls opposed to the Connecticut policy requiring transgender inclusion adamantly denied such bias. As one student-athlete expressed: "I think it's a very important thing for people to really understand where we're coming from, instead of just immediately going to, 'We're transphobic.'"[68] Another student explained:

> We live in such a cruel world, and society is just so hard to figure out sometimes... You never know what the reaction is going to be. It's so hard because you want your voice to be heard ... but, how can you know what to say that will affect things positively, instead of people twisting what you're saying and turning it against you?[69]

The girls struggled to explain that their pain stemmed from their belief that transgender girls have an unfair competitive advantage in sports, thereby diminishing their own chances for competitive victories, public attention and college scholarships. As Selina Soule explained: "It's very frustrating and heartbreaking when us girls are at the start of the race and we already know that these [transgender female] athletes are going to come out and win no matter how hard you try."[70] Another cisgender student-athlete explained: "It's not like we're saying that we don't like transgender people... It's just an equality issue where these [cisgender] girls are trying their absolute hardest to try and get those good things on their college resumes, and then it just gets completely taken away from them because there's a biological male racing against them."[71]

One may find the concerns of cisgender girls overblown. Selina Soule may have lost the chance to compete in the New England regionals in

---

[67] SHEILA L. CAVANAGH, QUEERING BATHROOMS: GENDER SEXUALITY, AND THE HYGENIC IMAGINATION 77 (2020). *See also* Marie-Amelie George, *Framing Trans Rights*, 114 Nw. U. L. Rev. 555, 610 (2019) (arguing in the context of transgender bathroom access that "[w]hat the responses to perceived gender transgression imply is that gender conformity is superior, and gender nonconformity is an illness requiring quarantine").
[68] See Bolar, *supra* note 53.
[69] *Id.*
[70] *Id.*
[71] *Id.*

the fifty-five-meter race because she was beaten by two transgender girls and finished eight rather than sixth, which would have qualified her for the regionals. But, given how few transgender girls there are in sports, how many cisgender girls really are likely to lose concrete opportunities because of transgender girls' participation? Cisgender girls may be empirically wrong in their estimations of how much they will lose as a result of transgender girls' participation. But even if cisgender girls' pain is based on empirically exaggerated estimations of harm, this would at most be an argument for discounting their pain. It does not suggest that the pain itself stems from anti-trans bias and is, as a result, invalid.

One may also find cisgender girls' concerns petty or narcissistic. One might want girls to participate in sports for the love of the sport, for the physical benefits, for the camaraderie. One might find the focus on winning, garnering attention and attracting college scholarship money unseemly.[72]

Yet even if one finds such an emphasis on winning to be unappealing, it seems difficult to disregard as somehow invalid. It is difficult, in other words, to argue that girls' pain stemming from their perceived competitive disadvantage should not count, particularly when Title IX itself values competitive glory, recognition and rewards for accomplishments.[73] But, if cisgender pain is not invalid, then it must be counted, which leads one back to the problems of balancing pain.

Subjective pain is a weak basis for transgender rights. Not only is the empirical basis for measuring pain and the normative basis for caring about pain uncertain, but it is far from certain that a hedonic utilitarianism would balance in favor of transgender inclusion. It is perhaps not

---

[72] *See, e.g.*, Buzuvis, *supra* note 57, at 54 ("Policies that include transgender athletes can promote educational values by mitigating the win-at-all-costs mentality that has crept into scholastic sports programs and undermines the educational purpose of athletics").

[73] Title IX 45 C.F.R. § 86.37(c) (1975) (codified at 34 C.F.R. § 106.37 (1991)); "1979 Interpretation" 44 Fed. Reg. 71, 413 (1979) issued by the Department of Health, Education, and Welfare's Office for Civil Rights require institutions to allocate athletic financial scholarships in proportion to the number of male and female participants in its athletic program. The 1979 Interpretation gave schools three ways to show they were providing female and male athletes with equal opportunities. The method most often used by schools was the proportionality test. *See also* Dionne L. Koller, *How the Expressive Power of Title IX Dilutes Its Promise*, 3 HARV. J. SPORTS & ENT. L. 103, 123 (2012) (explaining that "Title IX has signaled two different, and ... arguably conflicting messages. The first message is one of equality and empowerment: that girls and women are entitled to participate in athletics on a basis equal to boys and men. The second, less-examined message is ... that the natural and expected goal of sports participation is to be a highly skilled athlete capable of winning").

surprising, then, that arguments against misgendering often seem to rely too on more objective claims.

3.2 Objective Arguments

It may be that arguments against misgendering focus on pain, not because of a belief that such pain is more intense than other kinds of pain, but because of a belief that the pain is caused by a particularly egregious type of harm or injustice. In other words, the argument against misgendering may not really be about avoiding subjective pain but may instead be about furthering objective goals. Indeed, arguments for transgender inclusion often seem to rest on two distinct objective claims: First, that gender identity expression is critical to human flourishing, and second, that cisgender normativity must be dismantled through the erasure of biological sex.

3.2.1 Individual Flourishing

At times, the argument against misgendering in sports sounds distinctly perfectionist. Misgendering must be prohibited not merely because it causes subjective pain, but because it burdens something that is necessary for human flourishing – namely, expression of one's gender identity. Gender, under this view, is like religion in terms of its centrality to individual identity and well-being.

Religion is treated differently than other interests. Indeed, it was the Supreme Court's effort to treat religious interests the same as other kinds of personal interests in *Employment Division, Department of Human Resources of Oregon v. Smith* that prompted Congressional action and correction.[74] In *Smith*, the Supreme Court held that the Free Exercise Clause of the First Amendment was not violated by neutral laws of general applicability even if they burdened some individuals' sincerely held religious beliefs.[75] In response to *Smith*, Congress passed the Religious Freedom Restoration Act (RFRA) in 1993.[76] RFRA prohibits the federal

---

[74] 494 U.S. 872 (1990).
[75] *See id.* at 879 (explaining that the Court's decisions "have consistently held that the right of free exercise does not relieve an individual of the obligation to comply with a 'valid and neutral law of general applicability on the ground that the law proscribes (or prescribes) conduct that his religion prescribes (or proscribes)'" (quoting *United States v. Lee*, 455 U.S. 252, 263 n.3 (1982))).
[76] 42 U.S.C. §§ 2000bb (1994).

government from substantially burdening a person's exercise of religion, even through neutral laws of general applicability, unless the government can demonstrate that its law furthers a compelling governmental interest and is the least restrictive means possible.[77]

In applying RFRA, courts are highly deferential both to individual assertions of what their religion entails and to assertions of the substantiality of the burden being imposed. In *Burwell v. Hobby Lobby Stores, Inc*,[78] for example, the Supreme Court said that courts "have no business addressing []whether the religious belief asserted in a RFRA case is reasonable[]," nor second-guessing whether the burden on religion was in fact substantial.[79] "[I]t is not for us to say," the Court explained, "that [claimant's] religious beliefs are mistaken or insubstantial. Instead, our 'narrow function ... in this context is to determine' whether the line drawn reflects 'an honest conviction.'"[80] The result, as law professor Frederick Gedicks notes, is that "[o]nce a claimant honestly pleads unacceptable religious costs – that complying with a law violates his or her religious convictions – there remains no justiciable question whose answer will make any difference."[81] Rather, "[c]ourts must defer to the claimant's construction of her beliefs, however implausible it may appear to others."[82]

Religion is treated differently under Title VII as well. Title VII prohibits discrimination in employment on the basis of race, sex, religion and national origin, but it is only in cases involving religion that employers have an obligation to try to accommodate their workers. Once a plaintiff has shown that a religious belief conflicts with an employment

---

[77] "Government may substantially burden a person's exercise of religion only if it demonstrates that application of the burden to the person – (1) is in furtherance of a compelling governmental interest; and (2) is the least restrictive means of furthering that compelling governmental interest." 42 U.S.C.S. § 2000bb-1(b)(1)-(2) (1993). RFRA was invalidated as against state and local governments by *City of Boerne v. Flores*, 521 U.S. 507 (1997).

[78] 573 U.S. 682 (2014).

[79] *Id.* at 724.

[80] *Id.* at 725 (quoting *Thomas v. Rev. Bd. of Ind. Emp. Sec. Div.*, 450 U.S. 707, 716 (1981)).

[81] Frederick Mark Gedicks, *"Substantial" Burdens: How Courts May (and Why They Must) Judge Burdens on Religion under RFRA*, 85 Geo. Wash. L. Rev. 94, 98 (2017). *See also* Kelman, *supra* note 17, at 54 ("It is hard to imagine a court finding that the state has enacted a regulation that does not put significant pressure on a party to obey the regulation, and existing case law does seem to suggest that threatening to impose even fairly trivial fines on those who wish to engage in religiously mandated activity or refuse to engage in religiously prohibited activity can substantially burden free exercise").

[82] Gedicks, *supra* note 81, at 112. *See also* Kelman, *supra* note 17, at 37 ("Right now, courts defer completely to the subjective judgment of the complaining party that forcing facilitation substantially burdens the complaining party's freedom to live in accord with her religious beliefs").

requirement, the burden of proof shifts to the employer to show that it offered the employee a "reasonable accommodation" or that doing so would cause the employer "undue hardship."[83] No such accommodation is necessary when a workplace rule burdens an employee's expression of racial or gender identity.[84]

Scholars have sought to explain, and in some cases defend, the distinctive treatment of religion. According to Andrew Koppelman, "[r]eligion is a distinctive kind of hypergood[] because it attempts to respond to the inadequacy of human existence as a whole."[85] Michael McConnell similarly opines that "[r]eligion is a special phenomenon, in part, because it plays such a wide variety of roles in human life."[86] The special treatment of religion is not without critics,[87] but as a matter of law it is settled.

Only in the context of religion do purely subjective expressions of pain establish legally cognizable claims for protection. The right to freely express one's religious beliefs is treated as important and central to human flourishing in a way that even the right to vote, the right to speech and the right to be free from workplace harassment are not.

[83] See 42 U.S.C. § 2000e(j) (2018) ("The term 'religion' includes all aspects of religious observance and practice, as well as belief, unless an employer demonstrates that he is unable to reasonably accommodate to an employee's or prospective employee's religious observance or practice without undue hardship on the conduct of the employer's business").

[84] See Deborah L. Rhode, *The Injustice of Appearance*, 61 STAN. L. REV. 1033, 1077 (2009) (noting that in the sex context courts have "failed to question the sex stereotypes underlying conventional 'community standards'" and in the race context "workers have generally not succeeded in challenging bans on dreadlocks or cornrows on the grounds that they are racially discriminatory").

[85] Andrew Koppelman, *Is it Fair to Give Religion Special Treatment?*, 2006 U. ILL. L. REV. 571, 594 (2006). For a more recent account of Koppelman's views, see Andrew Koppelman, *How Could Religious Liberty Be a Human Right?*, 16 INT'L J. CONST. L. 985, 986 (2018) (arguing that "[r]eligion is not uniquely valuable" but it is a "class[] of ends that many people share").

[86] See Michael W. McConnell, *The Problem of Singling Out Religion*, 50 DEPAUL L. REV. 1, 42 (2000); see also Jared A. Goldstein, *Is There a "Religious Question" Doctrine? Judicial Authority to Examine Religious Practices and Beliefs*, 54 CATH. U. L. REV. 497, 497–98 (2005); Kent Greenawalt, *Hands Off! Civil Court Involvement in Conflicts over Religious Property*, 98 COLUM. L. REV. 1843, 1844, 1856 (1998).

[87] See Gedicks, *supra* note 81, at 149 ("Allowing churches and believers to claim RFRA exemptions without the check of meaningful judicial review is bad for both law and religion"); Micah Schwartzmann, *What if Religion Is Not Special?*, 79 U. CHI. L. REV. 1351, 1355 (2012) (arguing that religion should not be singled out for special treatment because religion is not ontologically distinct from other deep and valuable concerns); BRIAN LEITER, WHY TOLERATE RELIGION? 63–64 (2013) (arguing there is no valid reason to give claims of religious conscience any special protection over claims based on deeply held secular beliefs); Christopher L. Eisgruber & Lawrence G. Sager, *The Vulnerability of Conscience: The Constitutional Basis for Protecting Religious Conduct*, 61 U. CHI. L. REV. 1245, 1315 (1994) (arguing it is unfair to privilege religion over other deep human commitments).

3.2 OBJECTIVE ARGUMENTS

Arguments for transgender inclusion often ascribe to gender identity the same centrality to human experience reserved for religious identity and describe gender in similar terms. Buzuvis, for example, claims that "[g]ender identity, a person's basic sense of being male or female, is something far from trivial, but is rather a deeply felt, core component of a person's identity."[88] She goes on to say that "[m]edical experts assert that gender identity is a 'fundamental part of being human' and 'the most important determinant of a person's sex' – even more important than other sex-determinant factors such as chromosomes, hormones, genitalia, and secondary characteristics."[89] Tobin and Levi make the comparison with religion explicit and argue that expressions of gender identity should be afforded the same deference as expressions of religious faith. They note that "[u]nder Title VII, an employer is generally expected to accept an employee's assertion of a sincere religious belief at face value, unless there is some objective reason to doubt it, such as behavior obviously inconsistent with that belief."[90] Similarly, they contend that "[a]bsent such a reason, there is no justification for a school to question a student's gender identity."[91]

---

[88] Buzuvis, *supra* note 10, at 352.

[89] *Id.* First quoting Brief of World Professional Association for Transgender Health, Pediatric Endocrine Society et al. as Amici Curiae Supporting Appellant at *12, G.G. ex rel. Grimm v. Gloucester Cty Sch. Bd., 822 F.3d 709 (4th Cir. 2015) (No. 15-2056), then quoting Brief for Maine Chapter of the American Academy of Pediatrics et al. as Amici Curiae Supporting Appellant at *8, Doe v. Reg'l Sch. Unit 26, 86 A.3d 600 (Me. 2013) (No. Pen-12-585).

[90] Tobin & Levi, *supra* note 10, at 328.

[91] *Id.* The idea that authentic gender expression is core to human flourishing seems undercut somewhat by arguments that transgender students should be entitled to play on whichever sex-based team they would like. Arguments for choice seem to reflect a concern about subjective discomfort rather than a conviction that having one's authentic gender identity recognized is important for human flourishing. *See, e.g.*, Buzuvis, *supra* note 15, at 30 ("For some transgender individuals assigned a female sex at birth, but who identify as male, being restricted from women's sports could be exclusive and isolating, especially if they have grown up playing women's sports and have cultivated a community in that context… Given that women's sports leagues often foster community not only among women, but among lesbians in particular, a requirement that 'you must identify as female to play' has the possibility to exclude someone who has been playing with women all along, but who eventually comes out as transgender"). *See also* Skinner-Thompson & Turner, *supra* note 12, at 296 ("For some transgender students, especially those in the early stages of transition, continuing to participate on a team based on their assigned sex may feel more comfortable. No current policy dictates that a transgender student *must* play on the team associated with their gender identity, nor should they. That decision should be made by the individual transgender student based on his or her needs including privacy, safety, and comfort"). If expressing one's gender identity is critical for human flourishing, then it is not clear why transgender boys/men should be permitted to deny their identity by playing on girls'/women's sports teams. If the idea is that transgender boys/men are still affirming their identity as boys/men while playing on female sports teams, then it is not clear why

As a normative matter, treating gender identity as central to personhood and gender expression as critical for human flourishing may seem jarring – perhaps even nonsensical – for those who believe that gender itself is nothing more than a social construction.[92] Law professor Nancy Knauer explains that such a reaction is probably most likely for progressives born in the 1960s and 1970s who, as she describes, grew up being told "that we could be anything we wanted to be and gender didn't matter."[93] The result, Knauer explains, is a tension: "On some elemental level, we were raised to believe that gender is not real and, therefore, it is difficult for us to fathom how one could take gender so seriously that it literally redefines the person."[94] Professor Terry Kogan describes the normative challenges posed by the elevation of gender more starkly. As Kogan explains:

> Given that [for gender critical theorists] gender is socially constructed, a transsexual's autobiographical statement that *he* (a male in the eyes of the critical gender theorist) senses *himself* to have been "born a member of the other gender" makes little sense. According to critical gender theory, while one *may* be born a sexed being, one is not born gendered. One must learn gender presentation.[95]

As a practical matter, if gender were treated like religion, transgender individuals would be entitled to protection or exemption from

---

transgender girls/women could not also affirm their gender identity as girls/women while still playing on boys'/men's teams.

[92] Susanna Rustin, *Feminists Like Me Aren't Anti-Trans – We Just Can't Discard the Idea of "Sex,"* THE GUARDIAN (Sept. 30, 2020), https://perma.cc/HB9F-ZFRB (arguing that the concept of gender identity "can't be forced on women like me who regard questioning gender roles, while advocating on behalf of our sex as the whole point of feminism").

[93] Nancy J. Knauer, *Gender Matters: Making the Case for Trans Inclusion*, 6 PIERCE L. REV. 1, 3 (2007). Probably no one is more associated with the idea of gender as a social construct than Judith Butler. *See* JUDITH BUTLER, GENDER TROUBLE: FEMINISM AND THE SUBVERSION OF IDENTITY 140 (1990) ("Gender ought not to be constructed as a stable identity or locus of agency from which various acts follow; rather gender is an identity tenuously constituted in time, instituted in an exterior space through a stylized repetition of acts" (emphasis omitted)).

[94] Knauer, *supra* note 93, at 3. Knauer argues that "the first step toward understanding transgender issues is to shed this utopian view of gender." *Id.* Ryan T. Anderson identifies a similar tension within transgenderism itself. Ryan T. Anderson, *Transgender Ideology Is Riddled with Contradictions: Here Are the Big Ones*, HERITAGE FOUND. (Feb. 9, 2018), https://perma.cc/MT62-YFS6 ("[Transgender activists] say there are no meaningful differences between man and woman, yet they rely on rigid sex stereotypes to argue that 'gender identity' is real, while human embodiment is not. They claim that truth is whatever a person says it is, yet they believe there's a real self to be discovered inside that person").

[95] Terry S. Kogan, *Transsexuals and Critical Gender Theory: The Possibility of a Restroom Labeled Other*, 48 HASTINGS L.J. 1223, 1229 (1997).

categorizations based on biological sex – whether for sports teams, locker rooms, bathrooms or changing rooms – whenever such categorizations burdened their gender identity by separating them from others of the same gender. Transgender individuals (as well as nontransgender individuals) would also be entitled to protection or exemption from unisex standards of dress or grooming to the extent they substantially burdened one's gender identity expression. Expressions of gender identity would, as a result, be treated better than other expressions of individual status – like race or national origin – where subjective burdens on identity alone do not create a cause of action. The result would be a hierarchy of oppression. This prioritization may be neither inadvertent nor unwelcome.

3.2.2 Social Justice

Arguments against misgendering in sport often rely on a second objective claim – one focused more on social justice than individual flourishing. Namely, transgender girls are girls, transgender women are women, and society must dismantle the cisgender normativity which suggests they are different or less than. Critical to this dismantling is the rejection of biological sex as a useful and meaningful social category.

In her article, "Disaggregating Gender from Sex and Sexual Orientation," Mary Anne Case nicely summed up the traditional distinction between sex and gender when she explained "gender is for adjectives, sex is for nouns."[96] What she meant was that "'sex' refers to the anatomical and physiological distinctions between men and women; 'gender' by contrast, is used to refer to the cultural overlay on those anatomical and physiological distinctions."[97]

This traditional distinction has fallen out of favor among those advocating for transgender rights. As Professor Naomi Schoenbaum explains, the "new view" of sex is "premised on an 'internal, deeply held sense' of one's identity. Under this view, sex 'comes from the brain, not the body,' from 'between your ears, not between your legs.'"[98] While sex and gender were once understood as distinct categories that might each be relevant for particular purposes, the biological definition of sex is now being rejected

---

[96] See Mary Anne Case, *Disaggregating Gender from Sex and Sexual Orientation: The Effeminate Man in the Law and Feminist Jurisprudence*, 105 YALE L.J. 1, 9 (1995).
[97] *Id.* at 10.
[98] Naomi Schoenbaum, *The New Law of Gender Nonconformity*, 105 MINN. L. REV. 831, 866–67 (2020) (first quoting GLAAD MEDIA REFERENCE GUIDE 19 (10th ed. 2016), then quoting Denise Grady, *Anatomy Does Not Determine Gender, Experts Say*, N.Y. TIMES (Oct. 22, 2018), https://perma.cc[D55P-MJRD).

and gender identity is being elevated in importance. Gender identity – which is now both one's "gender" and one's "sex" – is the only categorization that matters.[99]

This new view of sex is at the core of arguments against misgendering. Transgender girls must be allowed to play on girls' sports teams because they are girls.[100] As Skinner-Thompson and Turner explain: "including transgender female athletes in sports consistent with their gender identity helps guarantee that Title IX's goal of providing athletic opportunities for all students (and *all* girls) free of discrimination is realized."[101]

It was this new definition of sex that drove the Obama administration's transgender policies. The 2016 Dear Colleague Letter explained that the Departments of Justice and Education should "treat a student's gender identity as the student's sex for purposes of Title IX and its implementing regulations."[102] "This means," the letter explained, "that a school must not treat a transgender student differently from the way it treats other students of the same gender identity."[103] Gender identity under this view defines both one's gender and one's sex. Biological sex, as a category with legal and social meaning, has simply been erased.[104]

The challenge this new definition of sex poses to cisgender normativity is direct and profound. Cisgender normativity relies on the idea that it

---

[99] See id. at 867 n. 165 ("[G]ender identity is the only medically supported determinant of sex when sex assignment as male or female is necessary… Gender identity does and should control when there is a need to classify an individual as a particular sex") (omission in original) (quoting Expert Decl. of Deanna Adkins, M.D. at 32–33, Carcano v. McCrory, 203 F. Supp. 3d 615 (2016) (No. 1:16-cv-00236), 2016 WL 4256691).

[100] See ACLU et al., *Statement of Connecticut Women's Rights and Gender Justice Organizations in Support of Full and Equal Access to Participation in Athletics for Transgender People* (June 24, 2019), https://perma.cc/CJE4-848L ("Transgender girls are girls and transgender women are women"); Shoshana K. Goldberg, *Fair Play: The Importance of Sports Participation for Transgender Youth*, CTR. FOR AM. PROGRESS (Feb. 8, 2021), https://perma.cc/K23X-A7MC ("These transphobic laws and policies … ignore[e] the reality that transgender women and girls are women and girls…"); *see also* Buzuvis, *supra* note 10, at 353 ("In all, the primacy and essential nature of gender identity means that a transgender girl is a girl, and a transgender boy is a boy"); Anderson, *supra* note 94 (quoting Dr. Deanna Adkins, Director of the Duke Center for Child and Adolescent Gender Care, as saying "From a medical perspective, the appropriate determinant of sex is gender identity").

[101] Skinner-Thompson & Turner, *supra* note 12, at 277 (emphasis added).

[102] 2016 Dear Colleague Letter, *supra* note 64, at 2.

[103] *Id.*

[104] *See, e.g.*, Mey Rude, *It's Time for People to Stop Using the Social Construct of "Biological Sex" to Defend Their Transmisogyny*, AUTOSTRADDLE (June 5, 2014), https://perma.cc/R5ET-B4QX (noting that "[t]here's actually a wide group of people, some 'allies,' some lawmakers and some just outright bigots who all rally behind the idea of using the social construct of 'biological sex' to misgender trans women").

is best for one's gender and biological sex to be aligned. If biological sex is erased as a meaningful category, then what it means to be cisgender loses any social significance. Biological markers may still exist, but biological sex as a social and legal category does not.[105] With the erasure of biological sex comes the eradication of any privilege from having one's gender identity and biology align. If all that matters is one's gender identity, alignment of identity and biological sex becomes unimportant, if not altogether meaningless.

It is not clear whether the demand for biological erasure is meant as a normative trump, an absolute demand which must be pursued at all costs, or whether the demand for biological erasure is subject to empirical balancing and counterweights. That is, are the normative ideals incommensurable with and immune to empirical side constraints, or might they at some point fall to them?

Often, advocates for transgender girls' inclusion in female sports downplay the potential harms such inclusion may cause to cisgender girls. They argue that cisgender girls are not likely to be denied opportunities to win, or at least that they will not be denied such opportunities unfairly. Erin Buzuvis, for example, urges that "policymakers should recognize that medical science does not support the conclusion that natal men have physical features presumed to be advantageous in athletics, nor does it support the conclusion that physical features associated with masculinity produce a competitive advantage."[106] Skinner-Thompson and Turner make the same point. They note that "[t]here is significant overlap between the range of size and strength of boys and girls thus making it likely that an individual transgender student would fit within the range of other team members and competitors."[107] They conclude that while "ensuring that young women are provided an opportunity to compete in sports is one of Title IX's most important objectives... [I]n the context of youth sports, the physical differences between males and females are not significant enough to justify a belief that a transgender female would inevitably prevail against cisgender female athletes."[108]

---

[105] *See Gender Unicorn*, TRANS STUDENT EDUC. RES., https://perma.cc/8UAE-AQSB (rejecting the "inaccurate term" biological sex and referring instead to "sex assigned at birth").

[106] Buzuvis, *supra* note 57, at 40.

[107] Skinner-Thompson & Turner, *supra* note 12, at 276.

[108] *Id.* at 277. *See also* Masha Gessen, *The Movement to Exclude Trans Girls from Sports*, NEW YORKER (Mar. 27, 2021), https://perma.cc/V6M2-5AXR (arguing that "[t]he goal of this campaign [to exclude trans girls from female sports teams] is not to protect cis-girl athletes as much as it is to make trans athletes disappear").

Moreover, they argue, given the small number of transgender girls, their inclusion is unlikely to cause any significant changes to female sports. As Skinner-Thompson and Turner contend: "There is no evidence or indication that the number of transgender girls desiring to participate on a given sport could be significant enough to deny cisgender girls meaningful athletic opportunities, even assuming arguendo that transgender girls have innate physical advantages."[109]

Indeed, it is not clear how many transgender girls and women may ultimately participate on female sports teams and displace biological girls from such teams. Even simple estimates of the percentage of the population that identify as transgender vary widely, making estimates about potential participation numbers on female sports teams by transgender girls mere guesses. A 2017 study by the Williams Institute found that 0.7 percent of youth ages thirteen to seventeen identify as transgender and 0.6 percent of adults identify as transgender.[110] A study published in 2018 based on a 2016 survey of almost 81,000 Minnesota teens found that almost 3 percent reported as transgender or gender nonconforming.[111] A 2016

---

[109] Skinner-Thompson & Turner, *supra* note 12, at 279. *See also* Sean Ingle, *British Olympians Call for IOC to Shelve "Unfair" Transgender Guidelines*, THE GUARDIAN (June 12, 2019), https://perma.cc/CK%K-9VVN (quoting transgender academic Joanna Harper: "Transgender women after hormone therapy are taller, bigger and stronger on average than cisgender women. But that does not necessarily make it unfair. In high levels of sport, transgender women are substantially underrepresented. That indicates that whatever physical advantages transgender women have – and they certainly exist – they are not nearly as large as the sociological disadvantages"); Turban, *supra* note 1 ("There is no epidemic of transgender girls dominating female sports"); David Crary & Lindsay Whitehurst, *Lawmakers Can't Cite Local Examples of Trans Girls in Sports*, ASSOCIATED PRESS, https://perma.cc/3YDV-5ABX ("Legislators in more than 20 states have introduced bills this year that would ban transgender girls from competing on girls' sports teams ... [y]et in almost every case, sponsors cannot cite a single instance in their own state or region where such participation has caused problems").

[110] Jody L. Jerman et al., *Age of Individuals Who Identify as Transgender in the United States*, WILLIAMS INSTITUTE (Jan. 2017), https://perma.cc/S75F-EDU9. *See also* Esther L. Meerwijk & Jae M. Sevelius, *Transgender Population Size in the United States: A Meta-Regression of Population-Based Probability Samples*, 107 AM. J. PUB. HEALTH 1, 4 (2017) (estimating the population of transgender adults in the US at 0.39 percent).

[111] *See* G. Nicole Rider et al., *Health and Care Utilization of Transgender and Gender Nonconforming Youth: A Population-Based Study*, 141 PEDIATRICS 1, 3 (2018). These numbers are similar to those reported by the Centers for Disease Control and Prevention (CDC) finding that nearly 2 percent of high school students in the United States identify as transgender. *See* Valerie Strauss, *CDC: Nearly 2 Percent of High School Students Identify as Transgender – And More than One-Third of Them Attempt Suicide*, WASH. POST (Jan. 24, 2019), https://perma.cc/U32P-WULZ (referring to findings published by the CDC in its Morbidity and Mortality Weekly Report).

survey of first year students at Evergreen College found that 12 percent of respondents self-identified as gender nonconforming or unsure of their gender identity.[112] A 2017 UCLA study of 796,000 California youth ages twelve to seventeen found that 27 percent reported they were viewed by others as gender nonconforming at school.[113] A recent study in Pittsburgh found that "nearly 1 in 10 students in over a dozen public high schools identified as gender diverse."[114]

Nonetheless, arguments about costs suggest that for at least some advocates of transgender inclusion there is a tipping point at which the costs of biological erasure to other groups or other social interests outweigh the benefits. It may be, for example, that if transgender girls have a 10 percent advantage over cisgender girls in a particular sport they should be included, but if they have a 50 percent advantage they should not be. Alternatively, it may be that transgender girls should be permitted to compose up to 10 percent of the positions on a girls' team but not more than that. If there is a tipping point, then costs matter and so does context. Misgendering in sports must be analyzed separately from misgendering in bathrooms, locker rooms or prisons because the counterweights, and hence the tipping points, in each context are likely to differ. Biological erasure may not always be required and the benefits of transgender girls' inclusion may sometimes be outweighed by the costs.

For other advocates, however, biological erasure seems more like a normative trump – an absolute requirement – not subject to balancing and without a tipping point.[115] It is, in other words, a moral commitment,

---

[112] See *New Student Study 2*, EVERGREEN STATE COLL. (2016), https://perma.cc/P4NL-NPL5 (the gender nonconforming students identified as transgender (2 percent), genderqueer (5 percent), not sure (2 percent) and another gender (4 percent); note the percentages in the study add up to 13 percent but the study lists gender nonconforming students as 12 percent).

[113] See Rachel Dowd, *27% of California Adolescents Say They Are Viewed as Gender Nonconforming, Study Finds*, UCLA NEWSROOM (Dec. 13, 2017), https://perma.cc/R7V2-J23J.

[114] See Dan Avery, *Nearly 1 in 10 Teens Identify as Gender-Diverse in Pittsburgh Study*, NBC NEWS (May 21, 2021), https://perma.cc/K5C5-FU3A (citing Kacie M. Kidd et al., 146 Prevalence of Gender-Diverse Youth in an Urban School District 2 (2021), https://perma.cc/WQF9-B9CG).

[115] See, e.g., Strangio & Arkles, *supra* note 1 ("Trans people are exactly who we say we are. There is no one way for women's bodies to be"); *Get the Facts: Trans Equity in Sports*, GENDER JUSTICE, https://perma.cc/WA87-XTPT ("Trans women are women and trans men are men. When trans women compete in women's sports, there are no men competing"); Will Hobson, *The Fight for the Future of Transgender Athletes*, WASH. POST (Apr. 15, 2021), https://perma.cc/9GZW-HY5K (quoting Cathryn Oakley, State Legislative Director at the

not a pragmatic one. But if biological erasure is an absolute requirement, then context does not matter. In all sex-segregated contexts, transgender girls (and women) must be treated as girls (and women) without exceptions or limitations. Male/female categorization need not be eliminated. Retaining such categories, but controlling access based on gender identity rather than biology, does far more to repudiate and reject the importance of biological sex than would eliminating the categories altogether. Indeed, if male/female categorization in sport were eliminated altogether – with all players competing together – a crucial opportunity to signal society's rejection of biological sex and embrace of gender identity would be lost.[116] For biological erasure absolutists, across contexts and regardless of costs, transgender girls and women must fall squarely and exclusively in the female category.

The prioritization of oppression is clear. For biological erasure absolutists, challenging cisgender normativity must always be prioritized over challenging the oppression of biological women. It is not simply the case that transgender girls' oppression is deemed more weighty or more legitimate than that of biological girls, it is instead that the latter is simply erased from view. One cannot both deny biological sex as a meaningful category and argue that biological women, as a social category, deserve greater respect, recognition and reward.[117] Given the conflict, efforts to elevate the status of biological women – traditionally at the heart of Title IX's application to sport[118] – must give way, logically and practically, to the challenges to cisgender normativity. Indeed, traditional arguments for

---

Human Rights Campaign, as calling a group favoring testosterone suppression requirements for transgender girls and women a hate group and saying "I don't know how you find a middle ground between a hate group and people pushing for equality").

[116] This may be one reason why transgender advocates rarely argue for eliminating male/female categorization in sport and focus instead on redefining access. But *see* Erin E. Buzuvis, *Attorney General v. MIAA at Forty Years: A Critical Examination of Gender Segregation in High School Athletics in Massachusetts*, 25 TEX. J. C.L. & C.R. 1, 15–20 (2019) (arguing in favor of more "gender-free" athletic opportunities for high school students).

[117] *See, e.g.*, Emrey Broyles, *Gender-Critical Feminists Are Anti Feminist*, TUL. HULLABALOO (Mar. 11, 2021), https://perma/cc/H3YG-2DUV ("If sex isn't real, the lived reality of women globally is erased" (quoting J.K. Rowling (@jk_rowling), TWITTER (June 6, 2020), https://perma.cc/RB83-6LK9)).

[118] *See* Deborah Brake, *Revisiting Title IX's Feminist Legacy: Moving Beyond the Three-Part Test*, 12 AM. U.J. GENDER SOC. POL'Y & L. 453, 459 (2004) ("[I]n the world of sport, despite massive shifts in female sports participation, there has been a good deal of 'preservation through transformation,' as the opportunity structures have regrouped to preserve the central features of male privilege in sport").

women's rights centered on biological women as a category become, at best, passé and, at worst, anti-trans.[119]

3.3 Conclusion

This chapter has focused on analyzing and critiquing the absolutist arguments for inclusion. It is not the case that all those in favor of transgender girls' inclusion in girls' sports hold absolutist positions, but nor are such arguments simply strawmen chosen for their ease of attack. Rather, absolutist arguments in favor of transgender girls' inclusion have dominated progressive political left discourse on transgender rights since the Obama administration. Moreover, their underlying beliefs about the centrality of gender to identity, the irrelevance of biology and the hierarchy of social oppressions have shaped, in often unseen ways, the broader debate about transgender girls' inclusion in girls' sports.

---

[119] The rise of the label TERF (trans-exclusionary radical feminist) to refer to feminists who oppose transgender girls' and women's participation in women's sports on the grounds that biologically female women should not have to compete against those with biologically male bodies reflects this view. *See* Britni De La Cretaz, *Biden Is Already Trying to Protect Trans Rights – & He Woke Up All the Twitter TERFS*, REFINERY 29 (Jan. 21, 2021), https://perma.cc/M4HB-97RF (noting that "when it comes to allowing trans girls to compete on girls' teams, TERFs argue that they have an advantage over cis girls because they were assigned male at birth. This sexist and transmisogynist claim ... not only underestimates the skill and athletic talent of girls, it isn't based in reality"); *see also* Hobson, *supra* note 115 (noting that "transgender and women's equality activist denounced" proposals to require transgender girls and women in high school sports and above to suppress testosterone for at least one year before competing on female teams "as transphobic and accused the women [supporting the proposals] of having a myopic focus on sports at a critical time for the transgender equality movement"); Michelle Goldberg, *What Is a Woman? The Dispute between Radical Feminism and Transgenderism*, NEW YORKER (July 28, 2014), https://perma.cc/3CL3-ZGPR (noting that "[t]o some younger activists, it seems obvious that anyone who objects" to challenges to treating biological womanhood as a meaningful social category "is simply clinging to the privilege inherent in being cisgender").

4

The Argument for Exclusion

While those advocating for inclusion argue that transgender girls are girls, those advocating for exclusion argue that transgender girls are biologically boys and must be treated as such. While those advocating for inclusion claim that transgender girls will die if they are not treated as girls, those advocating for exclusion argue that women's sports will die if transgender girls are treated as girls.[1] Behind the rhetoric are claims about athletic fairness and personal dignity. The claims, like those undergirding arguments for inclusion, are often empirically dubious and normatively controversial, providing weak justification for an absolute bar on transgender girls' participation in girls' sports.

Excluding transgender girls from girls' sports, as well as from other female-only spaces, became both a rallying cry, and a litmus test, for Republican politicians in the lead-up to the 2024 presidential election. In sharp contrast to President Biden's call for transgender girls' inclusion in sports, Republicans made transgender girls' exclusion from female athletic teams a centerpiece of their political agenda.

Donald Trump, while on the campaign trail in 2024, pledged that as president he would take steps to exclude transgender girls and women from women's sports. Trump argued that transgender girls' and women's inclusion in women's sports harmed individual female athletes and women's sports more generally. According to Trump: "'Young girls and women are incensed that they are now being forced to compete against those who are biological males. It's not good for women. It's not good for women's sports which worked so long and so hard to get to where they are.'"[2] Using intentionally inflammatory rhetoric, Trump said repeatedly

---

[1] See Jo Yurcoba, *Trump Promises to Ban Transgender Women from Sports if Re-Elected*, NBC News (last updated Feb. 1, 2022, 8:17 AM), (quoting former President Trump: "'If this [transgender girls' inclusion in women's sports] does not change, women's sport as we know it will die'"), https://shorturl.at/Nl2kQ.

[2] Kelsey Vlamis, *Trump Rants in CPAC Speech that Women's Sports "Will Die" if Trans Athletes Are Allowed to Compete*, Business Insider (Feb. 21, 2021, 5:24 PM), https://shorturl.at/pdy2W.

that he would "'ban men from participating in women's sports.'"[3] Indeed, Trump went so far as to say that he was running for president in order to "'defeat the cult of gender ideology.'"[4] His advertising bore this out. In the final days before the election, Trump's campaign and affiliated political action committees spent millions of dollars targeting the left's positions on transgender issues. The strategy was successful. One particularly notable advertisement proclaiming: "Kamala is for they/them. President Trump is for you," is widely credited with having significantly impacted the election result.[5]

Florida governor, and 2024 Republican presidential candidate, Ron DeSantis, holds similar views. Like Trump, DeSantis has argued that including transgender girls and women in women's sports is unfair to individual athletes and threatens to "destroy women's athletics."[6] In 2021, he signed into law the Fairness in Women's Sports Act, which barred transgender girls and women in Florida from playing on public school teams designated for females.[7] In 2022, he leaned into controversy when he signed a proclamation declaring that the collegiate swimmer who had placed second to transgender swimmer Lia Thomas in a National Collegiate Athletic Association (NCAA) title race was in fact the true winner of the event. "'In Florida, we reject these lies and recognize Sarasota's Emma Weyant as the best women's swimmer in the 500y freestyle,'" DeSantis declared.[8] In the lead-up to the 2024 presidential election, DeSantis, like Trump, made transgender exclusion, as well as an attack

---

[3] Andrew Kacqynski, *Trump Repeatedly Celebrated the Inclusion of Transgender Women in His Beauty Pageant*, CNN POLITICS (June 16, 2023, 9:03 PM), www.cnn.com/2023/0616/politics/trump-transgender-women-pageants-kfile/index.html.

[4] Kelly McClure, *Trump Targets "Cult of Gender Ideology" during Campaign Event in South Carolina*, SALON (Jan. 29, 2023, 10:17 AM), https://shorturl.at/jW3m0.

[5] Shane Goldmacher, et al., *How Trump Won, and How Harris Lost*, N.Y. TIMES (last updated Nov. 16, 2024), www.nytimes.com/2024/11/07/us/politics/trump-win-election-harris.html; *Why Anti-Transgender Political Ads Are Dominating the Airwaves This Election*, PBS News (Nov. 2, 2024, 5:35 PM), https://shorturl.at/CiLLY; Sarah Fortinsky, *Chris Christie: Most Effective Trump Ad Was "Kamala Harris is for They/Them,"* THE HILL (Nov. 11, 2024, 8:59 AM), https://thehill.com/homenews/campaign/4983706-chris-christie-donald-trump-win/; Jamie Joseph, *Trump's "They/Them" Ads Combined Culture War, Economic Worries to Make Effective Pitch*, FOX NEWS (Nov. 10, 2024, 2:33 PM), https://shorturl.at/VBbaM.

[6] Steve Contorno and Paul LeBlanc, *DeSantis Courts Further Controversy By Honoring Swimmer Who Finished Second to Lia Thomas*, CNN POLITICS (Mar. 22, 2022, 9:52 PM), https://shorturl.at/0EpiM.

[7] Bobby Caina Calvan, *Florida Governor OKs Limits on Transgender Student Athletes*, AP (June 2, 2021, 2:41 PM), https://apnews.com/article/florida-religion-government-and-politics-health-sports-38ef69813259d68ca84308fd884e5669.

[8] *Id.*

on "woke" politics more broadly, a centerpiece of his campaign. During a speech at Liberty University, DeSantis went so far as to call transgender swimmer Lia Thomas a "fraud," stating that "it is wrong to have a swimmer compete for three years on the men's swim team, switch to the women's team and win the women's national championship... That is fraud. That is wrong."[9] DeSantis later defended his comments, stating that "'we need to protect the integrity of women's sports and ensure that female athletes have a fair playing field."[10] DeSantis continued his inflammatory rhetoric. After Bud Light partnered with transgender activist Dylan Mulvaney on an Instagram video, sparking outrage among many on the political right, DeSantis released a video mocking transgender females who participate in women's sports, calling them "the men who hacked the system. Once mediocre in the men's division, now cream of the crop in the women's."[11]

The exclusionary rhetoric of the 2024 Republican presidential frontrunners reflected the position of the Republican Party more broadly. Indeed, in April 2023 and again in January 2025, House Republicans passed a bill that would ban transgender athletes from female sports teams at schools that receive federal funds. The bill would require that students be assigned to teams based solely on "reproductive biology and genetics at birth."[12] Although there is little chance the bill will pass the Senate, Republicans clearly believe that taking a stand against transgender girls' inclusion in girls' sports is a winning position for them. Several polls suggest they are right. A May 2023 poll of 1,365 adults conducted by the *Daily Mail* found that 67 percent of Republicans as well as 51 percent of Democrats believe that transgender athletes should only be allowed to play on the sports team that matched their birth sex.[13] A May 2023 Gallup

---

[9] *Florida Governor Ron DeSantis Calls Transgender Swimmer Lia Thomas a "Fraud,"* MARCA (Apr. 14, 2023, 8:15 PM), www.marca.com/en/ncaa/2023/04/15/6439fa7c46163f549d8b4598.html.

[10] *Id.*

[11] David Hookstead, *Ron Desantis' Team Drags Bud Light, Mocks Transgender Athletes with New Ad*, OUTKICK (Apr. 18, 2023, 10:11 AM), https://shorturl.at/W8Ah5.

[12] Clare Foran and Shawna Mizelle, *House Passes Anti-Trans Sports Bill*, CNN POLITICS (Apr. 20, 2023, 11:08 AM) www.cnn.com/2023/04/20/politics/house-transgender-sports-bill/index.html; Kyle Stewart et al., *House Passes Bill to Ban Transgender Student-Athletes from Women's Sports*, NBC NEWS (Jan. 12, 2025, 5:14 PM) https://shorturl.at/u0P0H.

[13] James Reinl, *Women's Rights Group Says Athena Ryan's 1600m Victory is "Not Isolated" and More Girls Will Lose Out to Trans Athletes from Biden's Title IX Changes – And Polls Show it Could Hurt the President's Chances in 2024*, DAILY MAIL (last updated May 22, 2023, 5:04 PM), https://shorturl.at/KssEf.

poll of 1,011 adults found a more stark party divide but still significant support for exclusion among both parties. According to the Gallup poll, 93 percent of Republicans compared with 48 percent of Democrats said that transgender athletes should play only on teams that matched their birth gender. Overall, the Gallup poll found, 69 percent of Americans, up from 62 percent in 2021, said that transgender athletes should play only on teams that matched their birth gender.[14]

Certainly, there are more nuanced public voices on the side of exclusion. Nancy Hogshead-Makar, former Olympic swimmer and founder of Champion Women, an advocacy organization for girls and women in sports, has publicly expressed her concerns about transgender girls' participation in female sports but has adopted a position short of absolute exclusion. She has argued that "[t]ransgender women should be allowed to compete in women's athletics, so long as these individuals can show that they've mitigated the athletic advantages that come with male puberty."[15] The Women's Sports Policy Working Group, cofounded by tennis legend Martina Navratilova, is also skeptical of inclusion but has adopted a position short of absolute exclusion. The group calls for transgender girls' exclusion from girls' sports only after fifth grade and urges for transgender women to be included in sports in other ways.[16]

Yet the voices receiving the most attention, and those having the greatest impact, are the most extreme – the most absolutist. As of October 2025, twenty-seven states have adopted legislation excluding transgender girls and women from female sports teams.[17] The laws typically define sex for the purposes of assigning students to sex-segregated teams either in

---

[14] Jeffrey M. Jones, *More Say Birth Gender Should Dictate Sports Participation*, GALLUP (June 12, 2023). *See also* John McCormack, *Gallup: Growing Super-Majority of Americans Agree with Conservatives about Transgender Athletes*, NATIONAL REVIEW (June 12, 2023, 9:57 AM), https://shorturl.at/Fgf7o.

[15] Nancy Hogshead-Makar, *It Was Not Fair When I Raced against Doped-Up East Germans and It Is Not Fair For Women to Compete against Transgender Swimmer Lia Thomas*, DAILY MAIL (last updated Dec. 19, 2021, 2:25 PM), https://shorturl.at/50yrx.

[16] *Our Position: Female Sports Are for Female Athletes*, WOMEN'S SPORTS POLICY WORKING GROUP (Mar. 3, 2025), https://womenssportspolicy.org/the-resolution/ ("Accommodations can include competing in the men's category or an 'open' category for everyone who is not female. Alternatively, schools and sport governing bodies could create new categories for transgender athletes who wish to compete based on their gender identity, *so long as there is no direct competition with females and no overall reduction of female athletes' right to their share of all participation opportunities and scholarships, as guaranteed by long-standing Title IX regulations*"); original emphasis.

[17] *Bans on Transgender Youth Participation in Sports*, EQUALITY MAPS, https://shorturl.at/hMm1o.

terms of biological characteristics or in terms of the sex indicated on the student's original birth certificate.

Kansas's Fairness in Women's Sports Act is an example of the first approach. According to the Kansas law: "'Biological sex' means the biological indication of male and female in the context of reproductive potential or capacity, such as sex chromosomes, naturally occurring sex hormones, gonads and nonambiguous internal and external genitalia present at birth, without regard to an individual's psychological, chosen or subjective experience of gender."[18] The law provides that "[i]nterscholastic, intercollegiate, intramural or club athletic teams or sports that are sponsored by a public educational entity or any school or private postsecondary educational institution whose students or teams compete against a public educational entity shall be expressly designated" as for males, for females or coed.[19] Teams that are "designated for females, women or girls shall not be open to students of the male sex."[20] North Dakota's law is similar. It provides that "'[s]ex' means the biological state of being female or male, based on an individual's non ambiguous sex organs, chromosomes, and endogenous hormone profile at birth,"[21] and it requires schools to designate their athletic teams as male, female or coed.

South Dakota's Protect Fairness in Women's Sports Act is an example of the second approach. Under South Dakota law, "biological sex is either female or male and the sex listed on the student's official birth certificate may be relied upon if the certificate was issued at or near the time of the student's birth."[22] Louisiana's law is similar, providing that for the purposes of sex-segregated sports, "'[b]iological sex' means a statement of a student's biological sex on the student's official birth certificate which is entered at or near the time of the student's birth."[23]

4.1 Fairness

The argument for exclusion is most often framed as an argument about fairness. Cisgender girls and women are treated unfairly, the argument goes, when they are required to compete against transgender female athletes because the latter have significant physical advantages.

---

[18] Kan. Stat. Ann. 2238, § 2(a) (2023).
[19] Kan. Stat. Ann. 2238, § 3(a) (2023).
[20] Kan. Stat. Ann. 2238, § 3(b) (2023).
[21] N.D. Cent. Code 1249, §1.2. (2023).
[22] S.D. Codified Laws, §1 (2022).
[23] 44 La. Stat. Ann. §1.1. (2022).

Cisgender girls and women are, as a result, unfairly deprived of opportunities, rewards and recognition.

Often the fairness argument focuses on individual athletes' opportunity to win. Transgender inclusion deprives cisgender athletes of victories that are rightfully theirs. This was the message Governor Ron DeSantis sought to convey when he celebrated Emma Weyant as the true winner instead of transgender swimmer Lia Thomas. It is also the argument made by the plaintiffs in the *Soule* case and emphasized publicly by the Alliance Defending Freedom (ADF), the advocacy group representing them. In their complaint, for example, the *Soule* plaintiffs argued that a transgender girl's "switch to competing in the girls' events immediately and systematically deprived female athletes of opportunities to advance and participate in state-level competition."[24] The ADF has repeated the argument numerous times in its own press releases. In a press release from June 18, 2019, the ADF claimed that "boys have consistently deprived Soule and the other female athletes of honors and opportunities to compete at elite levels."[25] Similarly, in a press release from May 26, 2021, the ADF argued that "Mitchell [a cisgender girl] … would have won the 2019 state championship in the women's 55-meter indoor track competition, but because two males took first and second place, she was denied the gold medal. Soule, Smith, and Nicoletti likewise have been denied medals and/or advancement opportunities."[26]

Implicitly, the individual fairness argument prioritizes athletics for its prizes over its more generalized health and wellness benefits. Transgender participation is unfair because it deprives cisgender girls of victories and elite competition, not because it deprives them of opportunities to participate in sports at all. The individual fairness argument also treats female sports as an ability category, the bounds of which necessarily exclude transgender athletes. Transgender inclusion is unfair because transgender girls' and women's physical advantages place them outside the relevant ability range.

Normatively, both assumptions are controversial. Certainly, sports are heavily valued for their scarce prizes and recognition. However, there are some contexts and some competition levels where sports are

---

[24] See Soule v. Connecticut Ass'n of Schools, Second Amended Verified Complaint for Declaratory and Injunctive Relief and Damages, Case 3:20-cv-00201-RNC (Aug. 11, 2020).
[25] *Female Athletes Challenge Connecticut Policy that Abolishes Girls-Only Sports*, ALLIANCE DEFENDING FREEDOM (June 18, 2019), https://shorturl.at/UqoE9.
[26] *Athletes Appeal Ruling that Allows CT Athletic Association to Abolish Girls-Only Sports*, ALLIANCE DEFENDING FREEDOM (May 26, 2021), https://shorturl.at/GTkJV.

valued primarily for their participation benefits rather than for their prizes – consider, for example, elementary school teams or Little League play. When sports are valued for their participation benefits, the argument that transgender participants should be excluded because they win too much loses its force. As long as cisgender girls and women continued to have opportunities to participate, transgender inclusion would not be "unfair." Concerns about "fairness" in such contexts would be less likely to prompt calls for transgender exclusion and more likely to prompt calls for expanded recreational leagues and noncut or lottery-based participation opportunities for all students. In short, in contexts in which the value of sports is viewed as less about winning and more about participation, arguments for transgender exclusion that focus on likely winners lose their force.

Similarly, conceiving of the female sports category as an ability category, while probably the dominant view, is not the only one. Indeed, at least some advocates for transgender inclusion in women's spaces contend that the female category should be defined in terms of gender marginalization and oppression. The student body president of Wellesley College, for example, argued in favor of transgender men's inclusion on the grounds that Wellesley, as a women's college, is "still, and always will be, a school to educate people who are of marginalized genders."[27] A professor at Wellesley who was also in favor of admission of transgender men explained that Wellesley "has always been a home for people who are 'not in positions of power in a patriarchal society.'"[28] To the extent the female category is understood in this way – as a refuge for the politically less powerful – there would be no reason to exclude transgender girls (or boys) from the category and no "unfairness" in their inclusion.

Even taken on its own terms, however, the argument that transgender inclusion unfairly deprives particular cisgender girls of opportunities to win is weak. Cisgender girls and women, like all athletes, have no right to have athletic eligibility lines drawn in a way that provides them with relative advantages over their competitors. Nor are they treated unfairly when lines are drawn in a way that disadvantages them.

Innumerable ability-relevant eligibility distinctions are possible and all benefit some athletes more than others. This does not make the eligibility

---

[27] Vimal Patel, *At Wellesley College, Students Vote to Admit Trans Men*, N.Y. TIMES (Mar. 14, 2023), www.nytimes.com/2023/03/14/us/wellesley-college-trans-nonbinary.html.
[28] *Id.*

rules unfair. Basketball leagues might, for example, divide female players based on height. Players might be divided into a less than 5 foot 10 inch category and an equal to or taller than 5 foot 10 inch category. Alternatively, players might be divided into a less than 6 foot 5 category and an equal to or taller than 6 foot 5 inch category. The first eligibility line will benefit players who are 5 foot 9 inches more than the latter eligibility line, but neither line is unfair to participants. No individual athlete has a right to victory, nor does any athlete have the right to have ability-relevant eligibility lines drawn in a way that favors them relative to their competitors. Individual cisgender girls are treated no more unfairly when they are required to compete against transgender girls than they are when required to compete against cisgender girls with significant physical advantages.

The response might be to pivot from claims based in rights to claims based in public policy. In other words, the argument might be that even if athletes are not entitled to particular eligibility rules as a matter of right – and, hence, cisgender athletes are not unfairly deprived of something to which they have a right when they compete against and lose to transgender athletes – as a matter of sound public policy, eligibility rules for athletic events should be drawn so as to tighten competition, reduce the risk of injury, and increase enjoyment for players and spectators alike. The argument is that drawing eligibility lines based on transgender status serves these goals because the status coincides with a range of ability-relevant advantages – for example, height, weight, testosterone level. In short, for policy reasons, transgender status is a good basis for ability-relevant eligibility rules because transgender status is a good proxy for ability.

The problem is that using transgender status as a proxy for ability is so wildly over- and underinclusive that it is not substantially related to the goal of achieving competitively tight athletic categories. Using transgender identity as a proxy for ability is overinclusive because many transgender girls and women do not have athletic advantages over cisgender girls and women. Particularly prepuberty, ability differences between biological boys and girls are small and many girls outperform boys in sports.[29] The same is true for cisgender girls and transgender girls. Even among

---

[29] See David J. Handelsman et al., *Circulating Testosterone as the Hormonal Basis of Sex Differences in Athletic Performance*, 39 ENDOCRINE REVIEW 803 (July 2018), at 805, 812; David J. Handelsman, *Sex Difference in Athletic Performance Emerge Coinciding with the Onset of Male Puberty*, 87 CLINICAL ENDOCRINOLOGY 68 (July 2017), at 68–72.

adults there is significant overlap between biological women and biological men on several ability-relevant traits. Consider, for example, the height distributions of biological women and men.[30] Although the mean height for men is taller than the mean height for women, there is significant overlap in the distributions, with some women taller than most men and some men shorter than most women.[31] The same is true for weight and for skeletal muscle mass.[32] Even when it comes to testosterone levels, some transgender women suppress their levels to numbers within the biological female range.[33] Given high levels of individual variation, many transgender girls and women will not in fact possess ability-relevant advantages over cisgender girls and women. Exclusion based on transgender status will, as a result, exclude girls and women who should not, for ability or competitiveness reasons, be excluded.

Using transgender status as a proxy for ability is similarly underinclusive in the sense that it allows cisgender athletes to be included even if they have rare and extreme ability advantages. Advocates for inclusion have made precisely this argument with regard to Michael Phelps and Simone Biles. For example, Gender/Justice, an advocacy group for gender equity, points out that Phelps excelled at swimming because "he is hyper-joined in the chest ... his double-jointed ankles bend 15 percent more than his rivals' and, coupled with his size-14 feet, help his legs act like flippers." They note that Biles, at 4 foot 8 inches, has a height-to-strength ratio that "enables her to do more flips/maneuvers in the same amount of time as other gymnasts who might be taller." The point, they emphasize, is that transgender athletes do not possess physical

---

[30] See *Transgender Women Athletes and Elite Sport: A Scientific Review*, CANADIAN CENTRE FOR ETHICS IN SPORT, at 5, 18 (noting that "[e]lite athletes tend to have higher than average height across genders"), https://shorturl.at/cd3i6.

[31] *See, e.g.*, Mark F. Schilling et al., *Is Human Height Bimodal?* 56 THE AMERICAN STATISTICIAN 223 (Aug. 2002).

[32] Ian Janssen et al., *Skeletal Muscle Mass and Distribution in 468 Men and Women Aged 18-88 yr*, 89 J. APP. PHYS. 81 (Feb. 2000), at 81–88, https://journals.physiology.org/doi/full/10.1152/jappl.2000.89.1.81.

[33] See CANADIAN CENTRE FOR ETHICS IN SPORT, note 29 at 30 (explaining that "[p]ost gonad removal, many trans women experience testosterone levels far below that of premenopausal cis women"). See also Jennifer J. Liang et al., *Testosterone Levels Achieved by Medically Treated Transgender Women in a United States Endocrinology Clinic Cohort*, 24 ENDOCRINE PRACTICE 135 (Feb. 2018), at 135–42 (finding that among transgender women undergoing testosterone suppression treatment, those in the highest suppressing quartile achieved testosterone levels in the female range while those in the second in the second highest suppressing quartile did not achieve female levels but remained below the male range).

advantages that are any more extreme than those possessed by Phelps and Biles over their same-sex peers.[34]

Of course, these same arguments about over- and underinclusiveness could be made about sex-based eligibility rules generally. Many men would lose to elite female athletes, so from a competitive standpoint there is no reason to exclude them from play. Meanwhile some female athletes are so exceptional that they come to dominate the female category and undermine its competitiveness.[35] In other words, from a policy perspective focused on competitive tightness, it is not only difficult to justify excluding transgender women from the female category, it is difficult to justify a female (and male) category altogether. Policy concerns about competitive tightness in athletic contests seem most sensibly and directly to suggest a move to gender-neutral ability categories.

A variant of the individual fairness argument focuses on individual safety, arguing that transgender girls must be excluded because of safety concerns for cisgender women. While such concerns are undoubtedly real in some contexts,[36] empirical evidence does not support a blanket exclusion of all transgender athletes from all sports at all levels. Safety concerns do not exist in noncontact sports – gymnastics, swimming, weightlifting, track and field. Moreover, even in contact sports, safety concerns seem far less real for younger children where height and weight differentials based on sex are smaller. The safety argument, as a reason to exclude all transgender girls and women from female sports, is too overinclusive to be persuasive.

It may be, however, that the fairness argument for transgender exclusion is not, at least not exclusively or even primarily, about an individual athlete's right to win, or even about the advantages of tight athletic competitions, but about participants' and nonparticipants' right to have the female category defined and understood in a particular way. Under this conception, the female sports category is not simply an

---

[34] *Get the Facts: Trans Equity in Sports*, GENDER/JUSTICE, www.genderjustice.us/get-the-facts-trans-equity-in-sports/.

[35] *See, e.g.*, Christina Capatides, *Greatest Female Athletes of All Time*, CBS NEWS (July 16, 2015, 11:20 AM), www.cbsnews.com/pictures/greatest-female-athletes-of-all-time/5/.

[36] See Alec Schemmel, *Injured Volleyball Player Speaks Out after Alleged Transgender Opponent Spiked Ball at Her*, ABC 13NEWS (last updated Apr. 20, 2023, 4:33 PM), https://wlos.com/news/local/volleyball-player-injured-after-transgender-opponent-spiked-ball-at-her-speaks-out; Anna Statz, *Trans-Identified Male Seen Injuring Female Player during Women's League Game*, REDUXX (May 31, 2023), https://shorturl.at/84UsH; *Tiyan Rugby Coach Calls for Ban on Transgender Players after Injuries at Weekend Match*, KUAM NEWS (Apr. 11, 2022, 7:11 PM), https://shorturl.at/OHgCD.

ability category, it is a social status category defined to serve certain social goals and provide certain social benefits. It is not fair to athletes or to society more generally to define the category in a way that undermines these goals and undercuts these benefits. Expressed in this way, the fairness argument is not solely, or even primarily, about individual competitors, but instead about groups.

It is this view of fairness that may be underlying and driving claims that transgender girls' and women's inclusion in female sports will kill women's sports. Inclusion is not unfair because of its effects on any particular cisgender female athlete, inclusion is unfair because it changes the nature and benefit of "female sports" in a way that is unfair to participants and nonparticipants alike. The fairness argument conceived of this way is about the social meaning of female sports for cisgender girls and women.

As an initial matter, it is difficult to justify a focus on cisgender girls and women as a group without ensuring a comparable focus on transgender girls and women. That is, as a normative matter, if group impact is to motivate policy decisions, it seems unjustifiable to prioritize group benefits for cisgender girls over group benefits for transgender girls (and boys). However, even taken on its own terms – with a focus on cisgender girls – the group fairness argument provides a weak basis for absolute exclusion.

Those arguing for exclusion do not make explicit what they understand the group benefits of female sports to be, though it seems implicit in the calls for exclusion of transgender girls that the benefits at issue accrue to biological girls and women because of the way society values and recognizes female bodies and physical accomplishments through sport. As I make clear in the last chapter, I find persuasive the argument that the female sports category is both a social category providing group benefits as well as an ability category meant to tighten competition. Moreover, I find persuasive that as a social category, female sports have traditionally, and certainly since the passage of Title IX, served to change the way society and cisgender girls think about female bodies. In particular, the celebration of elite female athletes serves to emphasize the power and agency of female bodies and to value these bodies for their strength as opposed to their objectified sex appeal.

There are two ways that transgender girls' participation in female sports might plausibly undermine the group benefits of female sports. First, transgender girls might dominate girls' sports in terms of overall participation numbers. If this were the case, female sports would cease to be a site where such bodies were seen and celebrated for agentic strength rather than objective beauty. Moreover, female sports would cease to be defined and determined by the distinct physicality of the female body. Second, transgender girls might dominate not the overall number of participants in female sports but the winners' circle for female sports. If this were the case, cisgender girls would no longer see those with their bodies celebrated and rewarded for their talent and achievement. However, neither concern about group benefits can justify the blanket exclusion of transgender girls and women from female sports.

Given the small numbers of transgender individuals in the population, there is no way that transgender girls will numerically dominate the female sports category. According to the Williams Institute at UCLA Law School, 0.52 percent of the US adult population identifies as transgender. Among those aged eighteen to twenty-four, 1.31 percent do and among those aged thirteen to seventeen, 1.43 percent do.[37] A recent Pew Center survey similarly found that 0.6 percent of all adults identified as transgender, while among those aged eighteen to twenty-seven the number was 2 percent.[38] Indeed, even in those schools that seem to have unusually high percentages of transgender students, transgender females will not numerically dominate cisgender females in sports. One of these outliers is Mills College, a historically women's college which was one of the first to embrace transgender students. At Mills, between 5 and 9 percent of the student body has identified as transgender in recent years[39] – a number considerably higher than the national average, but still not high enough to displace cisgender girls from significant amounts of playing opportunities.

Whether transgender women will dominate cisgender ones in the winner's circle is a different question. Transgender women may dominate the winner's circle for a sport or particular event even if they make up a

---

[37] Jody L. Herman et al., *How Many Adults and Youth Identify as Transgender in the United States?*, WILLIAMS INSTITUTE (June 2022), https://williamsinstitute.law.ucla.edu/publications/trans-adults-united-states/.

[38] The Pew Research Center Survey found significantly higher numbers when it combined those who identified as transgender or as nonbinary. Among all adults it found 1.6 identified as trans or nonbinary and, among those aged 18–29, 5.1 percent so identified. *See* Anna Brown, *About 5% of Young Adults in the U.S. Say their Gender Is Different from Their Sex Assigned at Birth*, PEW RESEARCH CENTER (June 7, 2022), www.pewresearch.org/short-reads/2022/06/07/about-5-of-young-adults-in-the-u-s-say-their-gender-is-different-from-their-sex-assigned-at-birth/.

[39] Moya Stone, *Transitions: The Transgender Policy*, MILLS QUARTERLY (June 22, 2022), https://quarterly.mills.edu/transitions-the-transgender-policy/.

miniscule proportion of the participants. Indeed, a transgender woman, even if she is the only transgender participant, might dominate a particular women's sporting competition and undermine the group benefits that cisgender girls and women would have gained from seeing those with similar bodies celebrated and rewarded. Indeed, for some time in 2022, Lia Thomas seemed to exhibit this kind of dominance in women's college swimming.[40] Other transgender women athletes who have achieved some measure of dominance in their sports include Fallon Fox in mixed martial arts,[41] and Kate Weatherly in mountain biking.[42] Yet there is no reason to exclude transgender girls at ages or in sports when their dominance is unlikely – consider, for example, gymnastics, figure skating, ultra distance running. Similarly, there is no reason to exclude transgender girls who, because of their age at transition or because of the nature of their medical intervention, are unlikely to dominate athletic competition. Categorical exclusion would harm transgender athletes with no physical advantages over their cisgender peers and is not necessary to ensure that cisgender girls receive the group benefits of female sports. The more sensible response, and the one endorsed by the major athletic governing bodies, would be to determine what factors give biological males an advantage over biological females in any given sport and to require that transgender girls and women undertake mitigation measures for these factors.[43]

---

[40] In the 2022 Ivy League Women's Swimming & Diving Championship, Lia Thomas won three individual events and broke six records. See Pat Ralph, *Penn Swimmer Lia Thomas Sets Six Records at Ivy League Championships*, PHILLY VOICE (Feb. 21, 2022), www.phillyvoice.com/lia-thomas-penn-transgender-swimmer-ivy-league-championships/.

[41] Prior to retiring, Fallon Fox had a professional mixed martial arts record of five wins (three via knockout and two via submission). She had one loss via technical knockout. See *Fallon Fox, Transgender MMA Fighter Who Broke the Skull of Her Opponent*, BJJ WORLD, https://shorturl.at/9OUBd.

[42] Weatherly won the elite women's division in New Zealand's downhill mountain bike national championship in 2018 and 2019. See Zachary Rogers, *"We are All Women": Trans Cyclist Dominating Women's Racing Slams New Trans Athlete Rule*, NBC 15NEWS (June 23, 2022, 12:33 PM), https://shorturl.at/pVckT; Daphna Witmore, *In Defence of Women's Sports*, REDLINE (Oct. 28, 2018), https://rdln.wordpress.com/2018/10/28/in-defence-of-womens-sports/.

[43] The NCAA in 2022 adopted a policy that called for transgender athletes' participation for each sport to be determined by the policy for the national governing body of that sport, or if there was no national governing body policy, by the sport's international federation, or if there is no international federation policy, by the policy criteria established by the International Olympic Committee (IOC). See Participation Policy for Transgender Student-Athletes, NCAA, www.ncaa.org/sports/2022/1/27/transgender-participation-policy.aspx. USA Swimming adopted a policy in 2023 that provides for transgender female athletes to compete in elite competitions they must show that the testosterone level is

4.2 Flourishing

The weakness of both individual and group-based fairness arguments to justify absolute exclusion of transgender athletes suggests that calls for absolute exclusion may in fact rest on other grounds. Calls for absolute exclusion may not in fact be about who wins any particular competition, but about how a meaningful life is understood and recognized. Calls for exclusion may, in other words, be grounded in a perfectionist claim of human flourishing rather than in an empirically grounded claim of fairness. Calls for categorical exclusion of transgender girls and women from female sports may at their core be claims about human flourishing and the necessary alignment of biological sex and gender. Respecting human dignity, in other words, may be viewed as requiring denial of the perceived delusion of transgenderism.

There is both a secular and a religious version of this argument. The secular version of the argument is that transgender girls and women are either mistaken or sick. They should not be included in the female category – in sports or in other contexts – because doing so indulges an untruth that is harmful to the possessor. Douglas Murray, author of *The Madness of Crowds: Gender, Race and Identity*, for example, argues that "[t]rans may, in years, turn out to be psychologically or biologically provable. But to date, no meaningful psychological differences have been shown to exist between trans and non-trans people. This lack of evidence is one reason

---

less than 5 nmol/L for a period of at least thirty-six months. See *19.0 Athlete Inclusion, Competitive Equity, and Eligibility Policy*, USA SWIMMING, https://shorturl.at/k9pvb. USA Cycling provides that in order to compete in elite competitions, transgender women must demonstrate testosterone levels below 2.5 nmol/L for a period of at least twenty-four months. See *Policy VII Transgender Athlete Participation*, USA CYCLING (Jan. 1, 2024), https://usacycling.org/about-us/governance/transgender-athletes-policy. FINA, the international federation for swimming and water sports, adopted a policy in 2022 that bans transgender women and girls from competing in the women's category unless they transitioned before age twelve and maintained their testosterone levels under 2.5 nmol/L. See *Policy on Eligibility for the Men's and Women's Competition Categories*, FINA. The National Women's Soccer League (NWSL) adopted a policy providing that transgender women are eligible to compete if their testosterone level is below 10 nmol/L for at least twelve months prior to competition. See *NWSL Policy on Transgender Athletes*, NWSL. The IOC's policy similarly requires that for a transgender woman to compete in the female category the athlete must demonstrate a testosterone level below 10 nmol/L for at least twelve months. See *IOC Meeting on Sex Reassignment and Hyperandrogenism*, INTERNATIONAL OLYMPIC COMMITTEE (Nov. 2015), https://stillmed.olympic.org/Documents/Commissions_PDFfiles/Medical_commission/2015-11_ioc_consensus_meeting_on_sex_reassignment_and_hyperandrogenism-en.pdf.

why some people believe the trans issue is a delusion."[44] Indeed, Murray has suggested that the trans rights discussion is an indication not just of the illness of some individuals but of society more broadly.[45]

Abigail Shrier, in her book, *Irreversible Damage*, does not deny that some individuals truly are transgender, nonetheless, she believes that many young people who believe they are transgender are confused and that society harms rather than helps them by facilitating their transition. According to Shrier, "many of the adolescent girls who fall for the transgender craze lead upper-middle-class, Gen-Z lives ... but they are in pain – lots of it. They are anxious and depressed ... awkward and afraid."[46]

Debra Soh's theory about the rise in transgender identification among young people is even more polarizing. She argues that progressive parents are actually pushing their gay teenagers to adopt a transgender identity because doing so gains both them and their children more currency and support in progressive circles. Soh argues that "[w]ith greater public awareness about gender dysphoric children and the difficulties and stigma that they face, parents will receive more admiration and support when raising a transgender child than a child who is gay... [T]ransitioning offers a promising solution..."[47] "What is most disturbing," she contends, "is that these parents will be praised as open-minded, examples of what true love and acceptance looks like ... when in actuality, some are homophobic and endorsing a repackaged, socially acceptable form of conversion therapy."[48]

There is a religious version to this delusion argument as well – namely that God does not make mistakes. God created two sexes and individuals act contrary to God's plan when they express a gender identity contrary to their biological sex. The Family Research Council (FRC), an advocacy organization advancing a "family-centered philosophy of public life," regularly espouses these views. The FRC explains: "We believe ... every person is defined by their immutable, in-born biological sex, which is

---

[44] *See* Douglas Murray, *It's Now Easier for a Teacher to Decide Your Little Girl is a Little Boy Than it is to Give Them Aspirin!*, DAILY MAIL (Sept. 14, 2019, 5:00 PM), https://shorturl.at/JU9bn.

[45] Brianna January, *Joe Rogan and Guest Discuss Whether Trans People Are a Sign of "the End of America,"* MEDIA MATTERS FOR AMERICA (Sept. 18, 2020, 3:18 PM), https://shorturl.at/kAd42.

[46] ABIGAIL SHRIER, IRREVERSIBLE DAMAGE: THE TRANSGENDER CRAZE SEDUCING OUR DAUGHTERS 20 (2020).

[47] DEBRA SOH, THE END OF GENDER: DEBUNKING THE MYTHS ABOUT SEX AND IDENTITY IN OUR SOCIETY, 175–76 (2020).

[48] *Id.* at 176.

present and identifiable in THE DNA of the human body. We believe our bodies are part of God's creation. This includes our gender – our maleness and femaleness."[49] With regard to the question of transgender inclusion in sports specifically, the FRC website asserts: "As Christians, we should not be silenced for not recognizing the 'fluidity' of gender. We should not be silenced for speaking up about the inappropriate and unfair nature of biological men competing with biological women. And we should never waiver on the sanctity and majesty of the God-given differences between genders."[50]

Neither human flourishing argument – secular or religious – is an appropriate basis for public policy. Relying on a religiously based conception of sex and individual identity for public policy raises Establishment Clause concerns. The Establishment Clause prohibits the state from endorsing one religious belief over another or endorsing religion over nonreligion.[51] To the extent that categorical exclusions of transgender girls from girls' sports have as their purpose or effect the endorsement of particular religious views, they are suspect.[52] The concerns are similar to those raised about same-sex marriage prohibitions motivated by religious beliefs.[53]

Secular human flourishing arguments, to the extent they are used as a justification for absolute exclusion, fail to give transgender individuals the respect and deference that all individuals are due within a liberal society. There may be valid reasons for a liberal society to limit certain kinds of transition care to adults, but there are not valid reasons for such a society to categorically reject transgender children's or adults' claims to self-expression, identity and flourishing. To do so is simply to treat transgender individuals as being less worthy of respect and recognition than others. It is, as Andrew Koppelman has argued, to try "to eradicate trans people altogether."[54]

---

[49] *Sexuality*, FAMILY RESEARCH COUNCIL, www.frc.org/sexuality.

[50] Caleb Seals, *How the Sexual Revolution Could End Women's Sports*, FAMILY RESEARCH COUNCIL (Jan. 24, 2019), www.frc.org/blog/2019.01.how-sexual-revolution-could-end-womens-sports.

[51] U.S. Const. amend. 1.3 § 1 ("Congress shall make no law respecting an establishment of religion").

[52] *See School Dist. of Abington Tp. v. Schempp*, 374 U.S. 203 (1963); *Allegheny Cnty. v. ACLU*, 492 U.S. 573, 592–94, 599–600 (1989); *Wallace v. Jaffree*, 472 U.S. 38, 56 & n. 42 (1985).

[53] *See, e.g.*, Gary J. Simson, *Religion by Any Other Name? Prohibitions on Same-Sex Marriage and the Limits of the Establishment Clause*, 23 COLUM. J. GENDER & LAW 132 (May 2012), at 132, 135–36.

[54] See Andrew Koppelman, *Gender Identity and Political Evil*, THE HILL (Sept. 7, 2023, 7:03 AM), https://shorturl.at/eWWsk.

4.3 Conclusion

This chapter has sought to understand and explain the current arguments in favor of excluding transgender girls and women entirely from female sports. It is, in other words, an effort to understand much of the contemporary conservative political agenda. I have suggested that fairness arguments may in fact mask religious and secular claims about human dignity and integrity and that such claims are far too controversial, and in some instances illiberal, to form the basis for antidiscrimination policy. Fairness arguments when taken on their own terms, by contrast, simply cannot justify the blanket exclusion of transgender girls from girls' sports.

The fact that categorical exclusion of transgender girls and women from female sports is unjustifiable does not, however, mean that more limited forms of exclusion are as well. The last chapter suggests a more nuanced framework for thinking about transgender girls' and women's inclusion in female sports. It focuses, in particular, on why participation in organized sports matters and explores how eligibility rules should be drawn to ensure that all girls and women – cisgender and transgender – like all boys and men, receive its benefits.

5

A Pragmatic Proposal for Women's Sports

Sports are social conventions through and through. There is nothing natural or predetermined about who gets to play and what one must do to win. But how sports are structured says a lot about what society values and whose interests it prioritizes. This chapter seeks to identify what society values about organized sports and what benefits flow from them. It then considers how these benefits should be distributed and what this means for how athletic eligibility rules should be drawn for different ages and levels of play.

5.1 What Is at Stake

The fight over access to athletic opportunities and resources is heated because much is at stake for participants and for the social groups with which they identify. There are three core benefits of organized sports. First, there are internal and individualistic health benefits that all participants receive simply from playing. I refer to these as basic benefits.[1] Second, there are external and individualistic benefits that a lucky few winners receive in the form of prizes, awards, recognition and scholarships. I refer to these as special benefits.[2] Third, there are benefits to nonparticipants because of their group membership. They include benefits that flow to those who socially identify with the winners. I refer to these as group benefits.

---

[1] I take this term from Jane English. Jane English, *Sex Equality in Sports*, 7 PHIL. & PUB. AFFS. 269 (1978).
[2] English refers to these as scarce benefits. *Id.* at 271 (referring to prizes and publicity as the scarce benefits of sport). I use the term "special" benefits to distinguish them more clearly from basic benefits, which I believe can also be scarce.

5.1.1 Basic Benefits

Organized sports are widely associated with a range of physical and psychological benefits for participants.[3] These basic benefits flow to all participants simply from playing. Skill level and competitive success are irrelevant.

Most direct are the benefits to participants' physical health. Moderate exercise has been shown, for example, to improve bone density and to lower the risks of heart disease, diabetes and some cancers.[4] Physical activity is also associated with improved mental health, specifically lower levels of depression and higher levels of creativity.[5] The health benefits of physical activity are so clear and extensive that some scholars have argued that women's athletic participation should be treated as a public health issue.[6]

Somewhat more tenuous are the benefits to participants' character. Participation in organized sports is widely thought to develop character

---

[3] According to English, basic benefits encompass "health, the self-respect to be gained by doing one's best, the cooperation to be learned from working with teammates and the incentive gained from having opponents, the 'character' of learning to be a good loser and a good winner, the chance to improve one's skills and learn to accept criticism – and just plain fun." English, *supra* note 1.

[4] *See* Matthew H. Specht, *Faster, Higher, Longer: International Development and the Olympic Games*, 14 VA. SPORTS & ENT. L.J. 300, 309 (2015) ("Physical inactivity is a major contributor to cancers, diabetes and heart disease"); *see also* WORLD HEALTH ORG., GLOBAL RECOMMENDATIONS ON PHYSICAL ACTIVITY FOR HEALTH 10 (2010)("[P]hysical inactivity is estimated as being the principal cause for approximately 21–25% of breast and colon cancer burden, 27% of diabetes and approximately 30% of ischaemic heart disease burden"); Ylva Trolle Lagerros et al., *Physical Activity in Adolescence and Young Adulthood and Breast Cancer: A Quantitative Review*, 13 EUR. J. CANCER PREVENTION 5, 5–12 (2004) (reviewing twenty-three studies and finding that individuals with the highest physical activity during adolescence and young adulthood were 20 percent less likely to get breast cancer later in life).

[5] *See* WOMEN'S SPORTS FOUNDATION, HER LIFE DEPENDS ON IT III: SPORT, PHYSICAL ACTIVITY, AND THE HEALTH AND WELL-BEING OF AMERICAN GIRLS AND WOMEN 3 (2015), https://shorturl.at/Vboy2 (noting that moderate levels of exercise are associated with lower levels of depression in girls and women); Christian Rominger et al., *Everyday Bodily Movement Is Associated with Creativity Independently from Active Positive Affect: A Bayesian Mediation Analysis Approach*, 10 SCI. REPS. 11985 (2020) (finding a positive correlation between bodily movement and creativity).

[6] *See* Nancy Leong & Emily Bartlett, *Sex Segregation in Sports as a Public Health Issue*, 40 CARDOZO L. REV. 1813, 1822–23 (2019) ("Participation in sports ... [has] vast implications for women's physical health. Cardiovascular disease, breast cancer, colorectal cancer, sexual health, and maternal health are all intimately connected with a woman's physical activity levels").

by teaching skills such as teamwork, leadership and discipline.⁷ The evidence for such benefits is more anecdotal and less rigorous than for the physical benefits. Nonetheless, they are widely ascribed to and are often cited as a reason to encourage children's participation in organized sports. Indeed, the International Charter of Physical Education and Sports adopted in 1978 by the United Nations Educational, Scientific and Cultural Organization (UNESCO) proclaimed that "[e]very human being has a fundamental right of access to physical education and sport" because such activity is "essential for the full development of [their] personality."⁸

More tenuous still are the benefits to participants' life choices. Although any causal link is unproven, much has been made of the correlation between athletic participation and better lifestyle choices and outcomes for children. Students participating in high school sports have higher grades, better attendance and higher graduation rates than their nonathlete peers.⁹ They are also more likely to attend and graduate

---

⁷ Norma V. Kantu, *Athletics Experience Vital to Both Sexes*, NCAA NEWS (Apr. 26, 1995), at 4, https://ncaanewsarchive.s3.amazonaws.com/1995/19950426.pdf (opining that "values we learn from participation in sports [include] teamwork, standards, leadership, discipline, work ethics, self-sacrifice, pride in accomplishment, [and] strength of character"); Erin E. Buzuvis, *Transgender Student-Athletes and Sex-Segregated Sport: Developing Policies of Inclusion for Intercollegiate and Interscholastic Athletics*, 21 SETON HALL J. SPORTS & ENT. L. 1, 46 (2011) ("Sports can foster such social skills as collaboration, trust, empathy and responsibility"). *But see* Suzanne Le Menestrel & David Perkins, *An Overview of How Sports, Out-of-School Time, and Youth Well-Being Can and Do Intersect*, 115 NEW DIRECTIONS FOR YOUTH DEV. 13, 16 (2007) (noting that "[a]necdotally, the assumption that playing a sport builds character has been part of American culture for many years," but that the research support for the belief is not clear).
⁸ UNESCO, INTERNATIONAL CHARTER OF PHYSICAL EDUCATION AND SPORT 3 (1978), https://shorturl.at/mjemR.
⁹ *See* Trevor Born, *High Standard for GPA*, STAR TRIB. (May 14, 2007) (reporting on a Minnesota State High School League survey finding that student athletes had higher grade-point averages than nonathletes and better school attendance); Dawn Podulka Coe et al., *Effect of Physical Education and Activity Levels on Academic Achievement in Children*, 38 MED. & SCI. SPORTS & EXERCISE 1515 (2006) (finding that elementary school-age students who participated in vigorous physical activity did approximately 10 percent better in math, science, English and social studies than students who did less exercise); Stephen Lipsomb, *Secondary School Extracurricular Involvement and Achievement: A Fixed Approach*, 26 ECON. EDUC. REV. 463 (2007) (finding participation in school sports "is associated with a 2 percent increase in math and science test scores"); Angela Lumpkin & Judy Favor, *Comparing the Academic Performance of High School Athletes and Non-Athletes in Kansas in 2008–09*, 4 J. SPORT ADMIN. & SUPERVISION 41 (2012) (reporting based on a study of nearly 140,000 Kansas high school students that "athletes earned higher grades, graduated at a higher rate, dropped out of school less frequently, and scored higher on state assessments than did non-athletes").

from college.[10] Teenage student-athletes are less likely to smoke cigarettes,[11] and teenage girls who participate in sports are less likely to engage in sexual activity or become pregnant.[12]

5.1.2 Special Benefits

Organized sports also provide some participants – those who win – with a distinct set of particularly valuable scarce benefits. Winners enjoy the excitement, pride and joy of victory. Sometimes, they also enjoy more concrete and tangible benefits. They may set records, win prizes, qualify for more prestigious teams or leagues, and garner attention and acclaim for their accomplishments.

For high school athletes, preferential treatment by colleges is a particularly valuable and sought-after special benefit for winners. The recent lawsuit against Harvard University alleging discrimination against Asian Americans revealed the magnitude of the preference.[13] According to the plaintiffs' analysis of Harvard's admissions data, athletes who were ranked 4 on a scale of 1 to 6 had a 70 percent chance of acceptance, while nonathletes with the same score had a 0.076 percent chance of admission.[14] This preference is consistent with that found almost twenty years earlier by James Shulman and William Bowen. In their book *The Game of Life*, Shulman and Bowen looked at admissions data for thirty

---

[10] *See Benefits of Youth Sports*, PRESIDENT'S COUNCIL ON SPORTS, FITNESS & NUTRITION SCIENCE BOARD (2020), https://shorturl.at/NWt2p. Betsey Stevenson has sought in her work to show a causal connection. *See* Betsey Stevenson, *Beyond the Classroom: Using Title IX to Measure the Return to High School Sports*, 92 REV. ECON. & STAT. 284, 294 (2010) ("[A] 10 percentage point increase in girls' sports participation generates an increase of 0.8 percentage points in the probability of attending at least four years of college... [A] 10 percentage point increase in girls' sports participation generates an increase of 1.9 percentage points in the probability of working full time").

[11] Luis G. Escobedo et al., *Sports Participation, Age at Smoking Initiation, and the Risk of Smoking among U.S. High School Students*, 269 J. AM. MED. ASS'N 1391 (1993); Paul W. Baumert et al., *Health Risk Behaviors of Adolescent Participants in Organized Sports*, 22 J. ADOLESCENT HEALTH 460 (1998).

[12] Donald F. Sabo et al., *High School Athletic Participation, Sexual Behavior and Adolescent Pregnancy: A Regional Study*, 25 J. ADOLESCENT HEALTH 207 (1999).

[13] *See Students for Fair Admissions, Inc. v. President & Fellows of Harv. Coll.*, 397 F. Supp. 3d 126 (D. Mass. 2019) (finding insufficient evidence of intentional discrimination against Asian Americans), *aff'd* 980 F.3d 157 (1st Cir. 2021).

[14] *See* Saahil Desai, *College Sports Are Affirmative Action for Rich White Students*, ATLANTIC (Oct. 23, 2018), https://shorturl.at/kGCv5.

selective colleges and found that athletes were given a 48 percent boost in admissions – a boost that was considerably higher than that for legacies (25 percent) and for racial minorities (18 percent).[15]

Moreover, the very best athletes receive not only admissions help but also financial rewards. Approximately 196,000 students annually, the top 1–3 percent of high school athletes, receive almost $4 billion in scholarship support from National Collegiate Athletic Association (NCAA) schools,[16] with an average scholarship amount of $18,000.[17] The best of this group, approximately 2 percent of college athletes, receive opportunities to play professionally.

5.1.3 Group Benefits

Even for those who do not play, organized sports confer benefits. Most general are the benefits – excitement and fun – that fans get from watching their favorite athletes and teams play and win. More discrete, and more significant from a social justice perspective, are the benefits that accrue to members of socially salient groups as a result of seeing members of their own group celebrated and rewarded. As Mark Kelman explains, nonparticipants who identify socially with athletic winners receive benefits from increased self-esteem, from role modeling and from the reduction of cultural subordination.[18]

---

[15] James Shulman & William Bowen, The Game of Life: College Sports and Educational Values 72 (2002); see also William G. Bowen & Sarah A. Levin, Reclaiming the Game: College Sports and Educational Values (2003) (finding that applicants to the Ivy League in the late 1990s with a combined SAT score between 1,300 and 1,400 had only a 15 percent chance of being admitted, but that recruited male athletes with scores in that range had a 60 percent chance of being admitted and recruited female athletes with scores in that range had a 70 percent chance of admission).

[16] See Scholarships, NCAA, www.ncaa.org/student-athletes/future/scholarships.

[17] See Deborah Ziff Soriano & Emma Kerr, 5 Myths about Athletic Scholarships, U.S. News (Mar. 24, 2021), https://shorturl.at/a91iZ.

[18] Kelman identified two additional group benefits that may flow from the allocation of resources to athletic winners. The first is a benefit resulting from interdependent utility functions between women as a group and female athletic winners. Because I agree with Kelman's skepticism that what women viewers share and celebrate is female winners' happiness, as opposed to the social meaning of their victories, I do not focus on this benefit. Kelman also identified a benefit in the preservation of a distinct subcultural identity. Because I am skeptical that either transgender or cisgender girls have a distinct subcultural identity that is tied to their participation in competitive athletics, I also do not focus on this benefit. See Mark Kelman, (Why) Does Gender Equity in College Athletics Entail Gender Equality?, 7 S. Cal. Rev. L. & Women's Stud. 63, 106–21 (1997).

Self-esteem is mediated both by one's own treatment as an individual and by the treatment received by members of one's group.[19] One's self-esteem may be enhanced by seeing members of one's group perform well and be treated with respect and adulation, as occurs when members of one's own group are athletic stars.[20] Conversely, self-esteem may be undermined by seeing members of one's group devalued and disrespected.[21] Moreover, associational self-esteem may be particularly important for members of subordinated groups.[22]

Role models encourage healthy behaviors and life choices by those who identify with them.[23] Individuals are more likely to "model

---

[19] *Id.* at 107. "[M]embers of historically subordinated groups," Kelman explained, "are linked in the sense that many may gain self-respect from the presence of highly visible successful people in their groups, since self-esteem grows in part out of how one's group is evaluated, as well as how one is treated personally." *See also* English, *supra* note 1, at 273 ("Members of disadvantaged groups identify strongly with each other's successes and failures. If women do not attain roughly equal fame and fortune in sports, it leads both men and women to think of women as naturally inferior").

[20] *See* Hart Blanton et al., *The Effects of In-Group versus Out-Group Social Comparison on Self-Esteem in the Context of a Negative Stereotype*, 36 J. EXPERIMENTAL SOC. PSYCH. 519 (2000) (finding female African American students' self-esteem was increased by comparisons with high-performing in-group members and decreased by comparisons with high-performing out-group members); Penelope Lockwood, *"Someone Like Me Can Be Successful": Do College Students Need Same-Gender Role Models?*, 30 PSYCH. WOMEN Q. 36 (2006) (finding that women reported higher increases in ratings of self-competence when exposed to successful women than when exposed to successful men).

[21] *See* English, *supra* note 1, at 273 ("When there are virtually no female athletic stars, or when women receive much less prize money than men do, this is damaging to the self-respect of all women").

[22] *See* Lockwood, *supra* note 20 (finding that women's self-competence ratings were affected by exposure to a successful woman whereas men's competence ratings were not affected by exposure to successful women or men, arguably because men's greater likelihood of success made such exposure less relevant); *see also* Kelman, *supra* note 18, at 107 (arguing that "[m]embers of historically subordinated groups, like women, require [group-mediated self-esteem], in ways that members of socially dominant groups do not, because the self-respect of individuals in these groups is below the social baseline enjoyed by dominant group members").

[23] The term "role models" is widely used and generally refers to individuals who serve as examples of a particular kind of behavior. *See, e.g.*, Lockwood, *supra* note 20 (describing role models as "individuals who provide an example of the kind of success that one may achieve, and often also provide a template of the behaviors that are needed to achieve such success"); DAVID GAUNTLETT, MEDIA, GENDER, AND IDENTITY 211 (2002) (defining a role model as "someone to look up to and base your character, values and aspirations on").

Ample research shows that under the right circumstances, role models can have many positive effects for role aspirants. *See, e.g.*, Nilanjana Dasgupta, *Ingroup Experts and Peers as Social Vaccines Who Inoculate the Self-Concept: The Stereotype Inoculation Model*, 224 PSYCH. INQUIRY 231 (2011) (showing that role models can reduce the effects of stereotype

themselves after members of their own groups than outsiders."[24] As a result, athletic nonparticipants benefit from having in-group role models who encourage athletic participation and healthy habits. As Kelman explains, female athlete role models not only encourage younger girls to participate in sports – and reap the accompanying health benefits – but also model and encourage a broader range of positive behavior – goal focus, intensity, competitiveness – that is advantageous for girls across contexts.[25] While the benefits to self-esteem probably require some parity in how female and male stars are treated, the benefits from role modeling seem to require only the existence of a critical mass of group-identified winners.[26]

Finally, the celebration of athletic stars enhances the status accorded to all members of their socially salient group and can change the social meaning of group membership. The celebration of female athletes, for example, reinforces a vision of women as autonomous agents that is at odds with more traditionally sexist conceptions of women as passive

---

threat); Anat BarNir et al., *Mediation and Moderated Mediation in the Relationship among Role Models, Self-Efficacy, Entrepreneurial Career Intention, and Gender*, 41 J. APPLIED SOC. PSYCH. 270 (2011) (role models can change aspirants' goals); Lockwood, *supra* note 20; Penelope Lockwood et al., *Motivation by Positive or Negative Role Models: Regulatory Focus Determines Who Will Best Inspire Us*, 83 J. PERSONALITY & SOC. PSYCH. 854–64 (2002) (role models can increase motivation); Michael E. Brown & Linda K. Treviño, *Do Role Models Matter? An Investigation of Role Modeling as an Antecedent of Perceived Ethical Leadership*, 122 J. BUS. ETHICS 587 (2013) (role models can prompt prosocial and moral behavior); Edith Chen et al., *Role Models and the Psychological Characteristics That Buffer Low-Socioeconomic-Status Youth from Cardiovascular Risk*, 84 CHILD DEV. 1241 (2013) (role models can lead to improved health); Gary Barker & Irene Loewenstein, *Where the Boys Are: Attitudes Related to Masculinity, Fatherhood, and Violence toward Women among Low-Income Adolescent and Young Adult Males in Rio de Janeiro, Brazil*, 29 YOUTH & SOC'Y 166 (1997) (role models can lead to a change in aspirant values).

[24] Kelman, *supra* note 18, at 108; *see also* Lockwood, *supra* note 20 (finding that female study participants identified more strongly with successful women than with men); J.G. Stout et al., *STEMing the Tide: Using Ingroup Experts to Inoculate Women's Self-Concept in Science, Technology, Engineering, and Mathematics (STEM)*, 100 J. PERSONALITY & SOC. PSYCH. 255 (2011) (finding that female students majoring in STEM who interacted with a female STEM expert attempted more math problems, showed a more positive attitude toward math and associated themselves more strongly with math than did female students who interacted with a male experimenter). *But see* B. Carrington et al., *Role Models, School Improvement and the "Gender Gap": Do Men Bring Out the Best in Boys and Women the Best in Girls?*, 34 BRIT. EDUC. RES. J. 315 (2008) (finding that teachers' gender had no impact on the math performance of boys and girls or their attitude toward math).

[25] *See* Kelman, *supra* note 18, at 108–09.

[26] *Id.* at 108 (explaining that what is necessary for role modeling is "absolute resource availability").

sexualized objects for a heterosexual male gaze.[27] Celebrating female athletes' strength and agency chips away at cultural sexism for all women and enhances women's social regard and status.

Because sports provide individuals and groups with important benefits, much is at stake in the distribution of athletic opportunities. The next three sections consider how the basic, special and group benefits of sport should be allocated – to whom, on what terms and for what social ends – and what these normative goals mean for the structure of girls' sports.

5.2 Allocating Basic Benefits

In theory, the basic benefits of sports are neither scarce nor rival.[28] All athletic participants receive the health and character benefits that flow from organized sports and one person's receipt of them does not deprive another of the same benefits. Nonetheless, because the basic benefits of sports flow from participation opportunities that are often limited, the basic benefits of sports become in practice both scarce and rival. This section considers how a society concerned about the basic benefits of sports should, under conditions of resource scarcity, structure and allocate athletic opportunities for transgender and cisgender girls.

One way to distribute scarce benefits is based on merit, where merit is defined by some relevant measure of ability or effort. Jobs, for example, are awarded based on qualifications and performance. Sometimes benefits are distributed in this way to achieve an independent external end. Imagine scarce spots in cardiac surgery residency programs or scarce government contracts for mechanical engineers to rebuild the nation's bridges. In both cases, there are external reasons related to public health and safety to allocate the scarce resources based on merit as measured by relevant performance. Other times, resources are distributed based on

---

[27] See id. at 119–20 ("By not affirming the importance of women's athleticism, women's bodies are 'affirmed' only as sexual (objects of heterosexual male gaze) and passive, rather than as self-directed, multi-faceted and active").

[28] Patrick Croskery explained: "A non-rival good is one where uses do not conflict. For example, we might distinguish between a text, that is, a pattern of words, and a book, that is, a particular physical object in which a text is instantiated. The text is a non-rival good – an unlimited number of people can be reading the same text without interfering with one another. The book, on the other hand, is a rival good – it is hard to imagine more than five or six people reading the same book, and certainly that many people would be interfering with one another as they tried to read it." Patrick Croskery, *Institutional Utilitarianism and Intellectual Property*, 68 CHI. KENT L. REV. 631, 632 (1993).

merit to encourage particular kinds of behavior. Consider a teacher trying to motivate her students to read. Allocating prizes based on numbers of books read – in other words, based on merit as measured by effort – would serve her goals well.

A merit-based distribution of sports' basic benefits – where merit is measured by athletic ability or performance – is difficult to justify on either ground. The basic benefits of sports are akin to core health and education resources. Distributing such health benefits to those who are most athletic – and likely healthiest – seems unlikely to further any important social goal. Instead, doing so would likely weaken society overall by degrading the status of the weakest and increasing the gap between the privileged and the poor. While awarding the basic benefits to those who are physically strongest probably would incentivize health-conscious behavior among some individuals, it would also punish and deprive those who are the weakest and most infirm. Awarding opportunities for health and well-being to those who already possess both, and denying opportunities to those who lack them, seems at best nonsensical and at worst unjust. As Jane English observed, "[i]f Matilda is less adept at, say, wrestling than Walter is, this is no reason to deny Matilda an equal chance to wrestle for health, self-respect, and fun."[29]

There is perhaps more normative appeal in allocating the opportunity for basic benefits based on need. Under this view, those who need such benefits to reach basic levels of health and functioning are most entitled to them. Martha Nussbaum and Amartya Sen are perhaps most strongly associated with this view. They have argued that a just society must distribute resources so as to guarantee that all individuals have the basic capabilities necessary for a good human life – chief among which are health and thought "as cultivated by an adequate education."[30]

---

[29] English, *supra* note 1.
[30] *See, e.g.*, AMARTYA SEN, EQUALITY OF WHAT? THE TANNER LECTURES ON HUMAN VALUES 195 (Sterling M. McMurrin ed., 1980), *reprinted in Choice, Welfare and Measurement* 353 (1982); AMARTYA SEN, Inequality Reexamined (1992); AMARTYA SEN, *Capability and Well-Being*, in THE QUALITY OF LIFE 30–31 (Martha Nussbaum & Amartya Sen eds., 1993) (for a definition of capabilities); Martha C. Nussbaum, *Human Functioning and Social Justice: In Defense of Aristotelian Essentialism*, 20 POL. THEORY 202 (1992); Martha C. Nussbaum, *Nature, Function, and Capability: Aristotle on Political Distribution*, 6 OXFORD STUD. ANCIENT PHIL. 145 (1988) (Nussbaum has offered the following as a working list of the most central human capabilities: (1) life, (2) bodily health, (3) bodily integrity, (4) senses, imagination, and thought, (5) emotions, (6) practical reason, (7) friendship and respect, (8) being able to live with concern for other species, (9) play and (10) control over one's environment); Martha C. Nussbaum, *Capabilities and Human*

Norman Daniels similarly has argued that health care must be distributed so as to give everyone the ability for "normal species functioning,"[31] with more resources going to those who need more to maintain or achieve normal functioning.[32]

As a practical matter, need does sometimes drive resource allocation decisions in education and health care. While state constitutions require that all children be given a basic minimum education, the federal Individuals with Disabilities Education Act (IDEA) requires that resources be allocated based on need.[33] The goal of the IDEA is to provide students with disabilities "a free appropriate public education" in the "least restrictive environment."[34] What this means in practice is that schools must devote extra resources to handicapped children to permit them to achieve the same basic educational goals that most nonhandicapped students can achieve with far fewer resources.[35] Disabled students who need more resources to achieve proficiency are given more resources – they are given preferential treatment as compared to other students who would benefit from the resources but "need" them less.

In health care, too, under both private and state-sponsored insurance plans, more resources and benefits go to those who need them to achieve basic levels of health and functioning. Indeed, rather than capping all individuals at the same level or expense of care, insurance programs direct far more resources to those whose impairments – from hearing loss to mobility problems to the need for dialysis – require more interventions to achieve basic levels of functioning.[36]

Transgender advocates, at times, seem to support a need-based distribution of athletic opportunities. Transgender girls, they emphasize, are an "'especially vulnerable population'"[37] with a particularly strong

---

Rights, 66 FORDHAM L. REV. 173, 287–88 (1997); *see also* JEAN DREZE & AMARTYA SEN, INDIA: ECONOMIC DEVELOPMENT AND SOCIAL OPPORTUNITY 13–16, 109–39 (1995).

[31] NORMAN DANIELS, JUST HEALTH CARE 26–28 (1985).

[32] *Id.* at 32.

[33] The IDEA provides states with financial assistance to educate students with disabilities. IDEA, 20 U.S.C. §§ 1400–1412 (2000).

[34] 20 U.S.C. § 1412(a)(1)-(5).

[35] Kimberly A. Yuracko, *One for You and One for Me*, 97 NW. L. REV. 731, 763–64 (2003).

[36] *See Risk Pooling: How Health Insurance in the Individual Market Works*, AM. ACAD. OF ACTUARIES (July 2017), https://shorturl.at/MzfSp; *see also Health and Economic Costs of Chronic Diseases*, CTRS. FOR DISEASE CONTROL & PREVENTION (CDC) (Sept. 8, 2022, 12:00 AM), www.cdc.gov/chronicdisease/about/costs/index.htm.

[37] *See* BUZUVIS, *supra* note 7 at 48 (quoting Arnold Grossman & Anthony R. D'Augelli, *Transgender Youth: Invisible and Vulnerable*, 51 J. HOMOSEXUALITY 111, 112–13 (2006)).

need for the basic benefits that sports confer.[38] Such need, they suggest, creates a privileged entitlement to athletic resources.

While perhaps intuitively appealing, need-based allocations of athletic resources are difficult for both conceptual and practical reasons. Conceptually, it is not clear whether the right deficit to focus on is relative physical health, psychological health or athletic skill. Nor is it clear if need should be assessed in terms of absolute deprivation – those who are most severely physically disabled are considered in most need – or in terms of capacity to benefit – those whose life trajectories would be most altered by additional resources are considered most in need. Practically, measuring individual need along any of these possible metrics would be burdensome and costly. Moreover, attempts to define individual need by looking at group membership is deeply flawed, both generally and in the particular context of transgender girls' participation in girls' sports. Even if some types of group membership may be associated with particular vulnerabilities, it does not follow that all members of a group are more vulnerable or needy than nongroup members. Individuals have varied group memberships, some associated with privilege and others with disadvantage. Such is certainly true with transgender identity. It is too simplistic to say that a transgender boy, by virtue of his gender identity, is more in need of the physical and mental health benefits of sport than a cisgender girl who is overweight or a cisgender boy suffering from depression. Yet individualized need assessments of all students seeking to participate in recreational school sports – even if there were agreement on what and how to measure – are not possible. Individually assessing and scaling the relative need of all students who might want to participate would be too costly and difficult.

Since a merit-based distribution is unappealing and a need-based distribution impractical, a third option is to give all students equal access to the basic benefits. Such a distribution is consistent with and bolstered by the widely shared view that all individuals have an equal moral entitlement to basic health care and education.

The idea that "everyone has a right to a minimum of 'decent,' 'reasonable,' 'basic,' 'essential,' or 'adequate' health care … commands widespread (though not universal) consensus,"[39] explains law professor Einer

---

[38] *See, e.g.*, Scott Skinner-Thompson & Ilona M. Turner, *Title IX's Protections for Transgender Student Athletes*, 28 WIS. J.L., GENDER & SOC'Y 271, 298 (2013) (arguing that the "social mental and physical benefits of interscholastic sports participation are even more necessary for vulnerable groups such as transgender students").

[39] Einer Elhauge, *Allocating Health Care Morally*, 82 CAL. L. REV. 1449, 1465–66 (1994).

Elhauge. Philosophers largely agree. In their book, *Social Justice: The Moral Foundations of Public Health and Health Policy*, Madison Powers and Ruth Faden argue that social justice requires that all individuals should be provided with a sufficient level of health and a reasonable life span.[40] According to John Rawls, a basic minimum of health care for all individuals is necessary for a stable democracy.[41]

A commitment to equal basic health care infuses public policy as well as political philosophy. As Erin Brown explains, a commitment to a basic minimum undergirds the patchwork of federal statutes that provide healthcare benefits for groups that might not be covered by employer-sponsored insurance, such as "Medicare, Medicaid, the Veterans Administration health system, TRICARE for active duty military and their families, the Emergency Medical Treatment and Active Labor Act (EMTALA), and, most recently, the ACA [Affordable Care Act]."[42] Indeed, Representative John Lewis, urging his colleagues to vote for the ACA, appealed to their sense of justice: "We have a mission. We have a mandate. We have a moral obligation to lead this nation into a new era where healthcare is a right and not a privilege."[43]

A similar commitment to a basic minimum exists in the context of education. Political theorists contend that a basic education is foundational to good citizenship. As Debra Satz explains, "[e]ducation has long been recognized as a 'foundation of good citizenship,' a necessary condition for full membership in the political community."[44] Schools teach "future citizens to evaluate different political perspectives that are often

---

[40] Madison Powers & Ruth Faden, Social Justice: The Moral Foundations of Public Health and Health Policy (2006); *see also Social Justice and Health*, Am. Pub. Health Ass'n (Nov. 27, 2022) https://shorturl.at/RA5Gx.

[41] John Rawls, The Law of Peoples 49–50 (1993). Rawls identified five conditions necessary for political stability: (1) "[a] certain fair equality of opportunity," (2) "[a] decent distribution of income and wealth," (3) "[s]ociety as employer of last resort," (4) "[b]asic health care assured for all citizens," and (5) "[p]ublic financing of elections and ways of assuring the availability of public information on matters of policy." *Id.*; *see also* Ani B. Satz, *The Limits of Health Care Reform*, 59 Ala. L. Rev. 1451, 1465 n.72 (2008) (arguing that "[t]he existence of universal health care schemes premised on basic minimums in most democratic western nations, including Canada, Australia, and Germany, is empirical support" for the claim that equal basic health care is necessary for democracy).

[42] Erin C. Fuse Brown, *Developing a Durable Right to Health Care*, 14 Minn. J.L., Sci., & Tech. 439 (2013).

[43] 111 Cong. Rec. H12857 (daily ed., Nov. 7, 2009) (Statement of Rep. John Lewis encouraging passage of the Quality Affordable Health Care for All Americans Act).

[44] Debra Satz, *Equality, Adequacy, and Educational Policy*, 3 Educ. Fin. & Pol'y 424 (2008).

associated with different ways of life."[45] Such civic education is critical, Amy Gutmann agrees, and "[t]he social stakes for liberal democracy ... are high. Absent mutual respect, citizens cannot be expected to honor the liberal principle of nondiscrimination."[46]

Access to a basic minimum education is in fact an individual right. Every state constitution includes an education clause obligating states "to establish and operate public schools that provide children with a basic minimum or adequate education."[47] Though the right to a basic minimum is not always realized, it is recognized.

While not going so far as to require that all students receive athletic opportunities, an equal-access approach recognizes and protects students' equal moral entitlement to the basic benefits of sport under conditions of scarcity. One way to ensure equal access to athletic opportunities would be to make sports unisex and to reconfigure them so that sports require and reward more equally the abilities of both girls and boys.[48] As Jane English has argued, "[w]e should develop a variety of sports, in which a variety of physical types can expect to excel."[49] Scholars focused on transgender athletes have made similar arguments. Irina Martinková, for example, has called for a shift to unisex sports that have been redefined to be "inclusive for athletes of all sexes."[50]

---

[45] Amy Gutmann, *Civic Education and Social Diversity*, 105 ETHICS 557, 561 (1995).
[46] *Id.* at 577.
[47] Kimberly A. Yuracko, *Education Off the Grid: Constitutional Constraints on Homeschooling*, 96 CAL. L. REV. 123, 136–37 (2008); *see also* Quentin A. Palfrey, *The State Judiciary's Role in Fulfilling Brown's Promise*, 8 MICH. J. RACE & L. 1, 6 (2002) ("Every state constitution contains an education clause requiring the state legislature to establish a system of free public schools"); James E. Ryan & Thomas Saunders, *Forward to Symposium on School Finance Litigation, Emerging Trends or New Dead Ends?*, 22 YALE L. & POL'Y REV. 403, 466 (2004) ("[E]very State constitution contains an education clause mandating the provision of a free, public education"). Some scholars argue that the federal constitution's Due Process Clause also creates a right to a basic minimum level of public education. Yuracko, at 138 n.69.
[48] English, *supra* note 1, at 276 ("Only where style of play is very different would groupings by weight, age, or sex be recommended").
[49] English, *supra* note 1, at 275.
[50] Irena Martinková, *Unisex Sports: Challenging the Binary*, 47 J. PHIL. SPORT 248, 251 (2020); *see also* TORBJÖRN TÄNNSJÖ, *Against Sexual Discrimination in Sports*, *in* VALUES IN SPORT: ELITISM, NATIONALISM, GENDER EQUALITY AND THE SCIENTIFIC MANUFACTURE OF WINNERS 102–03 (Torbjörn Tännsjö & Claudio Tamburrini eds., 2000) (arguing that men's and women's categories in sports should be eliminated and new sports should be created in which women and men can compete against each other as equals).

In the real world, creating sports that equally recognize and reward the aptitudes of women and men is likely to be challenging. The very small number of sports that currently fall into this category – perhaps dressage, riflery, long-distance swimming and car racing – hints at the difficulty of this endeavor. Encouraging people to adopt these newly configured sports is also likely to be challenging. Certainly, new sports do arise and gain popularity,[51] but there is also a lot of stickiness in people's athletic preferences. Indeed, the ten most popular sports in the world have been the same for the last ninety years.[52] The process of modifying or creating new sports and shifting athletic preferences, if possible at all, would take time.

A more practical, though less perfect, way to ensure equal access to athletic opportunities would be to shift existing sports to a unisex model and have spots allocated by lottery rather than performance. Existing sports tend to favor and reward male attributes and abilities, and this may explain in part why men are more drawn to sports than women. Nonetheless, if schools were to create robust unisex athletic offerings that were open to all without regard to performance, girls and boys – both transgender and cisgender – would have access to the basic benefits of sports to a degree that is functionally and practically equal, even if not perfectly so.

It may be, though, that participants prefer sex-segregated teams – at least at times – even when participation is not performance based. Boys may prefer playing with boys and worry that girls will change the nature of their game. Girls may prefer playing with girls and worry that boys will marginalize or condescend to them. Girls may also feel that rules designed to protect them or the fairness of play in coed competitions are patronizing.[53]

Conceding to this reality, however, makes ensuring that participants have equal access to the basic benefits of sports more challenging. Jane

---

[51] See, e.g., Billy Baker, *Pickleball Is Growing at an Almost Unprecedented Rate in the History of American Sports*, BOSTON GLOBE (Sept. 24, 2021), www.bostonglobe.com/2021/09/24/metro/boomers-have-created-pickleball-phenomenon.

[52] See *Most Popular Sports in the World (1930–2020)*, STAT. & DATA, https://statisticsanddata.org/most-popular-sports-in-the-world/.

[53] A move to unisex athletic teams would probably be easiest and best received for young children of elementary school age, in whom physical differences between the sexes are least pronounced. Espen Tonnessen et al., *Performance Development in Adolescent Track and Field Athletes According to Age, Sex and Sport Discipline*, 10 PLOS ONE 1 (2015) (noting that the performance sex difference evolves from <5 percent to 10 percent–18 percent in all the events from ages eleven to eighteen).

English has argued that under conditions of sex segregation, equal funding is key to equal access for girls.[54] "Rights to the basic benefits dictate immediate changes in the distribution of our sports resources," English explained, requiring "equal facilities – everything from socks to stadiums" and "equal incentives."[55] Girls and boys teams must, in other words, be the same in terms of the number of opportunities they provide students and the nature of these opportunities.

Most important when it comes to transgender students is category assignment. For transgender girls, equal access to the basic benefits of sports requires their access to and inclusion on girls' sports teams. Requiring transgender girls to compete on boys' teams would stigmatize them by labeling them as boys. It would also undermine the emotional health benefits of sport and likely discourage play.[56] Requiring transgender girls to play in their own category would likely have similar effects. While segregation of cisgender girls and cisgender boys in sports is generally not viewed as stigmatic to girls, segregation of cisgender and transgender girls is, often, viewed as stigmatic to transgender girls.[57] For transgender girls relegated to a "separate-but-equal" trans category, the basic benefits of sports would be undermined and diminished by the message that they are not in fact "real" girls.

For cisgender girls, transgender inclusion might affect their access to the special benefits of sport, but it should have no meaningful effect on their access to the basic benefits. Opposition to transgender

---

[54] English argued that athletic resources should be divided equally between men's and women's teams following a separate-but-equal model. English, *supra* note 1.
[55] *Id.* at 277. Writing in the 1970s, English focused on biological women. Equal resources for sex-segregated teams meant equal basic benefits for biological women and men. English did not focus explicitly on transgender girls and the question of how to ensure that they too receive equal basic benefits.
[56] *See* Chase Strangio & Gabriel Arkles, *Four Myths about Trans Athletes Debunked*, ACLU (April 30, 2020), www.aclu.org/news/lgbtq-rights/four-myths-about-trans-athletes-debunked/ ("Excluding trans people from any space or activity is harmful, particularly for trans youth... 'When a school or athletic organization denies transgender students the ability to participate equally in athletics because they are transgender, that condones, reinforces, and affirms the transgender students' social status as outsiders or misfits who deserve the hostility they experience from peers.'") *Id.* (quoting Dr. Deanna Adkins).
[57] *See* Shoshana K. Goldberg, *The Importance of Sports Participation for Transgender Youth*, AM. PROGRESS (Feb. 8, 2021), www.americanprogress.org/article/fair-play/ (arguing that policies that "ban transgender students from participating and competing on sports teams in accordance with their gender identity, or make it difficult for them to do so – can do substantial harm to the mental health, well-being, and lives of transgender youth, athletes and nonathletes alike").

girls' inclusion in girls' sports centers on the claim that if transgender girls compete directly against cisgender girls, the latter will lose. When it comes to the basic benefits, however, winning does not matter and prizes are not the point. The basic benefits come from playing and flow as readily from recreational sports as from elite-level sports. It is possible, if transgender girls' athletic ability is more comparable to cisgender boys' than cisgender girls', that some cisgender girls might be discouraged from participating for the same reasons they might be discouraged from participating in coed sports leagues – the game is different and/or the risk of injury is higher. However, given the low numbers of transgender individuals, it seems unlikely that the inclusion of transgender girls on sex-segregated recreational teams will change the nature of play or increase risk of injury across girls' sports in a significant way. It seems unlikely, in other words, that cisgender girls' access to the basic benefits of sport would be meaningfully affected by transgender girls' inclusion.

In sum, if society cared about organized sports only because of the basic benefits participants derived from them, there would be no reason to deny transgender girls access to girls' sports, and the issue of transgender girls' inclusion would probably not be terribly fraught.[58] Transgender girls would need access to girls' sports teams to have equal access to the physical and psychological benefits of sports. Meanwhile, cisgender girls would lose little, if anything, by having girls' sporting opportunities randomly distributed among a pool of potential participants that included both transgender and cisgender girls.

---

[58] There would still be those who as a matter of principle – whether moral or religious – believe that sex can never be changed and transgender girls must always be treated as boys. The political power and size of this contingent would certainly vary geographically. However, it seems clear from the controversy over transgender swimmer Lia Thomas's participation in women's swimming that much of the opposition to inclusion stems not from principle but from concern about access to the special benefits and rewards of sport. *See, e.g.*, Matt Bonesteel, *Sixteen Penn Swimmers Say Transgender Teammate Lia Thomas Should Not Be Allowed to Compete*, WASH. POST (Feb. 2, 2022), www.washingtonpost.com/sports/2022/02/03/lia-thomas-penn-swimming-teammates/ (quoting Penn swimmers who explain that they "fully support Lia Thomas in her decision to affirm her gender identity and to transition from a man to a woman" but arguing that "[i]f she were to be eligible to compete against us, she could now break Penn, Ivy, and NCAA Women's Swimming records"); John Lohn, *Allowing Lia Thomas to Compete at NCAA Championships Would Establish Unfair Setting*, SWIMMING WORLD (Dec. 9, 2021), https://shorturl.at/yyIC3 (noting that "Thomas is stalking Ledecky's 500 freestyle record, a chase that reveals the unfairness in her racing against cisgender women").

5.3 Allocating Special Benefits

What is at stake with athletic opportunities is not, however, only the basic benefits of sports. Indeed, the fight over transgender girls' inclusion in sports is not primarily about access to the basic benefits; it is instead about who gets the special benefits of sports – the prizes, recognition and rewards that go to only a few. When it comes to these benefits, distributions based on principles of equality or need hold little appeal. Only allocations based on merit – where merit is determined by performance – allow the special benefits to retain their meaning and symbolic value. On this, both sides of the culture war seem to agree.[59] What is less clear is who should compete against whom.

This section considers three distinct eligibility categories within which merit-based allocations of special benefits could be made: unisex open categories, unisex ability categories and sex-based categories. I argue that while a move to unisex categories – both open and ability-based – has advantages, and avoids the difficulty of categorizing transgender athletes, such categories also have distinct problems, both practical and legal. To the extent that society instead maintains sex-based categories,

---

[59] Those arguing for exclusion contend that direct competition between transgender and cisgender girls is unfair. Those arguing for inclusion contend that direct competition is fair. But for both, the spoils must go to the (fair) victors. *Compare* Chelsea Mitchell, *I Was the Fastest Girl in Connecticut: But Transgender Athletes Made It an Unfair Fight*, USA TODAY (May 22, 2021), https://shorturl.at/Y60sV; Eric Spitznagel, *Trans Women Athletes Have Unfair Advantage over Those Born Female: Testosterone*, N.Y. POST (July 10, 2021), https://shorturl.at/1e7DB (drawing on a recently published book and outspoken athletes to highlight that trans women have an unfair advantage in sports based on their testosterone); Martina Navratilova, *The Rules on Trans Athletes Reward Cheats and Punish the Innocent*, SUNDAY TIMES (Feb. 17, 2019), https://shorturl.at/HvvQe; Dan Avery, *Trans Women Retain Athletic Edge after a Year of Hormone Therapy, Study Finds*, NBC NEWS (Jan. 5, 2021), https://shorturl.at/KEsKl; *and* John Stossel, *Transgender Athletes Have an Unfair Advantage*, TIMES NEWS (Aug. 5, 2021), https://shorturl.at/cfQAC; *with* Jack, *Trans Girls Belong on Girls' Sports Teams*, SCI. AM. (Mar. 16, 2021), www.scientificamerican.com/article/trans-girls-belong-on-girls-sports-teams/ (arguing there is no scientific case for excluding transgender girls from girls' sports teams); Tinbete Ermyas & Kira Wakeam, *Waves of Bills to Block Trans Athletes Has No Basis in Science, Researcher Says*, NPR SPORTS (Mar. 18, 2021), https://shorturl.at/AzKDm; Ashley Schwartz-Lavares, *Trans Women Targeted in Sports Bans, But Are They Really at an Advantage?*, ABC NEWS (Apr. 7, 2021), https://shorturl.at/X5eEx; James Factora, *Trans Inclusion in School Sports Doesn't Hurt Cisgender Girls, New Report Finds*, THEM (Feb. 8, 2021), www.them.us/story/trans-inclusion-school-sports-study; *and* Risa Isard, *Discriminatory Sports Laws Hurt Trans Girls – And Cis Girls, Too*, GLOB. SPORTS MATTERS (May 31, 2021), https://shorturl.at/0ULqm (arguing there is no evidence that trans girls are better at sports than cis girls).

it must enforce them fairly. This section concludes by considering what fair enforcement of the "female" category means and how it affects transgender and cisgender girls.

5.3.1 Unisex Open Competition

The simplest and cleanest way to draw an eligibility category in sports is to allow all interested individuals to compete directly against each other in an open "best in show" competition. Merit is determined by ability and achievement. At least formally open competitions of this sort are the norm for jobs and academic prizes, but they are rare in sports.[60]

Often there are strong objective and external reasons to want open competitions. When hiring heart surgeons, for example, hospitals have strong incentives to use open competitions: patients' lives are at stake. Rather than choosing the best surgeon in an over-200 pound division and the best surgeon in an under-200 pound division, hospitals and patients want the best overall surgeon. The same is true when choosing pilots. Airlines want the best possible pilots rather than the best pilots from among different narrower eligibility groupings. In these contexts, and many others, there is something important at stake apart from the distributional benefit to individual candidates or the associational benefit to members of their social identity groups. Allocation of rewards based on open competition best serves these external interests.

This is not the case in sports. Open competition in sports is not required by external interests. Indeed, such external interests do not exist in the context of sports. Society neither suffers any great cost nor incurs any great risk if it eschews open competition in this context. There is nothing inherently valuable that is lost or endangered if society awards athletic prizes to the best athletes in narrower eligibility categories rather than to the best athletes in open competition. Lives will not be lost or endangered if athletic prizes are given to the best wrestlers weighing under 150 pounds and to the best wrestlers weighing over 150 pounds, rather than to the best overall wrestlers. Nor will any

---

[60] While a few sports are currently unisex, the vast majority of sporting competitions are not. Indeed, the only Olympic sport that is unisex is equestrian. Martinková, *supra* note 50. There are "mixed sports." They include mixed doubles in tennis, 4x400m relays in track and field, and four-person teams in Alpine skiing parallel slalom. However, mixed sports are not the same as unisex sports. In unisex sports, the sex of the participants is irrelevant to their participation, while in mixed sports, the sex of the participants is an element of their eligibility to participate on the mixed team.

important knowledge be forgone, or social advance missed, if prizes are awarded to the best female and male tennis players rather than to the best overall tennis players.

There are, moreover, good reasons to eschew open competitions in sport. Biological girls and women would do far worse in open competitions than they currently do in sex-segregated competitions.[61] Their share of the special benefits of sports would be significantly diminished.[62] Transgender girls too would lose out. Certainly, they would win less often in open competitions than in sex-segregated competitions in which they were assigned to the "female" category. But additionally, and importantly, in open competitions transgender girls would lose out on the opportunity to signal through sports their social standing and acceptance as girls.

A move to open competition might even be legally impermissible. Although Title IX's implementing regulations suggest that sex-segregated teams may not be required,[63] a school that eliminated them altogether would likely face a disparate-impact claim. The Supreme Court "has not yet decided whether Title IX allows for liability based on a

---

[61] *See Olympian Nancy Hogshead Fires Back at Trans Athlete Lia Thomas … "It Isn't Fair,"* TMZ Sports (May 31, 2022), www.tmz.com/2022/05/31/nancy-hogshead-lia-thomas-trans-athletes-evidence/ ("After somebody has been through male puberty, you cannot roll that back," and in the absence of sex segregation in sports, women would "have to be gracious losers to somebody that has a biological advantage that you can't train for, you can't eat better, you can't find better coaching" (quoting Nancy Hogshead Makar)); Doriane Lambelet Coleman, *Sex in Sport*, 80 L. & Contemp. Probs. 63, 87 (2017); Steve Magness, *There's Good Reason for Sports to Be Separated by Sex*, Atlantic (Sept. 29, 2022), www.theatlantic.com/culture/archive/2022/09/why-elite-sports-should-remain-separated-by-sex/671594/ (describing the gap between males' and females' performances in track and swimming).

[62] *See* Jessica A. Clark, *They, Them, and Theirs*, 132 Harv. L. Rev. 894, 973 (2019) ("At elite levels, gender neutrality would reduce the number of women who qualify for national teams and win medals. If only a few women succeed, they will be written off as 'outliers' and their small numbers will be used as evidence of women's natural athletic inferiority rather than 'an indictment of society's suppression of female athleticism'"). As discussed previously, while some scholars argue in favor of creating new sports or modifying existing ones to achieve a more proportional distribution of wins for male and female athletes, I am skeptical that existing preferences can be easily changed and wary of the state or institutional suppression of existing sports that would probably be required to do so. In any event, creating new sports and shifting participant preferences would take time. In the meantime, girls and women would receive significantly fewer prizes and awards than they do under a system of sex-segregated sports.

[63] *See* 34 C.F.R. § 106.41(b) (2020) (stating that a recipient of federal funds "may operate or sponsor separate teams for members of each sex").

disparate impact theory,"[64] but some lower courts have recognized such claims.[65] To the extent that a move to open competition resulted in girls and women as a group having a significantly smaller share of the special benefits of sports than boys and men, the move would be vulnerable to challenge.[66] There is, in short, little to recommend the use of open unisex categories in sports and much to discourage it. Distributing special athletic benefits within ability-based eligibility groupings is an alternative.

5.3.2 Unisex Ability Categories

Increasingly, there have been calls for a move to unisex ability categories under which special benefits are awarded not to the best overall athlete but to the best athlete in a narrower category defined by ability-relevant characteristics – for example, height, weight or age.[67] As a general matter,

---

[64] *See* Zoe Seaman-Grant, *Title IX and the Alleged Victimization of Men: Applying Twombly to Federal Title IX*, 28 MICH. J. GENDER & L. 281, 296 (2022); Guardians Ass'n v. Civ. Serv. Comm'n N.Y.C., 463 U.S. 582, 602 (1963) (holding that Title VI supports a private right of action for declarative and injunctive relief for unintentional violations).

[65] *See* Haffner v. Temple Univ., 678 F. Supp. 517, 539 (E.D. Pa. 1988) (holding in a Title IX action that "plaintiffs need not prove discriminatory intent to succeed on their claim"); Horner v. Ky. High Sch. Athletic Ass'n, 206 F.3d 685, 692 (6th Cir. 2000) (recognizing a disparate-impact claim under Title IX but holding that discriminatory intent "is a prerequisite for money damages under Title IX when a facially neutral policy is challenged under a disparate impact theory"); *but see* Doe v. Univ. of Cincinnati, 173 F. Supp. 3d 586, 608 (S.D. Ohio 2016) (holding that "since recovery under Title IX under a disparate impact theory is not permitted, Plaintiffs' [sic] cannot state a claim by alleging that UC's otherwise gender-neutral disciplinary procedures disproportionately affect men").

[66] Indeed, according to the Office for Civil Rights (OCR): "an institution would not be effectively accommodating the interests and abilities of women if it abolished all its women's teams and opened up its men's teams to women, but only a few women were able to qualify for the men's team." *See* U.S. Dep't of Health, Educ., and Welfare, OCR, Sex Discrimination in Athletic Programs, 40 FR 52655, 52656 (Nov. 11, 1975).

[67] *See* Leong & Bartlett, *supra* note 6 (arguing that under Equal Protection Clause analysis, the health consequences of segregation should be taken into account to determine when sports should or should not be segregated by sex); Adrienne Milner & Jomills Braddock, Sex Segregation in Sports: Why Separate Is Not Equal (2016) (arguing in favor of dismantling Title IX's sex-segregation structure); Maggie Mertens, *Separating Sports by Sex Doesn't Make Sense*, ATLANTIC (Sept. 17, 2022), www.theatlantic.com/culture/archive/2022/09/sports-gender-sex-segregation-coed/671460/ ("Old notions of sex as a marker of physical capability are changing, and more research is making clear that sex differences aren't really clear at all"); Flick Haigh, *Don't Segregate Female Athletes: Celebrate Them.*, N.Y. TIMES (Dec. 6, 2019), www.nytimes.com/2019/12/06/opinion/women-sports-segregation.html (arguing that lack of encouragement rather than disparity in physical abilities drives differences in sports performance between the sexes).

ability categories have several advantages over open competition.[68] Ability-based eligibility categories can make play more enjoyable for athletes by tightening contests and ensuring that competitors are evenly matched. They can also decrease the risk of injury.[69] For fans, ability-based groupings can make contests more fun to watch.[70]

Advocates for unisex ability categories see them as a means of challenging the gender binary and perceived stereotypes of female athletic inferiority. As Maggie Mertens argued in the *Atlantic*, "[m]aintaining this binary in youth sports reinforces the idea that boys are inherently bigger, faster, and stronger than girls in a competitive setting – a notion that's been challenged by scientists for years."[71] A move to unisex ability categories also eliminates the challenge of categorizing transgender athletes – transgender athletes, like all athletes, simply compete in their ability category.

Ability categories can be drawn in innumerable ways. In a sport such as basketball, where height is relevant to performance, players can be divided into those under 5 feet, under 5 foot 5 inches, under 5 foot 10 inches and under 6 foot 3 inches. Alternatively, players could simply be divided into those under 5 foot 10 inches and those equal to or greater than 5 foot 10 inches in height. Weight too is an ability-relevant characteristic in many sports. Players could be divided into those who weigh less than 100 pounds, less than 150 pounds, less than 200 pounds and equal to or more than 200 pounds. Alternatively, players could be divided into fewer weight categories or many more. Wingspan, lung

---

[68] Ability categories, by controlling to some degree for natural advantages, crystallize the distinction between ability and effort and define merit, to a greater degree than in open competition, in terms of the latter.

[69] *See* Cruz v. Pa. Interscholastic Athletic Ass'n, Inc., 157 F. Supp. 2d 485 (E.D. Pa. 2001) (explaining that the reason for age-based eligibility rules was to ensure that teams were evenly matched and to protect younger athletes from injury).

[70] *See* Henry T. Greely, *Disabilities, Enhancements, and the Meanings of Sports*, 15 STAN. L. & POL'Y REV. 99, 124 (2004) (opining that "closer contests are usually more entertaining").

[71] Mertens, *supra* note 67; *see also* SARAH JANE TEETZEL, A PHILOSOPHICAL ANALYSIS OF OLYMPIC ELIGIBILITY, VALUES, AND AUXILIARY RULES 215 (2009) (Ph.D. dissertation, University of Western Ontario) (noting that "[w]hile dividing sports into men's and women's events is socially convenient, doing so upholds outdated stereotypes about women being less powerful and more fragile athletes" and arguing that "[a]lternatives to the current categories that divide most competitions into separate men's and women's events could include divisions not based on sex but on competitors' weight and height, which is already done in boxing, wrestling, and to some extent rowing").

capacity, strength, flexibility and speed are all ability-relevant characteristics that can be demarcated in any number of ways.[72]

All ability categories necessarily benefit some athletes more than others, and all are to some extent arbitrary. If height categories in basketball divide those who are shorter than 5 foot 10 inches from those who are equal to or taller than 5 foot 10 inches, those who are 5 foot 9 will be advantaged by playing in the shorter league. They will be more likely to excel and to stand out. Players who are 5 foot 10 inches will be disadvantaged. Being the shortest in their league will make it more difficult for them to dominate play. Malcolm Gladwell documented just this phenomenon and its impact in his study of age cutoffs for youth hockey players in Canada. Those players whose birthdays were just shortly after the age cutoff, and hence were the oldest in their competition category, fared better. The relatively older players scored more and received more attention, more encouragement and ultimately more opportunities to play college and professional hockey.[73]

The fact that ability categories will necessarily favor some athletes more than others does not make them unfair to the losers. Individual athletes do not have an entitlement to categories drawn in a particular way. Categories need not, and indeed cannot, equalize the chances of winning for all individual participants.

Nonetheless, unisex ability categories may be unfair to women as a group for the same reason that open competition is. Although ability categories can be drawn with an eye to increasing wins by female athletes, it will be difficult, if not impossible, to draw such categories so as to equally advantage women and men.[74] To the extent that men dominate unisex

---

[72] See Rosalyn Kerr, *Why It Might Be Time to Eradicate Sex Segregation in Sports*, CONVERSATION (Jan. 14, 2018), https://theconversation.com/why-it-might-be-time-to-eradicate-sex-segregation-in-sports-89305 (describing a range of ability-based categories in sports and arguing that sex-based categories should be replaced with discrete ability categories).

[73] MALCOM GLADWELL, OUTLIERS: THE STORY OF SUCCESS 3–4 (2011).

[74] It is more possible with ability categories than it is with open competition to draw eligibility rules so as to reduce the disparity between men's and women's victories. For example, ability-based eligibility lines for basketball that separate those athletes who are shorter than 5 foot 5 inches from those who are taller than 5 foot 5 inches will more evenly distribute special benefits to women and men than would eligibility lines that divide between those athletes who are shorter than and taller than 6 feet. Nonetheless, it is likely that most common ability categories – e.g., those divided by height or weight – will be dominated by men. See Sandro Bartolomei et al., *A Comparison between Male and Female Athletics in Relative Strength and Power Performances*, 6 J. FUNC. MORPH. & KINESIOLOGY 17 (2021); Lincoln E. Ford et al., *Gender- and Height-Related Limits of Muscle Strength in World Weightlifting*

ability categories, the categories will be vulnerable to the same disparate-impact challenge as are open athletic competitions. In short, moving to unisex ability categories to distribute the special benefits of sport is unlikely to be quick, simple or uncontroversial.

5.3.3 Sex-Based Categories

To the extent that society continues to use sex-segregated competition categories as the framework for distributing the special benefits of sports – either on a permanent or interim basis – participants have a right to their fair enforcement. What "fair" looks like in this context is, of course, at the heart of the current debate over transgender girls' inclusion in girls' sports.

Thomas Pogge has offered three morally universal principles for assessing the fairness of social rules or states of affairs.[75] According to Pogge, a morally universal framework must (1) "subject[] all persons to the same system of fundamental moral principles,"[76] (2) "assign the same fundamental moral benefits ... and burdens to all,"[77] and (3) formulate the fundamental moral benefits and burdens "in general terms so as not to privilege or disadvantage certain persons or groups arbitrarily."[78] William Morgan has offered a more contextually based framework for assessing fairness. According to Morgan,

> fairness in sport demands that everyone in sport be treated equally, in other words, that the rules of sport apply to all in relevantly similar ways, and that the distribution of benefits and responsibilities in sport be determined by a competition open to all on the basis of the relevant talent and capabilities of would-be participants and in such a way that does not diminish the goods that sport delivers that draws people to them.[79]

Together Pogge's and Morgan's works suggest three core requirements for fair categories and eligibility rules in sports. The first is a requirement of consistency across contexts and contests. Consistency across contexts

---

Champions, 89 J. App. Phys. 1061 (2000); Allison Jack, *The Comparison of Vertical Jump Height between Gender and Body Fat Percentage* (2013) (University of Texas Arlington Libraries), https://rc.library.uta.edu/uta-ir/handle/10106/24194.

[75] Thomas W. Pogge, *Moral Universalism and Global Economic Justice*, 1 Pol., Phil. & Econ. 29 (2002).
[76] *Id.* at 30.
[77] *Id.*
[78] *Id.*
[79] William J. Morgan, *Fair Is Fair, Or Is It? A Moral Consideration of the Doping Wars in American Sport*, 9 Sport in Soc'y 177, 180 (2006).

means that eligibility rules across sports must be based on the same underlying principles. Consistency across contests means that rules within sports must remain consistent enough over time to provide predictability and protect reasonable reliance interests. As Professor Sarah Teetzel has argued in the context of an examination of Olympic eligibility rules, "the rules that specify precise eligibility requirements must be fair, just and consistently applied."[80] The second requirement is that those who are similar be treated similarly and those who are dissimilar be treated differently. As Professor Sigmund Loland has explained, "[r]elevantly equal cases ought to be treated equally, cases that are relevantly unequal can be treated unequally, and unequal treatment ought to stand in reasonable accordance with the actual inequality between cases."[81] The third requirement is that rules further the same moral or social goals for all individuals or groups. Eligibility rules must, in other words, promote the same social goals and provide the same goods for members of all social groups.

This section examines three distinct conceptions of the "female" sports category. It explores which conception is most fair in light of the three principles and it considers what such a conception of the category means for transgender girls' inclusion.

5.3.3.1 "Female" as a Gender Category

Sometimes the "female" sports category is conceived of as a gender identity category. According to this view, transgender girls must always be included because the limits of the category are determined by self-identification.[82] This was, effectively, the position of the Obama administration. In a Dear Colleague letter written by the Department of Justice and the Department of Education on May 13, 2016, the agencies explained that they "treat a student's gender identity as the student's sex for purposes of Title IX and its implementing regulations."[83] What this means, they advised, is that "a school must not treat a transgender

---

[80] Teetzel, *supra* note 71 at 180–81.
[81] SIGMUND LOLAND, FAIR PLAY IN SPORT: A MORAL NORM SYSTEM 29 (2002).
[82] *See* Nicholas Chadi, *Gender Identity*, MEDSCAPE (Nov. 14, 2022), https://emedicine.medscape.com/article/917990-overview ("Gender identity, as it develops, is self-identified, as a result of a combination of inherent and extrinsic factors"); *Myths about Transgender Girls in Sports*, ACLU IOWA, www.aclu-ia.org/en/myths-about-transgender-girls-sports ("The bottom line is that trans girls *are* girls and should participate in girls' sports. They are not boys and they are not an 'other' that should be excluded").
[83] Dear Colleague Letter on Transgender Students, U.S. DEP'T OF EDUC. & U.S. DEP'T OF JUST. (May 13, 2016), www.ed.gov/ocr/letters/colleague-201605-title-ix-transgender.pdf.

5.3 ALLOCATING SPECIAL BENEFITS

student differently from the way it treats other students of the same gender identity."[84] "When a school provides sex-segregated activities and facilities," the departments emphasized, "transgender students must be allowed to participate in such activities and access such facilities consistent with their gender identity."[85] Moreover, a student's gender identity, the agencies explained, was simply a matter of self-assertion – "there is no medical diagnosis or treatment requirement that students must meet as a prerequisite to being treated consistent with their gender identity."[86] The Biden administration endorsed a similar approach.[87]

---

[84] *Id.*

[85] *Id.* at 3.

[86] *Id.* at 2. The Trump administration rescinded the Dear Colleague Letter. *See* Dear Colleague Letter, U.S. Dep't of Educ. & U.S. Dep't of Just. (Feb. 22, 2017), www.cmu.edu/title-ix/2-22-17-guidance_letter1.pdf.

[87] President Biden, while on the campaign trail, promised to reinstate the Obama-era guidance. *See* The Biden Plan to Advance LGBTQ+ Equality in America and Around the World, Democratic Nat'l Comm., https://joebiden.com/lgbtq-policy/#. He did not do so, but he did, upon taking office, issue a broad executive order to protect transgender children that provided: "Children should be able to learn without worrying about whether they will be denied access to the restroom, the locker room, or school sports." *See* Exec. Order No. 13988, 86 Fed. Reg. 7023–25 (2021), www.whitehouse.gov/briefing-room/presidential-actions/2021/01/20/executive-order-preventing-and-combating-discrimination-on-basis-of-gender-identity-or-sexual-orientation/. This rather vague executive order instructed the head of each agency to promulgate any new actions necessary to further the policy of the order. In response to the order, the Department of Education issued a Notice of Interpretation explaining that Title IX's prohibition of discrimination on the basis of sex includes discrimination based on gender identity. *See* U.S. Department of Education Confirms Title IX Protects Students from Discrimination Based on Sexual Orientation and Gender Identity, 86 Fed. Reg. 32637 (proposed June 16, 2021), www.govinfo.gov./app/details/FR-2021-06-22/2021-13058. In addition, on June 23, 2022, the Department of Education released for public comment proposed changes to Title IX regulations that would strengthen protections for transgender students. The proposed regulations "would make clear that preventing any person from participating in an education program or activity consistent with their gender identity would subject them to more than de minimis harm on the basis of sex and therefore be prohibited, unless otherwise permitted by Title IX or the regulations." *See* Nondiscrimination on the Basis of Sex in Education Programs or Activities Receiving Federal Financial Assistance, 87 Fed. Reg. 41390, 41534 (proposed Jul. 12, 2022) (to be codified at 34 C.F.R. pt. 106), www.govinfo.gov/content/pkg/FR-2022-07-12/pdf/2022-13734.pdf. On April 6, 2023, the Department of Education issued a Notice of Proposed Rulemaking on Title IX dealing particularly with athletes. The proposed rule provides that if a school adopts criteria that would limit a student's eligibility to participate on the athletic team consistent with their gender identity, the criteria must be substantially related to an important educational objective and must minimize harm to the affected student. *See FACT SHEET: U.S. Department of Education's Proposed Change to Its Title IX Regulations on Students' Eligibility for Athletic Teams*, U.S. Dept. of Educ. (Apr. 6, 2023), https://shorturl.at/YaC85.

As a historical, rather than normative, matter, reading the category "female" in sports as a category of gender self-identification is clearly erroneous. As Lindsay Pieper explained in *Sex Testing: Gender Policing in Women's Sports*, the International Olympic Committee (IOC) has been engaged in sex testing of female athletes since the 1920s.[88] She described a range of different tests used – from anatomical exams to chromosomal checks.[89] All focus on the body and involve an external evaluator. Indeed, as Ruth Padawer explained in the *New York Times*, "[n]o governing body has so tenaciously tried to determine who counts as a woman for the purpose of sports as the I.A.A.F. [International Association of Athletics Federations] and the International Olympic Committee (I.O.C.). Those two influential organizations have spent a half-century vigorously policing gender boundaries."[90]

It is not surprising, then, that the NCAA's initial policy regarding transgender athletes, adopted in 2010, focused on biological markers rather than self-identification. The NCAA's Inclusion of Transgender Student-Athletes policy provided that "[a] trans female (MTF) transgender student-athlete who is not taking hormone treatments related to gender transition may not compete on a women's team."[91] With regard to trans athletes undergoing hormonal treatment, the policy provided: "A trans female (MTF) student-athlete being treated with testosterone suppression medication for Gender Identity Disorder or gender dysphoria and/or Transsexualism, for the purposes of NCAA competition may continue to compete on a men's team but may not compete on a women's team without changing it to a mixed team status until completing one calendar year of testosterone suppression treatment."[92]

In 2022, the NCAA revised its transgender inclusion policy in response to controversy over transgender swimmer Lia Thomas's success competing for Penn's women's team.[93] The NCAA's revised policy calls

---

[88] *See* LINDSAY PIERPER, SEX TESTING: GENDER POLICING IN WOMEN'S SPORTS 1 (2016).
[89] *Id.* at 2; *see also* Cheryl Cooky & Shari L. Dworkin, *Policing the Boundaries of Sex: A Critical Examination of Gender Verification and the Caster Semenya Controversy*, 50 J. SEX RSCH. 103 (2013); Haley K. Olsen-Acre, *The Use of Drug Testing to Police Sex and Gender in the Olympic Games*, 13 MICH. J. GENDER & L. 207 (2007).
[90] Ruth Padawer, *The Humiliating Practice of Sex-Testing Female Athletes*, N.Y. TIMES (June 28, 2016), www.nytimes.com/2016/07/03/magazine/the-humiliating-practice-of-sex-testing-female-athletes.html.
[91] *NCAA Inclusion of Transgender Student-Athletes*, NCAA OFF. OF INCLUSION (Aug. 2011), at 13, https://ncaaorg.s3.amazonaws.com/inclusion/lgbtq/INC_TransgenderHandbook.pdf.
[92] *Id.*
[93] *See* Alan Blinder, *Lia Thomas Wins an N.C.A.A Swimming Title*, N.Y. TIMES (Mar. 17, 2022), www.nytimes.com/2022/03/17/sports/lia-thomas-swimmer-wins.html.

for transgender participation to be determined by the governing bodies of each individual sport.[94] Yet the policy also provides for deadlines by which transgender student athletes need to document their "sport-specific testosterone levels."[95] In other words, although the NCAA has moved to a more sport-specific approach, it continues to view and define the female category in terms of objective, measurable biological criteria.

In response to the new NCAA policy, USA Swimming published its own policies for transgender inclusion.[96] USA Swimming distinguishes between non-elite-level events and elite-level events. For the former, the governing body emphasizes the importance of sport as a "vehicle for positive physical and mental health"[97] and allows swimmers to compete in the category consistent with their gender identity and expression. At the elite level, however, where the special benefits of sport are substantial, USA Swimming states its express concern with "providing a level-playing field for elite cisgender women."[98] Its policy requires transgender female athletes to present "[e]vidence that the concentration of testosterone in the athlete's serum has been less than 5 nmol/L ... continuously for a period of at least thirty-six (36) months before the date of Application."[99] Moreover, the policy provides that decision-making about eligibility will be made by a panel of "three independent medical experts."[100] When it comes to elite swimming, USA Swimming makes clear, "female" is not a gender-identity category. It never has been, in swimming or other elite athletic competitions.

Conceiving of the "female" athletic category as a gender-identity category would violate at least two of the three fairness principles for eligibility categories. It would violate the first fairness principle requiring consistent and predictable interpretations of the category. This ahistorical and atypical conception of the category would undermine the reasonable reliance interests that female athletes have in competing in a category determined and defined to some degree by biological markers.

---

[94] See *Board of Governors Updates Transgender Participation Policy*, NCAA (Jan. 19, 2022), https://shorturl.at/tHU07.
[95] *Id.*
[96] See *USA Swimming Releases Athlete Inclusion, Competitive Equity and Eligibility Policy*, USA SWIMMING (Feb. 2, 2022), https://shorturl.at/ENg75.
[97] *Id.*
[98] *Id.*
[99] *19.0 Athlete Inclusion, Competitive Equity, and Eligibility Policy*, USA SWIMMING (adopted/last revised Mar. 10, 2023), https://shorturl.at/BB6cy.
[100] *Id.*

This is not to say that it is impossible or impermissible to change the meaning of a category, but fairness does demand some notice to participants and a period of transition. The conception would also violate the second fairness principle requiring that, to the extent distinctions are drawn, they treat those who are similar in relevant ways the same and those who are dissimilar in relevant ways differently. Defining the "female" category exclusively in terms of gender self-identification draws boundaries and distinguishes individuals only in terms of a criteria irrelevant to athletic performance.

5.3.3.2 "Female" as an Ability Category

More often, the "female" sports category is treated as a type of biologically based ability category. Under this conception, the "female" category is considered a proxy for a range of ability-relevant physical characteristics. This view of the "female" category as an ability category – in contrast to the view of it as an identity category – permeates both the public debate about transgender inclusion and the eligibility lines drawn by athletics' governing bodies.

Those arguing both for and against transgender girls' inclusion focus on whether transgender girls have physical advantages that take them outside the category's appropriate ability range. Those arguing for transgender girls' inclusion, for example, emphasize the wide variation of physical characteristics within the "female" sports category and contend that transgender girls are no more outliers than are certain cisgender girls.[101] In a similar vein, but from a different vantage point, those arguing for transgender exclusion contend that transgender girls are too distinct in terms of ability-relevant characteristics from those in the girls' category to be included. They focus on the nonoverlapping levels of testosterone between women and men and the importance of male puberty for athletic performance.[102]

---

[101] See e.g., *Get the Facts: Trans Equity in Sports*, GENDER/JUSTICE (Jan. 12, 2021), www.genderjustice.us/get-the-facts-trans-equity-in-sports/ (focusing on the wingspan of Michael Phelps, the height-to-strength ratio of Simone Biles and the height of Manute Bol and explaining that "[t]here's no scientific evidence that the average trans athlete is any bigger, stronger, or faster than the average cis athlete"); Dirk Smith, *Do Transgender Athletes Have a Performance Advantage? Let's Look at the Results*, COMPETE NETWORK (June 7, 2021), https://shorturl.at/6vY4W (contending that "all the arguments debating 'biology' and 'physiology' in regard to performance advantages of trans athletes vs cisgender athletes on the basis of biological sex are moot given there is no statistical evidence to support any such conclusion").

[102] See, e.g., Frank Mir & Terry Schilling, *Not a Fair Fight: Our Athlete Daughters Shouldn't Have to Compete with Transgender Women*, USA TODAY (Feb. 26, 2021, 2:06 PM)

Transgender girls, according to this argument, have ability-relevant attributes that take them outside the female category.

In line with this broader public debate, athletic governing bodies have for years defined the "female" category in terms of biological markers deemed relevant to athletic ability. Of particular focus have been testosterone levels. In 2015, the IOC enacted a policy that limited eligibility to compete in the "female" category to athletes whose "total testosterone level ... has been below 10nmol/L for at least 12 months prior to her first competition."[103] In doing so, the IOC made clear that its objective was to "guarantee ... fair competition" and that, toward this aim, "[r]estrictions on participation are appropriate to the extent that they are necessary and proportionate to the achievement of that objective."[104] In the same policy, the IOC rejected prior policies requiring anatomical changes as a requirement for "female" category inclusion because it found that such requirements were "not necessary to preserve fair competition."[105] The IOC's new policy allows more deference to individual sports' governing bodies to determine their own eligibility rules for female athletes, but both the IOC and the individual governing bodies continue to define the category in terms of ability-relevant criteria.[106]

---

https://shorturl.at/zPlyj (arguing that "[b]iological male athletes have an insurmountable physical advantage over biological female athletes. They have greater muscle mass, bigger and stronger bones, and larger hearts and lungs than women"); Sean Ingle, *Sport's Trans Issue Is Here to Stay: But at Last, the Debate Is Starting to Change*, GUARDIAN (Dec. 13, 2021), https://shorturl.at/nhiI3 (contending that "male puberty provides such a categorical advantage – in terms of muscle mass, strength, lean body mass and bone density – that it far exceeds the advantage of a few centimeters in arm length" that Michael Phelps may have had over other cisgender males); Nancy Hogshead-Makar, *It Was Not Fair When I Raced Against Doped-Up East Germans and It Is Not Fair for Women to Compete Against Transgender Swimmer Lia Thomas; Here's Why*, DAILY MAIL (Dec. 24, 2021), https://shorturl.at/TpvLP (arguing that that "[a]llowing transgender women to change the meaning of the women's category makes as much sense as allowing 180-pound athletes into the 120-pound weight category ... or allowing adults to compete against children").

[103] *IOC Consensus Meeting on Sex Reassignment and Hyperandrogenism*, INT'L OLYMPIC COMM. (2015), https://tinyurl.com/mvj6fnsf.

[104] *Id.*

[105] *Id.*

[106] *See, e.g.,* Frankie De La Cretaz, *The IOC Has a New Trans-Inclusion Framework, but Is the Damage Already Done?*, SPORTS ILLUSTRATED (Mar. 23, 2022), https://shorturl.at/jwDQQ (describing female eligibility rules for the IOC and for several different athletic governing bodies); *see also supra* note 96; *IOC Framework on Fairness, Inclusion and Non Discrimination on the Basis of Gender Identity and Sex Variations*, INT'L OLYMPIC COMM. (2021), https://shorturl.at/7GeIy; Katie Barnes, *NCAA Updates Policy on Transgender Participation, to Let Each Sport Set Eligibility Requirements*, ESPN (Jan. 19, 2022), https://shorturl.at/F02Jf; *NWSL Policy on Transgender Athletes*, NAT'L WOMEN'S SOCCER

Given this history, conceiving of the "female" athletic category as an ability category satisfies both the first and second principles of fairness. First, defining the boundaries of the sex category with regard to ability-relevant criteria is consistent with widely shared expectations of how the boundaries should be, and are being, drawn. Such an interpretation is, as a result, predictable (at least in terms of its general contours if not its specifics) and consistent with settled expectations about when one will be included in or excluded from the category. Second, treating the "female" category as an ability category treats those who are dissimilar differently and those who are similar similarly. Sex-based athletic categories, broadly conceived, do map onto and encompass a range of ability-related characteristics that are particularly pronounced post puberty. Those who have gone through male puberty have on average taller heights and longer wingspans, larger bones, a larger heart and greater lung capacity than those who have not.[107] As evolutionary biologist Carole Hooven explains, with regard to sports, "[m]en don't have an advantage over women because of one of these factors, but all of them put together."[108]

Indeed, if the "female" and "male" athletic categories did not map onto and reflect real and relevant physical differences, it is likely that sex segregation in sports would be far more widely viewed as stigmatic. Imagine, for example, an employer that requires male employees to wear blue shirts and female employees to wear pink shirts and offers awards to the best female and male employee of the week. The distinction seems at best silly and at worst marginalizing and demeaning. The same holds for race and religion categories in sport. Awarding medals to the fastest Black swimmer and the fastest white swimmer would stigmatize Black swimmers in a way that awarding medals to the fastest female swimmers does not. Drawing categories without ability-based differences seems to reflect views of social inferiority, distaste, or at best protectionism – all

---

LEAGUE (2021), https://shorturl.at/xzBkc; *Athletes Unlimited Policy on Participation of Transgender and Non-Binary Athletes: Women's Sports*, ATHLETES UNLIMITED (2021), https://shorturl.at/89tf8. *But see* Paul Krotz, *PHF Updates Transgender and Non-Binary Inclusion Policy*, PREMIER HOCKEY FED'N (Oct. 15, 2021), https://shorturl.at/Cplwe (removing all hormone requirements for transfeminine athletes).

[107] *See* David J. Handelsman, *Circulating Testosterone as the Hormonal Basis of Sex Differences in Athletic Performances*, 39 ENDOCRINE REV. 803, 805 (2018); Antonella LoMauro & Andrea Aliverti, *Sex Differences in Respiratory Function*, 14 BREATHE 131 (2018).

[108] *See* Suzy Weiss, *Watching Lia Thomas Win*, COMMON SENSE (Feb. 21 2022), https://bariweiss.substack.com/p/watching-lia-thomas-win?utm_source=url.

of which can serve to stigmatize and marginalize the group already viewed as less socially powerful.[109]

It seems both accurate and fair, then, to conceive of sex categories in sports as biologically based ability categories. Nonetheless, treating the "female" category as exclusively an ability category is a mistake, both descriptively and normatively. The "female" athletic category must also be defined and conceived of as a status category.

5.3.3.3 "Female" as a Status Category

Sex-based athletic categories are drawn not only to make contests closer – by narrowing ability differences – but, more critically, to ensure that women, like men, receive the group benefits of sport. The categories reflect social salience as much as athletic prowess and they further antisubordination as much as close competition. Indeed, at least since the passage of Title IX, women's sports have become an explicit tool of female empowerment and gender equality.[110]

---

[109] Interestingly, while ability differences may be necessary to keep categories from being viewed as stigmatic, their existence may not always be sufficient to prevent such a perception. Indeed, sometimes even when there are likely sex-based ability differences, as is the case with math aptitude at the highest level, making sex an eligibility criteria for awards and prizes and having different prizes for women and men may be viewed as stigmatic because it reinforces a distinction with which we are not as a society comfortable and would seemingly like to ignore.

For example, when Larry Summers, then president of Harvard University, suggested that innate ability differences between girls and boys at the highest levels of math ability might be in part responsible for women's underrepresentation on math and engineering faculties, his comments received widespread criticism. *See* Sam Dillon, *Harvard Chief Defends His Talk on Women*, N.Y. TIMES (Jan. 18, 2005) www.nytimes.com/2005/01/18/us/harvard-chief-defends-his-talk-on-women.html; Marcella Bomvardieri, *Summers' Remarks on Women Draw Fire*, BOST. GLOBE (Jan. 17, 2005), https://shorturl.at/FsHfC; Daniel J. Hemel, *Summers' Comments on Women and Science Draw Ire*, HARV. CRIMSON (Jan. 14, 2005), www.thecrimson.com/article/2005/1/14/summers-comments-on-women-and-science/; *see also* Diane F. Halpern et al., The Science of Sex Differences in Science and Mathematics, 8 Psych. Sci. Pub. Int. 1 (2007).

[110] *See* Note, *Cheering on Women and Girls in Sports: Using Title IX to Fight Gender Role Oppression*, 110 HARV. L. REV. 1627 (1997); *Title IX and the Rise of Female Athletes in America*, WOMEN'S SPORTS FOUND. (Sept. 2, 2016), https://shorturl.at/vvX0F; Ruth Igielnik, *Most Americans Who Are Familiar with Title IX Say It's Had a Positive Impact on Gender Equality*, PEW RSCH. CTR. (Apr. 21, 2022), https://shorturl.at/ezvUr; *Sport for Generation Equality: Advancing Gender Equality in and Through Sport*, UN WOMEN (Mar. 10, 2020), www.unwomen.org/en/news/stories/2020/3/news-sport-for-generation-equality; *Women, Gender Equality and Sport*, UNITED NATIONS (2007), www.un.org/womenwatch/daw/public/Women%20and%20Sport.pdf; LYNDSAY M.C. HAYHURST ET AL., INTRODUCING SPORT, GENDER AND DEVELOPMENT: A CRITICAL INTERSECTION (2021).

If the "female" athletic category were solely an ability category, elite female athletes would have no greater claim to resources or social recognition than would mediocre male athletes who could, very likely, beat them in direct competition. As ability categories, "elite women" and "mediocre men" look similar. Yet there is virtually no serious political or social argument that these two groups should be treated the same. Ability categories, when they exist, are mapped onto sex categories but rarely replace them. Elite female athletes' claims of entitlement are to parity with elite male athletes, not with the male second string. The "female" category may be an ability category, but it is not only an ability category. It is also a social category drawn with the purpose of providing particular social rewards and recognition to a particular social group – women.

Such a focus on groups and social status is essential. Indeed, the third requirement of fairness is that eligibility rules be drawn with the goal of providing all individuals and groups with access to the same social benefits. The boundaries of the "female" category must, then, be drawn with an eye to their effect on women as a group and with the goal of elevating women's social status to equality with men's. In other words, the category must be defined not only with regard to ability markers but also with regard to the group benefits the category provides girls and women. With this definition of and requirement for the "female" category in mind, the next section considers what eligibility rules for female sports maximize the group benefits of sport for all girls, transgender and cisgender.

5.4 Allocating Group Benefits

This section explores several possible framings of the "female" sports category with the goal of optimizing group benefits for both transgender and cisgender girls and women. It begins by considering the effects of exclusion – that is, the separation of transgender and cisgender girls into different athletic categories – and explains why the kind of separate-but-equal framework used by Title IX to equalize group benefits between girls and boys is neither desirable nor feasible when it comes to transgender and cisgender girls. It next considers the effects of inclusion – that is, the direct competition of transgender and cisgender girls in one athletic category. More specifically, it considers the effects of inclusion under three different plausible empirical realities: (1) transgender girls perform no better than cisgender girls on average and are no more likely to win prizes (mean and tail equivalence), (2) transgender girls perform better than cisgender girls on average but are no more likely to win prizes (mean superiority), and (3) transgender girls are significantly more likely than cisgender girls to win prizes and other scarce benefits (tail superiority).

5.4.1 Exclusive Categories

As between female and male athletes, separate-but-equal athletic opportunities and resources ensure that women and girls receive group benefits from sports that are comparable to those received by men and boys.[111] Female athletes necessarily win special benefits and in doing so convey reflective benefits on girls and women generally. Some commentators on girls' sports have argued for a similar separate-but-equal approach for transgender and cisgender girls.[112] When it comes to transgender and cisgender girls, however, separate-but-equal is inherently unequal.

Even under the best-case scenario – one in which transgender girls were able to field robust and diverse athletic teams and competitions – transgender girls would not receive group benefits from sports comparable to those received by cisgender girls. Critically, they would not receive increased self-esteem and social status as girls. Under a separate-but-equal framework, cisgender girls would benefit from having athletic role models and from seeing those with biologically female bodies recognized and celebrated for their strength and agency. Transgender girls too would have athletic role models and would benefit from seeing transgender athletes celebrated and rewarded in ways comparable to those of cisgender athletes. What transgender girls would not receive, however, no matter how well transgender girls were treated under a separate-but-equal model, is affirmation of their status as girls. Separation, and its

---

[111] This is what is required by Title IX. *See* 34 C.F.R. 106 (2001); *see also* Title IX of the Education Amendments of 1972; a Policy Interpretation; Title IX and Intercollegiate Athletics 44 Fed. Reg. 71,413 (Dec. 11, 1979).

[112] Nancy Hogshead-Makar, for example, has suggested that one possible remedy for what she perceives as the unfair inclusion of transgender girls in girls' sports is to have transgender girls compete in their own leagues. *See* Louisa Thomas, *The Trans Swimmer Who Won Too Much*, NEW YORKER (Mar. 17, 2022), https://shorturl.at/fAv2E ("Hogshead-Makar has suggested that, in some sports, trans women should occupy their own classification, apart from women, and proposed to me that Thomas be allowed to swim in a separately demarcated lane, next to the eight set aside for cisgender women, and have her own podium"); *see also Sports Should Have Two Categories: Open and Female*, ECONOMIST (Mar. 19, 2022), https://shorturl.at/pZo5q; Joanna Haper et al., *Implication of a Third Gender for Elite Sports*, 17 CURR. SPORTS MED. REPS. 42 (2018); Niamh Lewis, *British Triathlon Creates Open Category for Transgender Athletes*, ESPN (July 6, 2022), https://shorturl.at/oxA6I.

message that transgender girls are not "real girls," would likely undermine any other self-esteem benefits that transgender girls would get from seeing transgender athletes celebrated.

Moreover, this best-case scenario is unrealistic. There are too few transgender athletes to field exclusively transgender teams or leagues. Precise data on the number of transgender girls playing sports at the elementary, high school or college level do not exist, but a series of estimates suggests that the number of participants is almost certainly extremely low. There are approximately 15 million high school students in the United States, of whom approximately 8 million participate in high school sports.[113] According to a Centers for Disease Control study, 1.8 percent of high school students are transgender.[114] Of those, the Human Rights Campaign has found that 14 percent of transgender boys and 12 percent of transgender girls play sports.[115] These numbers suggest that 0.44 percent of high school athletes are transgender. Even if these numbers are off tenfold, transgender athletes would not be able to field teams and leagues in the range of sports or with the depth of talent that cisgender athletes enjoy. Separate-but-equal athletic categories for cisgender and transgender girls are impractical as well as undesirable.

5.4.2 Inclusive Categories

Transgender girls' inclusion in girls' sports – to some degree, and under some conditions – seems essential to ensuring that transgender and cisgender girls receive comparable self- and social-esteem benefits from sport. The next three subsections explore the effects that transgender girls' inclusion in girls' sports would have on the allocation of group benefits under a range of different empirical assumptions.

Critical to the analysis in each section are two assumptions: first, that transgender girls identify more closely with transgender girls and, as a result, reap more group benefits from transgender girls' victories than from cisgender girls' victories, and second, that cisgender girls identify more closely with cisgender girls and, as a result, reap more group

---

[113] See Katie Barnes, *Young Transgender Athletes Caught in the Middle of States' Debates*, ESPN (Sep. 1, 2021), https://shorturl.at/mCEIF.

[114] Michelle M. Johns et al., *Transgender Identity and Experiences of Violence Victimization, Substance Use, Suicide Risk, and Sexual Risk Behaviors among High School Students: 19 States and Large Urban School Districts, 2017*, 68 CDC Morbidity & Mortality Weekly Rep. 67 (2019), www.cdc.gov/mmwr/volumes/68/wr/mm6803a3.htm.

[115] *Play to Win: Improving the Lives of LGBTQ Youth in Sports*, Hum. Rts. Campaign, https://assets2.hrc.org/files/assets/resources/PlayToWin-FINAL.pdf.

benefits from cisgender girls' victories than from transgender girls' victories. To the extent that transgender girls identify equally strongly with cisgender girls as with transgender girls and are equally strongly identified socially with each group (and that the same is true for cisgender girls), the benefits received by both groups will be the same regardless of whether transgender or cisgender girls win particular contests. There would be no reason to care, or even keep track of, whether the special benefits of sports were being awarded disproportionately to transgender or cisgender girls within sex-segregated athletic competitions. Both the theory of role modeling and the political fight over transgender inclusion strongly suggest that this is not the case.

Studies have shown that individuals are more likely to use those who are similar to themselves "as a source of information about themselves" and look for comparisons to those who are "similar to them in terms of their overall performance level on various ability-related tasks."[116] Moreover, it seems that the effects and importance of intragroup role modeling are particularly strong for members of minority and disadvantaged groups.[117] Given the arguable physical-ability differences between transgender and cisgender girls and the enduring social status differences between the two groups,[118] it seems likely that transgender

---

[116] Lockwood, supra note 20, at 2; see also George R. Goethals & John M. Darley, *Social Comparison Theory*, in SOCIAL COMPARISON PROCESSES: THEORETICAL AND EMPIRICAL PERSPECTIVES 259 (Jerry M. Suls & Richard L. Miller eds., 1977) and Karl L. Hakmiller, *Need for Self-Evaluation, Perceived Similarity and Comparison Choice*, 1 J. EXPERIMENTAL SOC. PSYCH. SUPPLEMENT 49 (1966) (both showing that individuals use those similar to themselves as a source of information). Ladd Wheeler, *Motivation as a Determinant of Upward Comparison*, 1 J. EXPERIMENTAL SOC. PSYCH. SUPPLEMENT 27 (1966) (showing that people compare to those who are similar in terms of overall performance level on ability-related tasks).

[117] See Lockwood, supra note 20, at 37 (showing that women were more inspired by outstanding female role models than male role models, but gender did not have the same effect for men); E.J. Parks-Stamm et al., *Motivated to Penalize: Women's Strategic Rejections of Successful Women*, 34 PERSONALITY & SOC. PSYCH. BULL. 237 (2008) (finding that in-group role models are more important for minority group members and less important for members of majorities or positively stereotyped groups).

[118] "According to the 2015 U.S. Transgender Survey:

- Nearly half (46%) of respondents were verbally harassed in the past year because of being transgender.
- Nearly one in ten (9%) respondents were physically attacked in the past year because of being transgender.
- Nearly half (47%) of respondents were sexually assaulted at some point in their lifetime and one in ten (10%) were sexually assaulted in the past year. In communities of color, these numbers are higher: 53% of Black respondents were sexually assaulted in their lifetime and 13% were sexually assaulted in the last year.

girls and cisgender girls will identify more strongly with transgender and cisgender athletic winners, respectively.[119] In other words, who wins will matter to transgender and cisgender girls alike. This section considers next the effect that several possible competitive realities would have on their respective group benefits.

5.4.2.1 Mean and Tail Equivalence

Imagine first that transgender girl athletes are both no better on average than cisgender girl athletes and no more likely to win. Cisgender girls dominate the winner's circle, but only because there are more of them competing; their odds of winning are the same as those for transgender girls.

Under such circumstances, nonparticipant transgender girls will experience self-esteem benefits from seeing transgender winners celebrated for their athletic accomplishments. They will also benefit from having transgender girl role models who encourage athletic participation and healthy choices generally. Finally, transgender girls will experience social-esteem benefits from the message of inclusion – namely that transgender girls are girls and should be treated and celebrated as such.

Cisgender girls will experience comparable benefits. They will experience self-esteem benefits from seeing cisgender girls celebrated for their strength and athleticism. They will benefit from having cisgender girl role models whose success encourages their own participation. Finally, cisgender girls' athletic success, and its celebration, boosts cisgender girls' social status by reinforcing their strength and agency and undermining society's sexualization and objectification of biological women.

- 72% of respondents who have done sex work, 65% of respondents who have experienced homelessness, and 61% of respondents with disabilities reported being sexually assaulted in their lifetime.
- More than half (54%) experienced some form of intimate partner violence, including acts involving coercive control and physical harm."

Sandy E. James et al., *The Report of the 2015 U.S. Transgender Survey*, NAT'L CTR. FOR TRANSGENDER EQUAL. (2016), https://shorturl.at/SCBfQ; see also *Transgender People over Four Times More Likely than Cisgender People to Be Victims of Violent Crime*, UCLA SCH. L. WILLIAMS INST. (Mar. 23, 2021), https://williamsinstitute.law.ucla.edu/press/ncvs-trans-press-release/; Brenda Alvarez, *Fair Play for Trans Girls and Women in School Sports*, NEA TODAY (June 21, 2021), https://shorturl.at/P9vi4.

[119] See Thekla Morgenroth, *How Role Models Affect Role Aspirants' Motivation and Goals* 33 (2015) (Ph.D. thesis, University of Exeter) (explaining that "shared group membership per se is not the characteristic that matters [for effective role modeling] but rather whether the person who might serve as a role model is *seen* as an ingroup member by the role aspirant").

Individual cisgender girls may still feel aggrieved if they lose to a transgender girl they believe exceeds the relevant ability metrics. Yet cisgender girls as a group will reap benefits from seeing cisgender girls' success within the "female" category as regular rather than exceptional.

Under conditions of equivalence, inclusion and integration of transgender and cisgender girls in sports makes sense. Inclusion provides transgender and cisgender girls with similar group benefits and does not involve significant trade-offs between the two. More specifically, inclusion of transgender girls does not entail group losses for cisgender girls. Inclusion under such conditions is also unlikely to be deeply controversial.[120]

5.4.2.2 Mean Superiority

Consider next a world in which transgender girls are slightly to moderately better than cisgender girls on average but no better at the extremes. As a result, transgender girls are no more likely to win athletic competitions than are cisgender girls. Despite the fact that transgender girls are somewhat more likely to make a competitive team, the winner's circle is, again, dominated by cisgender girls, simply because there are so many more cisgender girls than transgender girls competing.[121]

Under such conditions, transgender girls would experience group benefits comparable to those received under conditions of mean and tail equivalence. Indeed, with no more winners, the role-modeling, self-esteem, and social-status benefits for transgender girls would effectively be the same.

---

[120] *See* Barnes, *supra* note 113 (describing how parents do not care about transgender girls' inclusion in sports when the transgender girls are not winning competitions). The fact that transgender boys are not seen as likely to beat cisgender boys in competitions probably also explains why there is little controversy over transgender boys competing against cisgender boys.

[121] There is not enough evidence or study of transgender athlete performance yet to know if, on average, transgender athletes will perform better than their cisgender peers, but at least some research suggests this might be the case in some sports. *See* T.A. Roberts et al., *Effect of Gender Affirming Hormones on Athletic Performance in Transwomen and Transmen: Implications for Sporting Organisations and Legislators*, 55 BR. J. SPORTS MED. 577 (2021) (finding in a study of forty-six transwomen in the United States Air Force that after two years of taking feminizing hormones, transwomen had lost their performance advantage over their female counterparts in push-up and sit-up tests but were still 12 percent faster than their female counterparts in a 1.5-mile run (down from being 21 percent faster before beginning hormone treatment)). *But see* Joanna Marie Harper, *Race Times for Transgender Athletes*, 6 J. SPORTING CULTURES & IDENTITIES 1 (2015) (finding, in a study of eight transwomen who were over thirty years of age and not elite runners, that, on average, after transitioning, in distance-running events the transgender women had similar age-graded performance scores as women as they had pre-transition as men).

Cisgender girls too would experience group benefits comparable to those received under conditions of mean and tail equivalence. The fact that transgender girls are on average somewhat better than cisgender girls and might hold disproportionate spots on any given team would do little to undermine the self-esteem benefits for cisgender girls. With cisgender girls dominating the winner's circle, nonparticipant cisgender girls would continue to have ample role models and would experience self-esteem and social-status benefits from society's celebration of cisgender girl victories.

There would be no meaningful trade-off or transfer of group benefits between cisgender and transgender girls. Inclusion of transgender and cisgender girls in the same athletic categories would produce substantial and equivalent benefits for both groups.

5.4.2.3 Tail Superiority

Consider, finally, a world in which transgender girls are disproportionately likely to be found at the tail end of the performance distribution for girls and are, therefore, disproportionately represented among athletic winners. Given how many more cisgender than transgender girls there are, it would still be the case that there are more absolute cisgender winners than transgender winners. Nonetheless, under this scenario, a disproportionate share of records, medals and awards would be won by transgender girls, and in certain discrete categories, transgender girls would dominate.

Certainly, nonparticipant transgender girls would benefit richly under such conditions – more richly even than they did under conditions of mean equivalence and mean superiority. With more winners, transgender athletes would be more frequently celebrated, transgender girls' social status would be elevated and transgender girl role models would be more plentiful.

Cisgender girls, however, would not fare as well as they did under conditions of equivalence or mean superiority. Indeed, the more transgender girls dominate the winner's circle, the more they deprive cisgender girls of the group benefits of sport. Cisgender girls would see fewer members of their subgroup celebrated, they would have fewer role models, and they would experience fewer reflective and associational self-esteem benefits. Additionally, with biologically female bodies dominated in girls' sports, the social script that female bodies are physically weak, sexualized objects would be less subject to challenge.

This sense that there is something particularly dangerous about transgender women winning explains the tone and tenor of the controversy over swimmer Lia Thomas.[122] Thomas competed for three seasons on Penn's men's swim team before transitioning to female and competing in 2021–22 on Penn's women's team. On the men's team, Thomas was a good but not great swimmer.[123] On the women's team, Thomas was great. She won races and set records.[124] At the Zippy Invitational, in December 2021, Thomas "won three events and swam the fastest time in the country in two of those races."[125] In the Ivy League Championship, Thomas won the 500 freestyle with a lead of more than seven seconds over the runner-up.[126] At the NCAA Championships in March 2022, Thomas again won the 500-freestyle event.[127]

Much of the opposition to Thomas's participation focused on her perceived dominance.[128] In a letter opposing her participation, sixteen of her teammates highlighted that Thomas's "'rankings have bounced from #462 as a male to #1 as a female.'"[129] They cautioned: "'If she were to be eligible to compete against us, she could now break Penn, Ivy, and NCAA Women's Swimming records.'"[130] Former Olympic swimmer Nancy Hogshead-Makar was even more direct in her identification of Thomas's "domination of the 'women's sports' category" as the problem.[131]

---

[122] See Les Carpenter, *Lia Thomas Broke No Records at the NCAA Championship but Left Plenty of Questions*, WASH. POST (Mar. 20, 2022), https://shorturl.at/Eyjk0 (discussing the controversy around testosterone levels sparked by Lia Thomas's performance at the NCAA championships).

[123] See Josh Moody, *Penn Swimmers Take Aim at Trans Teammate in Anonymous Letter*, INSIDE HIGHER ED (Feb. 4, 2022), https://shorturl.at/nlwJL.

[124] *Id.* (noting that Lia set school records in both the 200 free and the 500 free).

[125] David Rieder, *Lia Thomas, Transgender Swimmer from Penn, Swims Fastest Times in Nation; Controversy Raging*, SWIMMING WORLD (Dec. 7, 2021), https://shorturl.at/DgB2a.

[126] See John Lohn, *Lia Thomas Saga: With NCAA Championships Now Here, Betrayal of Female Athletes Continues*, SWIMMING WORLD (Mar. 16, 2022), https://shorturl.at/mtjtC.

[127] Importantly, however, Thomas did not win the two other individual events in which she competed at the NCAA Championships. She placed eighth in the 100 freestyle and tied for fifth in the 200 freestyle. See Katie Barnes, *Lia Thomas Finishes 8th in 100-Yard Freestyle, Final Race of Collegiate Swimming Career*, ESPN (Mar. 19, 2022), https://shorturl.at/y41WS.

[128] Luke Gentile, *Transgender Swimmer Dominates since Joining Penn's Women's Swimming and Diving Team*, WASH. EXAM'R (Dec. 1, 2021), https://shorturl.at/o8Xr2 (describing Thomas as "dominating in the pool" and "beating the competition by significant margins").

[129] Bonesteel, *supra* note 58.

[130] *Id.*

[131] Hogshead-Makar, *supra* note 102.

She argued that transgender women should be allowed to compete in women's athletics only if they "can show that they've mitigated the athletic advantages that come with male puberty."[132] While concerns about Thomas's dominance were often framed or read as being about unfairness to other competitors,[133] they are better understood as revealing a deeper and broader worry – namely that athletic dominance by transgender girls and women will harm all biological girls and women by deflating or undermining the esteem, role-modeling and status benefits that biological girls get from biological girls' and women's victories.

Indeed, it is under conditions of transgender girls' superiority at the tail of the female performance curve that transgender and cisgender girls' interests are most directly in conflict. Under such conditions, group benefits for transgender girls come at a cost for cisgender girls. It is, as a result, on such conditions that policymakers must focus, and only under such conditions that transgender girls' inclusion in girls' sports should be limited and made conditional.

5.5 Conclusion

Sports, as social conventions, should be structured to optimize individual well-being and to further social goals. This chapter has sought to identify the individual and group benefits of sport and to suggest eligibility rules for girls' sports that optimize the benefits of sports for both transgender and cisgender girls.

However, moving from an identification of the benefits of sports to a prescription for policy is complicated. Different benefits are furthered by different, and incompatible, organizational structures. A society that cares only about the basic benefits of sports, would, for example, organize sports in a very different way than a society that cares only about the special benefits or group benefits of sports. In practice, society cares about all three.

---

[132] *Id.*; *see also* Robert Sanchez, *"I am Lia": The Trans Swimmer Dividing America Tells Her Story*, SPORTS ILLUSTRATED (Mar. 3, 2022), https://shorturl.at/oCOJd (describing Thomas as becoming, after her transition, "one of the most dominant college athletes in the country and, as a result, the center of a national debate").

[133] Aubri Spady, *Swimmer Riley Gaines Trusts Gov Noem to "Fight for Girls" after Competing against Biological Male Lia Thomas*, FOX NEWS (Oct. 11, 2022), www.foxnews.com/politics/swimmer-riley-gaines-trusts-gov-noem-fight-girls-competing-against-biological-male-lia-thomas; *see also* Brooke Migdon, *Conservative Group Files Title IX Complaint against UPenn over Lia Thomas Controversy*, HILL (Mar. 17, 2022), https://shorturl.at/gdXd8.

5.5 CONCLUSION

Prescriptions are made even more complicated by the fact that the three benefits exist, to varying degrees, at every level of play. Recreational players care about the (largely intangible) special benefits that come with winning. Elite players reap basic benefits from sport along with the (many tangible) special benefits of play. Young girls may find role models at every level.

Nonetheless, it is the case that particular benefits are more pronounced in particular athletic contexts. For recreational and early childhood leagues, the dominant benefits of play, and often the main reasons for playing, are the basic benefits of sports. At the varsity level of high school and college play, the special and group benefits of play are far more significant. Elite athletes work incredibly hard to play at a high level because of the prizes, recognition and rewards that come from victory. As a result, group benefits are most likely to flow from these high-profile athletic wins.

The context dominance, though not exclusivity, of particular benefits suggests a path for optimizing athletic eligibility rules for transgender and cisgender girls. At the recreational and early childhood levels, the values governing the basic benefits of sports should drive eligibility rules. Such leagues and opportunities should be open to all without regard to ability – though ability-based groupings may best further the health, safety and enjoyment goals of recreational play. Whether such leagues and opportunities are sex-segregated or unisex is largely immaterial, and there is no reason to distinguish between transgender and cisgender girls in either case. At the elite level of varsity high school and college sports, the values furthered by the special and group benefits should drive eligibility rules. At least in the short term, sex segregation most directly furthers those goals by ensuring and celebrating female winners and elevating the status of women as a group. Moreover, including transgender women in women's sports optimizes the special and group benefits of sports for both, except in those cases in which transgender athletes dominate the winning of special benefits.

Conclusion

On his first day in office in 2025, President Trump signed an executive order making it the policy of the United States to recognize two sexes, male and female, which, the order explained, were not changeable and were defined in terms of reproductive biology at birth. The order went on to require that all federal agencies enforce sex-based rights and make sex-based distinctions on the basis of biology not gender identity. To make the president's intentions with regard to sex-segregated sports crystal clear, in February 2025, President Trump issued another executive order, prohibiting transgender girls and women from participating in women's sports.

Perhaps in an attempt to leave nothing to chance, the Republican-controlled House of Representatives has taken steps to amend Title IX so as to explicitly bar transgender girls from girls' sports. Moreover, as of October 2025, twenty-seven states have passed their own laws defining eligibility for female sports teams in terms of biological sex at birth and categorically excluding transgender girls from girls' teams.[1] The Supreme Court is poised to rule on the constitutionality of two such categorical state bans in the spring of 2026.

Despite these actions, the social debate over transgender girls' inclusion in girls' sports is far from over and the legal issues inclusion raises are far from settled. Instead, positions seem increasingly partisan and antagonistic. Stakes seem increasingly high.

During the 2025–2026 term, the Supreme Court heard two cases raising constitutional challenges to state laws categorically excluding transgender girls from girls' sports. If the categorical exclusions are deemed unconstitutional, political and legal questions will remain. New lines will need to be drawn and innumerable variations are possible. All pose relative advantages and disadvantages to transgender and cisgender girls. All

---

[1] *Bans on Transgender Youth Participation in Sports*, EQUALITY MAPS, https://shorturl.at/hMmlo.

will be subject to legal challenge. If the categorical exclusions are deemed permissible, they may not be constitutionally required. States that do not want to categorically exclude transgender girls will continue to struggle with the question of how much inclusion is politically and legally feasible.

There is nothing magical about the categories we draw, but they do say a lot about us. They reveal what we think matters and who we value. Categories are empirical – showing the distinctions we think are relevant – and, often, they are aspirational – showing the groups we are trying to elevate. We distinguish wrestlers by weight because we think weight matters – that heavier wrestlers will almost always win against those who are significantly lighter – and because we want to recognize and reward the skills of the lighter wrestlers. We distinguish youth tennis players by age because we think age matters – that high school players will almost always beat those in elementary school. We may not think the younger players are as skillful as their more mature counterparts, but we want to reward their efforts and encourage their development.

Distinguishing athletes based on biological sex sends the message that biological sex matters to performance. In practice, it is likely that those who are biologically male will be, and are, those who are most celebrated. Nonetheless, the categorization provides recognition, respect and resources for biologically female athletes. Transgender athletes are overlooked and unrecognized.

Distinguishing athletes based on gender identity sends the message that identity matters for sports, and for society more broadly. In practice, those who identify as male and have male bodies are likely to continue to be the most celebrated. Nonetheless, the categorization elevates the importance of gender identity and provides recognition and resources for those who identify as female. Biological womanhood, however, is denied importance and salience.

Were we to divide athletes based on characteristics such as muscle mass or testosterone levels, rather than biological sex or gender identity, we would send the message that these characteristics matter for sports. In practice, the most celebrated groupings – the high muscle mass, high testosterone divisions – would be populated heavily (perhaps exclusively) by biological men. Yet the categorization would increase recognition and support for low muscle mass and low testosterone athletes – at least some of whom would probably be cisgender and trans women. Women – as a biological or identity category – would be invisible.

The point is that there is no neutral categorization. There is no categorization in sports, or otherwise, that does not say something about what and who we value. More specifically, there is no categorization that does not send a message about the value that we put on biological sex and gender identity. To be sure, the fight over eligibility rules is over opportunities and rewards, but it is also, perhaps more importantly, about respect. Hence, the culture war.

Courts and policymakers will ultimately need to decide how eligibility rules should or must be drawn. In answering these questions, they will need to decide what the social goal of sex-segregated sports is and which eligibility rules best serve those ends. This book started from the premise that transgender and cisgender girls are entitled to equal concern and respect. It then offered a pragmatic and workable framework for optimizing both the individual and group benefits of sports for all girls.

Yet it is worth recognizing – perhaps in a moment of ceasefire – that this a war over the leftovers, not the spoils. Whatever eligibility rules policymakers draw and courts allow for women's sports, cisgender men are likely to continue to be the winners. Their access to resources, rewards and recognition is unchallenged. It is women and girls (biological and trans) who are fighting over the remains.

INDEX

5-alpha reductase deficiency (5-ARD), 38, 49

Affordable Care Act (ACA), 110
Alliance Defending Freedom (ADF), 87
A.M. v. Indianapolis Public Schools, 33–34
American Civil Liberties Union (ACLU), 3, 55–56
American Psychological Association (APA), 41
androgen insensitivity syndrome (AIS), 38, 49–50
Athlete Ally, 56

Biden, Joe (administration), 1, 23–25, 123
Biles, Simone, 90–91
Bostock v. Clayton County, 14, 23
B.P.J. by Jackson v. West Virginia Board of Education, 32–33, 35
Brown, Erin, 110
Burwell v. Hobby Lobby Stores. See Religious Freedom Restoration Act (RFRA)
Buzuvis, Erin, 58, 66, 73, 77

California Education Code, 27
California Interscholastic Federation (CIF), 28
Case, Mary Anne, 75
Centola v. Potter, 12
Chevron Defense. See *Chevron v. Natural Resources Defense Council*
Chevron v. Natural Resources Defense Council, 31–32
chromosome, 37–39

Civil Rights Restoration Act of 1988, the, 16
Coleman, Doriane, 39–41, 45–46, 52
Concerned Women for America, 22–23
Connecticut Interscholastic Athletic Conference (CIAC), 29. See also *Soule v. Connecticut Association of School*

Department of Education, 20, 23. See also Letter to Dear Colleague, 2016
  Office for Civil Rights (OCR). See also Letter to Emily Prince; Letter of Impending Enforcement Action, Revised
  proposed regulations, 24–25
Department of Justice (DOJ). See also Letter to Dear Colleague, 2016
DeSantis, Ron, 83–84, 87. See also Fairness in Women's Sports Act, Florida
Diagnostic and Statistical Manual of Mental Disorders (DSM), 42–43
disparate impact, 14, 117–18
D.N. v. DeSantis, 35
Doe by Doe v. City of Belleville, 12
Dreger, Alice, 37–39

Employment Division, Department of Human Resources of Oregon v. Smith, 70
English, Jane, 107, 111–13
Equal Protection Clause, 34–35
  heightened scrutiny. See Equal Protection Clause, intermediate scrutiny

INDEX

Equal Protection Clause (cont.)
  intermediate scrutiny, 32–34
  rational review, 35
erasure, biological, 76–77, 79–80
Establishment Clause, 97

Fairness in Women's Sports Act, Florida, 28, 83. *See also D.N. v. DeSantis*
Fairness in Women's Sports Act, Kansas, 86
Family Research Council (FRC), 96–97
framing effect, 61–62
Franklin Pierce University, 22–23

gametes, 37–38, 40
Gay & Lesbian Alliance Against Defamation (GLAAD), 55
Gedicks, Frederick, 71
Grove City College v. Bell, 16

Handelsman, David, 43–44, 48, 52
Hecox v. Little, 5, 34–35, 57
Hogshead-Makar, Nancy, 85, 137–38
Hohfeld, Wesley, 64
Holloway v. Arthur Anderson, 10–11
Hooven, Carole, 37, 40, 47, 52–53, 128
Hopkins, Ann. *See Price Waterhouse v. Hopkins*
Human Rights Campaign, 55, 132
hyperandrogenism, 49

Individuals with Disabilities Education Act (IDEA), 108
INS v. Chahda, 15
International Association of Athletics Federations (IAAF), 124
International Olympic Committee (IOC), 50, 124, 127–28
intersex, 38–43

Jespersen v. Harrah's Operating Company, 13
Jordan-Young, Rebecca, 37–38, 48–49, 51–52
Joyce, Helen, 40

Kahneman, Daniel, 62–63
Karkazis, Katrina, 37–38, 48–49, 51–52

Kelman, Mark, 65, 103–4
Kilborn, Jason, 61
Klinefelter syndrome, 38
Knauer, Nancy, 74
Kogan, Terry, 74
Koppelman, Andrew, 72, 97

Letter of Impending Enforcement Action, Revised, 21–23. *See also* Connecticut Interscholastic Athletic Conference (CIAC)
Letter to Dear Colleague, 2016, 19–21, 67, 76, 122–23
Letter to Dear Colleague, 2017, 21
Letter to Emily Prince, 18–19
Levi, Jennifer, 57, 67, 73–74
Lewis, John, 110
Loper Bright Enterprises v. Raimondo, 31

McConnell, Michael, 72
Mills College, 93
Missouri State High School Transgender Participation Policy, The, 29
Morgan, William, 121
Murray, Douglas, 95–96

National Collegiate Athletic Association (NCAA), 30, 124–25
National Organization for Women, 3–4
National Women's Law Center, 3
Nussbaum, Martha, 107

Obama, Barack (administration), 1, 18–21, 67, 76, 122–23

Patton, Greg, 60–61
Phelps, Michael, 90–91
Pogge, Thomas, 121
polycystic ovary syndrome (PCOS), 49–50
Price Waterhouse v. Hopkins, 11–14
priming effect, 60–61
Prince, Emily. *See* Letter to Emily Prince
Protect Fairness in Women's Sports Act, South Dakota, 86
puberty, 43–44, 47–48

Religious Freedom Restoration Act (RFRA), 70–71
Rhode Island Interscholastic League (RIIL), 28–29
Roe v. Utah High School Activities Association, 34–35
Rowling, J.K., 4

Save Women's Sports Act, South Carolina, 27
Save Women's Sports Bill, West Virginia. *See B.P.J. by Jackson v. West Virginia Board of Education*
Schoenbaum, Naomi, 75
Sen, Amartya, 63–64, 107
Shinohara, Chika, 60
Shreve, Wickliffe, 45–46
Shrier, Abigail, 96
Skinner-Thompson, Scott, 57, 65–66, 76–78
Smith v. City of Salem, 13
Soh, Debra, 37, 39–40, 96
Soule, Selina. *See Soule v. Connecticut Association of School*
Soule v. Connecticut Association of School, 64–65, 68, 87

testosterone suppression, 29, 124
Thomas, Lia, 2, 83–84, 87, 94, 124, 137–38
Tobin, Harper, 57, 67, 73–74
Trump, Donald (administration), 2, 22–23, 25–26, 34, 82–83, 140. *See* Letter to Dear Colleague, 2017; Letter of Impending Enforcement Action, Revised
Turner syndrome, 38
Turner, Ilona, 57, 65–66, 76–78

Uggen, Christopher, 60
Ulane v. Eastern Airlines, 11
USA Gymnastics, 31
USA Swimming, 30–31
USA Volleyball, 31

Van Anders, Sari, 38, 48, 50–51
Virginia High School League, 29

Washington State Interscholastic Activities Association, 28
Wellesley College, 88
Weyant, Emma, 83, 87. *See also* DeSantis, Ron; Thomas, Lia
Wisconsin Interscholastic Athletic Association, 29–30
Women's Sports Policy Working Group, 85
World Aquatics, 30

For EU product safety concerns, contact us at Calle de José Abascal, 56–1°,
28003 Madrid, Spain or eugpsr@cambridge.org.

www.ingramcontent.com/pod-product-compliance
Lightning Source LLC
LaVergne TN
LVHW011836060526
838200LV00053B/4062